THE FURNITURE FACTORY OUTLET GUIDE

BY KIMBERLY CAUSEY

HOME DECOR PRESS

Published by: Home Decor Press
                PMB 312
                11770 Haynes Bridge Rd., Suite 205
                Alpharetta, GA 30004

To order single copies of this book, or any other books published by Home Decor Press, please call (800) 829-1203 or use the order form given in the back of this book. All major credit cards are accepted.

Quantity discounts are available. Please call the publisher at (678) 947-1750 for a discount schedule. Our titles are also available through Ingram Book Co. and Baker & Taylor Books.

If you have any questions or comments regarding this book, please write to the author in care of the publisher at the above address.

Publisher's Cataloging-in-Publication Data

Causey, Kimberly,

    The Furniture Factory Outlet Guide

    Includes index.
    1. Interior decoration--United States   2. Consumer education--United States 3. Shopping--United States

ISBN 1-888229-41-1

    The author and publisher have made every reasonable effort to ensure the accuracy and completeness of the information contained in this book. However, we assume no responsibility for any errors, inaccuracies, or omissions herein. Also, we are not responsible for any changes in the information given in this book that may occur after the book has been printed. We shall have no responsibility or liability to any person or entity with respect to any loss or damage caused, or alleged to have been caused, directly or indirectly, by the information and advice contained in this book.
    This book is designed to provide information about the home furnishings industry based upon the personal experience and research of the author. The information and recommendations given in this book strictly reflect only the author's opinions and personal knowledge of the products, services, people, companies, and all other topics discussed herein.
    The author's sole purpose in writing this book is to present information and consumer advice that may benefit readers. The author and publisher do not intend to provide legal, accounting, or medical advice. If expert assistance is required, please consult a qualified professional.

TABLE OF CONTENTS

FACTORY OUTLETS AND DISCOUNTERS (CONT.)

FACTORY OUTLETS AND DISCOUNTERS (CONT.)

FACTORY OUTLETS AND DISCOUNTERS (CONT.)

FACTORY OUTLETS AND DISCOUNTERS (CONT.)

BRAND INDEX

FREQUENTLY ASKED QUESTIONS

What are "factory outlets" and "discounters"?

The term "factory outlet", in this book, refers to any factory-owned store that sells floor samples, overstock furniture, photography samples, customer returns, discontinued styles, and seconds. These outlets are set up by most major furniture manufacturers to sell off furniture that can't be sold to their regular wholesale customers, primarily furniture stores and interior designers.

Except for seconds, the vast majority of the furniture in stock at a typical factory outlet is in new first-quality condition. Factory outlet furniture is normally just as high-quality and in just as good condition as the furniture sold by your local furniture retailer. Seconds do have small flaws, but they are very clearly identified as such and usually make up a very small percentage of the furniture in stock at a typical factory outlet.

"Discounters", such as Boyles and Furnitureland South, are not factory-owned stores. They are retailers that buy furniture from the factories and resell it to the public.

Unlike your local furniture retailer, however, discounters have made a conscious decision to drastically lower their prices by reducing their overhead. They typically don't offer "free" design services in your home, as your local furniture retailer usually does, nor do they have large advertising budgets or big brightly-lit stores in the high-rent district of every major city. Discounters cut costs even further by having just one central location, usually just a few miles from the furniture factories in North Carolina, instead of having multiple stores all over the country.

By eliminating the huge budget a typical local furniture retailer spends on rent, advertising, utilities, and a staff of interior designers, a furniture discounter is able to pass those savings on to you. Typically, the very same piece of furniture made by the very same manufacturer will cost you about half as much if you order it through a discounter as it would if you ordered it through a local furniture retailer.

Simply put, local furniture retailers attempt to get more customers by offering more "free" services while keeping prices at or near full retail. Furniture discounters attempt to get more customers by cutting overhead costs and reducing prices to near-wholesale. Factory outlets exist to sell off furniture that can't be sold through the normal retail channels, at prices below the normal wholesale price.

How much money will I save if I buy my furniture from a factory outlet or discounter?

The typical savings at a factory-owned factory outlet run from 50%-80% off the normal retail price you would pay at your local furniture retailer for the very same furniture. New first-quality furniture normally runs 50%-75% less than the prices you would pay at a local furniture retailer. Discontinued styles, floor samples, photography samples, overstock furniture, and customer returns are usually new first-quality and account for the vast majority of the furniture at a typical outlet.

Seconds, or furniture with small flaws, normally costs 75%-80% less than the prices you would pay for the same style if you purchased it through a local furniture store. Most outlets have very few second-quality pieces, and many outlets have none at all.

The typical savings on new first-quality furniture ordered through a discounter run from 40%-70% off retail, with most brands discounted about 50% off the prices charged by local furniture retailers.

My local furniture retailer is having a big sale. Does this mean that I'll get just as good a deal from the local retailer as I would from a true factory outlet or discounter?

No. It is an unfortunate fact that many local furniture retailers misrepresent the discounts on their furniture. It is a common practice for local furniture retailers to mark the regular price of a piece of furniture up right before a sale, and then mark it right back down, leading their customers to believe that they're getting a big discount when they really aren't. In the industry, this is called "marking it up to mark it down".

In fact, one major furniture retail chain was recently sued by the California State Attorney General and seven other states over exactly this practice. As reported in the Los Angeles Times, Levitz Furniture Co. paid $1.2 million dollars in 1996 to settle charges brought by the State of California that it "misled consumers with phony discounts". Arizona, Connecticut, Maryland, Missouri, Pennsylvania, Texas, and Washington also took part in the suit against Levitz. Levitz admitted no wrongdoing in its settlement of the lawsuit, although it should be noted that the company was also sued by the State of California on similar false-advertising charges back in 1973.

According to the CBS Morning News, in its reporting of the same lawsuit, Levitz "was accused of posting false regular prices on sale items to give consumers the impression they were getting a great deal when they were actually paying full price".

According to the allegations by the State of California, "Levitz duped customers by comparing 'sale' prices to 'regular' prices that never existed". As a part of the settlement, Levitz agreed not to advertise "regular" prices unless the item is available at that price at least 60% of the time and is sold at that price at least 20% of the time.

California Deputy Attorney General Albert Shelden told the Los Angeles Times, "We are hoping these standards will lead [furniture retailers] to not engage in as much phony advertising. It is a problem we see a lot and we are concerned about".

It is a problem that I, and many of the consumers I've spoken with all over the U. S., have seen frequently as well. My family owned a factory that sold to local furniture retailers all over the U. S. for over twenty years. We saw this problem contantly among local furniture retailers in every state. The problem of phony discounts is so prevalent in the home furnishings industry that it even has a special name: "borax pricing", named after similar shady practices in the mining industry.

Occasionally, I speak with consumers at my seminars who have seen this type of phony pricing first hand. Typically, these are consumers who check and record prices over several months before making a purchase. One man related this story at a seminar:

> *"I saw a chair I wanted at a local retailer and wrote the price down: $500.00. Then, a few weeks later, I noticed that the store was having a "40% off sale". I went to buy the chair expecting it to be marked 40% off of the original $500.00 price. When I got to the sale, I found that the chair's original retail price had been marked up, and the new SALE price was $515.00!"*

Research is the best defense. Although some local furniture retailers do advertise their sales honestly, many don't. Don't take any chances. Always compare the ACTUAL PRICE among many different retailers, including the factory outlets and discounters in North Carolina, before you buy. Completely ignore any claims of percentages off and focus on the actual dollar amount, including freight and sales tax, that you'll actually have to pay for the furniture. As long as you do this every time you shop, you can't be fooled into paying more than you should.

Can I use a professional interior designer and still get my furniture at a discount?

Certainly. I've found that some consumers believe that they must make a trade-off between price and service. They think that if they choose to buy their furniture from a factory outlet or discounter which doesn't provide an in-home design service, they can't have any in-home design help. This isn't at all the case.

There are many interior designers who work on an hourly basis. It is a simple matter to hire a designer at an hourly rate for her design advice only, and then go buy your furniture directly from the factory outlets and discounters. In this way, you still get the best possible price, and you can get the service you need.

Another advantage to hiring a designer this way is that you only pay for the help you actually need and no more. If you buy your furniture through a local retailer and use their "free" in-home design help, what you're actually doing is paying a large mark-up on everything you buy to compensate the designer for his or her time. Everyone pays the same mark-up whether they need to consult with the designer for an hour, a week, or a month. So, customers who only need a little help choosing their colors and arranging their furniture pay the same hefty commission as those customers who need far more assistance. This is hardly a fair system.

You can't go wrong hiring a designer by the hour. This way, you only pay for exactly the help you actually need and receive.

For detailed information on locating a reputable and qualified designer in your area, negotiating a fair hourly rate, putting together a contract, and making sure the job is done properly, please read chapter 14 of my book, _The Insider's Guide To Buying Home Furnishings_.

If I see a piece of furniture I like at a local furniture retailer, how can I get the accurate item number so I can compare the price with factory outlets and discounters?

This is, unfortunately, a growing problem. Some local furniture retailers will actually hide, remove, or alter the original manufacturer's item numbers and names to prevent customers from comparing prices with factory outlets and discounters. This is hardly what could be called a "fair trade practice".

Fortunately, there are several ways around this problem:

1. Ask to see the manufacturer's catalog. Most furniture stores do have the original manufacturer's catalog and will bring it out on request. One customer told me that she always gets the store salespeople to bring out the catalog by asking them what other items the manufacturer has that match the one she is considering buying. Usually, the manufacturer's catalog has all of the correct item numbers and names.

2. Ask for a product sheet. Many furniture manufacturers provide stores with color product sheets for their furniture. Often, these sheets have the accurate item number, or at least the accurate style name. If the product sheet doesn't have the item number shown, you can usually fax or mail the entire sheet to a discounter and get them to properly identify the product for you so they can give you a comparison price.

3. Take a photograph of the furniture. Many local furniture retailers won't object to photographs. Many people do take photographs of furniture to show their husbands, wives, children, etc., when shopping for furniture alone. Then, send the photograph to a discounter and let them help you identify the product.

Never allow a local furniture retailer's hiding or falsification of product information to cause you to pay too much for your furniture. No customer would tolerate this practice at a car dealership, computer store, or electronics store, so why should anyone put up with this from furniture stores? Consumers deserve accurate product information, and they have every right to compare prices among different sources before they buy.

What brands and types of furniture are available at a discount?

Nearly every brand of furniture at your local furniture retailer is also available through factory outlets and discounters.

There are factory-owned factory outlets for most major furniture brands, including Baker, Century, Hickory White, Pennsylvania House, Drexel-Heritage, Henredon, Hickory Chair, Councill Craftsmen, Clayton Marcus, Maitland-Smith, La Barge, and many more. They are all listed in this book. If there is a factory-owned factory outlet for the brand of furniture you want, you'll normally get the best deal there.

About 99% of the other brands sold by local furniture retailers and interior designers are available through one or more of the discounters listed in this book. Most of the individual discounter descriptions in this book include a list of the brands they carry. If you don't find the brand you want listed with any discounters in this book, call several of the largest discounters, such as Shaw Furniture Galleries or Boyles. Frequently, discounters can also order brands other than those listed here, and many discounters add new brands all the time.

If you can't find the brand you want through any of the discounters listed here, and this will happen with about 1% of the brands on the market, there are a couple of alternatives:

1. Let the discounters help you find an identical product from another brand.

    A few brands greatly restrict the availability of their products in order to keep prices high. For instance, Ethan Allen furniture is normally carried only by Ethan Allen's corporately-owned retail stores. No discounter carries that line, so Ethan Allen stores have no price competition and can charge full retail for their furniture.

    Fortunately, there are other brands that have identical or nearly identical furniture to Ethan Allen's that are available through discounters and factory outlets. You might particularly want to check out Pennsylvania House, which is Ethan Allen's biggest competitor nationwide, and Hitchcock Chair, which specializes in early American furniture. Both of these brands have factory-owned factory outlets and are widely available through discounters.

    Stickley is another brand that can be difficult to find at a discount, although they do have periodic sales at their old factory building (see *Stickley Factory Sale* in this book for more information). Several other brands manufacture furniture in the same style and quality as Stickley: Kincaid, Arts & Crafts Industries, and Richardson Brothers, to name a few. Each of these lines produces furniture that is identical in looks and quality to many Stickley products, and they're all a lot cheaper. As with many designer products, sometimes you really do pay more for the name.

    If you can't find the brand you want from a factory outlet or discounter, contact several discounters and let them identify other brands that have the same look and quality you want. Frequently, you can find a product from another manufacturer that is absolutely identical to the one you originally picked out.

2. Shop wholesale. There are some lines that aren't available through discounters or factory outlets that are available through wholesale showrooms. There are wholesale showrooms in most major cities that sell primarily to interior designers and interior decorators. Many members of the public get into these show-rooms to shop, too. This is a very common practice in the industry.

    For many years, my family's factory had showrooms at the world trade centers in Atlanta and Dallas, and we also showed at the International Home Furnishings Market in High Point, NC. During all the years I worked in those showrooms, I watched many consumers come in and shop for themselves. Some were friends and relatives of furniture store owners and others in the trade, but many had simply figured out how to get in on their own.

    The Los Angeles Times recently interviewed Elaine M. Redfield, president of the American Society Of Interior Designers (ASID) for the Los Angeles area, about consumers getting into design centers and wholesale showrooms to buy directly from manufacturers. She had this to say: "It's a simple matter for someone to get a resale number and go shop at the showrooms, and many do."

The Los Angeles Times also interviewed Pat Stamps, the former head of the ASID for the Los Angeles area. She had this to say about retail customers getting into the wholesale showrooms to shop: "We all know it happens because our customers tell us they've shopped here. I've seen women who come in who use their husband's resale number, and he sells plants."

In my experience, about 3/4 of the manufacturers out there will sell directly to consumers at their wholesale showrooms. Of course, it is important to know how to get into the showrooms and how to properly conduct business once you get there. Wholesale shopping is not at all like shopping at a local retail store. It's also important to have the proper credentials, including a resale number.

For more detailed information on how to get into wholesale showrooms and design centers, and how to shop properly once you get there, please read chapter 19 of my book, _The Insider's Guide To Buying Home Furnishings_.

Do I have to travel to North Carolina to save a lot of money on furniture?

Not necessarily. It is true that you'll get the very best deals if you go in person. If you want to save 75% to 80% off retail on new first-quality furniture, you'll have to go in person to the factory outlets and clearance centers, the vast majority of which are located in North Carolina where most of the furniture factories are. There are a few factory outlets in other states, including New York, Missouri, Wisconsin, and Virginia.

If you do decide to travel to North Carolina to shop, be sure to contact the discounters and outlets you intend to visit in advance of your trip. Some offer travel discounts from time to time. A few discounters will rebate all or part of your travel expense up to a certain amount if you buy your furniture from them. Other discounters have arranged for package deals on airfare and hotel rooms that can save you quite a bit. Please read the individual listings in this book for more information.

If you aren't able to travel to North Carolina, you can still save around 50% off retail on most brands by ordering your furniture from those discounters who accept phone orders and having it shipped to you. This is how most people buy their furniture from North Carolina. This is a very safe and reliable way of buying your furniture, and it can save most people thousands of dollars on their purchases.

If I order my furniture over the phone, do I have to pay sales tax on it?

If you order your furniture over the phone from outside of North Carolina, you will not have to pay any North Carolina sales tax.

Whether or not you will have to pay sales tax to your own home state depends on the laws where you live. In many states, you don't have to pay sales tax on purchases made by phone. In other states, you do. It's best to ask the particular discounter you're ordering your furniture from about this when you make your purchase. They usually have up-to-date lists of those states that require you to pay sales tax on purchases shipped to you from another state.

How can I make sure I'm buying high-quality furniture?

It is important to make sure you are choosing the correct type of wood, and the correct type of fabric in the case of upholstered furniture. Making sure your furniture is made from the highest-quality and most appropriate materials is the best way to make sure it will last for a long time.

This is too broad a subject to go into here. For detailed information on furniture construction, wood types, and fabric types, please read chapters 2 and 3 of my book, _The Insider's Guide To Buying Home Furnishings_.

If I do decide to visit a factory outlet in person, what should I be sure to bring with me?

1. Simple sketches of each room you intend to decorate, with the basic room dimensions shown. Snapshots of each room are very useful, as well.

2. Measurements of all doorways and hallways that your furniture will have to go through to reach the correct room. Before you buy that unreturnable entertainment center at the factory outlet in North Carolina, it's very important to make sure it will fit through the door when you get it home.

3. Swatches of any fabrics, carpeting, or paint that you'll need when choosing upholstered furniture.

4. Photographs torn from magazines or copied from books that show the basic styles you like (and those you hate). This can be a very useful way to narrow down the look you want (and the looks you want to avoid).

5. Tape measure to measure any furniture you are considering buying. Outlets generally don't have any to lend.

6. A camera to take snapshots of furniture before you buy. It can be very helpful to take snapshots of everything that appeals to you as you shop around the various outlets, and then spread out the pictures back at your hotel room to make your final decision before going back to make your actual purchases. You may also want to be able to fax a picture of a piece of furniture to a relative back home for a second opinion.

How long will it take to receive my furniture?

If you're shopping in person at the factory outlet or discounter, you can normally have your furniture shipped to you the same day. This is another big advantage to going to North Carolina in person. Not only do you get substantially better discounts, there's no wait for your furniture.

If you order your furniture over the phone from a discounter, you will normally have to wait 8-12 weeks for your furniture to be delivered. Just like local furniture retailers, furniture discounters custom-order your furniture directly from the manufacturer. Medium to high-end furniture is just too expensive for any store to keep in stock waiting for a buyer.

How will my furniture be shipped to me?

Most factory outlets and discounters use special furniture delivery services that will unpack your furniture and set it up in the correct place in your home, including carrying it up or down stairs if needed. It's important to be aware, though, that there are some things you need to do before your new furniture arrives.

1. Move your old furniture. It's important to have the spot where your new furniture is to go already cleared.

2. Remove pictures and other items from hallway walls. It's too easy for them to be bumped or broken as the deliverypeople carry your furniture down the hall. It's a good idea to remove any nails from the walls, too. Yes, this is a nuisance, but not nearly as much of a nuisance as having your brand-new upholstery repaired.

Furniture deliverypeople will generally not provide the following services: moving your old furniture, taking away packing materials, and putting electronic equipment into entertainment centers.

How much will the freight charges be to have my furniture shipped home?

The freight charges will depend on the weight of the furniture. The factory outlet or discounter will be able to give you a written quote at the time you place your order or buy your furniture in person.

Occasionally, I am asked if the cost of having furniture shipped to you from North Carolina will outweigh or cancel out the savings. No.

The normal savings on furniture purchased from factory outlets and discounters is 50% to 80% off retail. The usual freight charge to have your furniture shipped home normally runs about 5% of the retail cost of the furniture. So, you are still far ahead to order your furniture directly rather than through a local retailer.

Another thing to bear in mind is that whether you order your furniture through a local furniture store or directly from a North Carolina factory outlet or discounter, it all has to be shipped from North Carolina either way. That's where the vast majority of the furniture factories are. No matter how you order it, the furniture will have to be shipped from North Carolina, and the cost of that freight will be passed on to you.

In many cases, sales tax will not have to be paid on furniture ordered over the phone. This savings can often completely cover the freight cost.

Can I buy custom draperies, fabrics, wallcoverings, carpeting, rugs, blinds, accessories, and other furnishings at a discount, too?

Absolutely. All of these things can be purchased directly from manufacturers, discounters, factory outlets, and local wholesale workrooms. For more information, please read chapters 3 through 18 of my book, _The Insider's Guide To Buying Home Furnishings_.

What do "case goods" and "upholstery" mean?

"Upholstery" simply refers to any upholstered chairs, sofas, lounges, and other furniture. "Case goods" refer to any all-wood furniture, such as entertainment centers, chests, beds, dressers, armoires, etc.

What do I do if there's a problem with my order?

Statistically, you are far less likely to have a problem with a factory outlet or discounter than you are with your local furniture dealer. Still, every year some problems do occur with furniture ordered from North Carolina.

The best defense is prevention. Avoiding problems before they happen and troubleshooting them after they happen is too broad a subject to go into here. For more information on this subject, please read chapter 20 of my book, _The Insider's Guide To Buying Home Furnishings_.

**FOR MORE INFORMATION ON
FURNITURE SHOPPING, MONEY-SAVING TIPS,
ANNOUNCEMENTS OF NEW OUTLET OPENINGS
AND SPECIAL SALES,
PLEASE CHECK OUR WEB SITE AT:**

WWW.SMARTDECORATING.COM

FACTORY OUTLETS AND DISCOUNTERS

A & H Wayside Furniture

1086 Freeway Dr.
Reidsville, NC 27320

Phone:	(336) 342-0717	**Hours:**	M-F 9:00-5:30, Sat 9:00-5:00
Toll Free:	(800) 334-0369	**E-mail:**	wayside@netmcr.com
Fax:	(336) 342-6524	**Web site:**	None

A & H Wayside Furniture has been discounting furniture by phone for nearly 25 years. They are a very well established company with a good reputation for service.

If you visit this source in person, don't forget to check out their clearance center about a mile down the road!

Lines carried:

A. Locke	Ashley Manor	Bevan Funnel, Ltd.	Capitol Leather
A. A. Laun	Athol Table	Blacksmith Shop	Carlton-McLendon
Action Recliners	Baldwin Brass	Black Hawk	Carolina Heritage
American Drew	Baldwin Clocks	Bradington Young	Sleepers
American Of High Point	Barcalounger	Brady	Carolina Mirror
American Impressions	Barclay	Braxton Culler	Carter Chair
American Of Martinsville	Barn Door	Brown-Jordan	Casa Bique
American Reproductions	Bassett	Broyhill	Casual Lamps
A. P. Industries	Bassett Mirror	Builtright Chair Co.	Charleston Forge
Arbek	Bean Station	Butler Specialty	Chatham
Ardley Hall	Benecia Beds	C. R. Laine	Chromcraft
Artistica Metal Design	Benchcraft	Cal-Style	Claridge Manor
Ashley	Berkline	Canal Dover	Clark Casual

Phone orders accepted:	Yes
Discount:	40%-50% off mfrs. suggested retail
Payment methods:	VISA, MC, Discover, personal checks
In-house financing available:	No
Deposits required:	50% deposit when order is placed, balance due when furniture is ready to be shipped
Catalog available:	No
Clearance center:	Yes - See *A & H Wayside Clearance Center*
Delivery:	Full service in-home delivery and set-up. Customer pays freight company directly for shipping costs.

Directions: From I-40, near Greensboro, NC, take Hwy. 29 north at exit #127. After about 30 miles you will come to the Reidsville area. Take the first Reidsville exit, and go west on Business 29. After about 8 miles, you will come to a major intersection where Business 29 will bear left. Stay on Business 29. About 1/2 mile after the intersection, you will see A & H Wayside on the right side of the road next to an Oldsmobile dealership.

A & H Wayside Furniture (cont.)

Lines carried (cont.):

Classic Leather
Classic Rattan
Clayton-Marcus
Cochrane
Colonial
Comfort Designs
Conant Ball
Conover Chair
Cooper Classics
Corsican Brass
Country Concepts
Country Manor
County Seat Dinettes
Cox Furniture Mfg.
Craftique
Craftmaster
Craftwork Guild
Crawford
Crestline
Dansen Contemporary
Decorative Arts & Crafts
Designer Wicker
Designmaster
Dillon
Distinction Leather
Dobbs
Eagle Craft Desks
Elliott's Design
Executive Leather
Fairfax
Fairfield Chair Co.
Fashion Bed Group
Fashion House
Ficks-Reed
Flexsteel
Florida
Franklin
Frederick Cooper
Frederick Edwards
Friendship
HTB
Hammary
Hekman
Henry Link
Heritage Leather
Hickory Hill
Hickory House
Hickory International
Hickory Leather Co.

Hickory Tavern
Highland House
Hollywoods
Hood Furniture
Hooker
Houston House
Howard Miller
Hukla Leather
Huntington House
Hyundai Furniture
International
JDI
J. Royale
Jasper Cabinet
Johnston Benchworks
Johnston Casuals
JTB
Keller
Kessler
Key City
Kimball
King Hickory
Kings Creek
Klaussner
Knob Creek
Lane
Lane/Venture
Lea Industries
Leathertrend
Legacy Leather
Leisters
Leonards
Lexington
Life Style California
Ligo
Link Taylor
Lloyd Flanders
Lyon-Shaw
Madison Square
Marlowe
Martinsville Novelty
Master Design
Masterfield
McKinley Leather
Meadowcraft
Mersman
Millenium
Mobel
Mohawk

Morgan Stewart
Morris Greenspan Lamps
National Of Mt. Airy
Nichols & Stone
North Hickory
Northwood
Null
Oak Craft
Ohio Table Pad Co.
Old Hickory Tannery
P & P Chair Co.
Pearson Co.
Pennsylvania Classics
Peoplelounger
Peters-Revington
Pine-Tique
Pinnacle
Pulaski
Reflections
Regency House
Rex
Richardson Bros.
Ridgeway Clocks
Ridgewood
Riverside
Rock City
Royal Patina
Saloom
Sam Moore
Schnadig
Sealy
Seay
Selig
Serta Mattress
Simply Southern
Skillcraft
Sleepworks
Sligh
South Sea Rattan
Southern Craftsmen's
    Guild
Southern Furniture
Southwood
Spring Air Mattress
Stakmore
Stanton-Cooper
Statesville Chair
Statton
Stiffel

Stoneville
Stratalounger
Stratford
Sumter Cabinet
Superior
Swaim
Swan Brass
Taylor-King
Taylorsville Upholstery
Telescope
Temple-Stuart
Temple Upholstery
The Chair Co.
Timberwood Trading Co.
Tradition France
Tropitone
Universal
Uttermost
Uwharrie Chair
Vanguard
Vaughn
Vaughn-Bassett
Veneman
Venture By Lane
Villageois, Inc.
Virginia House
Virginia Metalcrafters
Walton
Wambold
Waterford
Webb
Weiman
Wesley Allen
Wesley Hall
Whitaker
Wildwood
Winston
Wisconsin
Woodard
Woodmark Originals
Yesteryear Wicker

A & H Wayside Clearance Center

1550 Freeway Dr.
Reidsville, NC 27320

Phone:	**(336) 342-4532**	**Hours:**	**M-F 8:30-5:30, Sat 9:00-5:00**
Toll Free:	**None**	**E-mail:**	**wayside@netmcr.com**
Fax:	**None**	**Web site:**	**None**

A & H Wayside Clearance Center carries discontinued styles, floor samples, and customer returns from A & H Wayside's main showroom and telephone sales center just up the street. They have a nice selection of contemporary and traditional furniture, the vast majority of which is in new first-quality condition.

This clearance center is definitely worth checking out if you are in the Greensboro, NC, area.

Lines carried:

A. Locke	Ashley Manor	Bevan Funnel, Ltd.	Carlton-McLendon
A. A. Laun	Athol Table	Blacksmith Shop	Carolina Heritage
Action Recliners	Baldwin Brass	Black Hawk	Sleepers
American Drew	Baldwin Clocks	Bradington Young	Carolina Mirror
American Of High Point	Barcalounger	Brady	Carter Chair
American Impressions	Barclay	Braxton Culler	Casa Bique
American Of Martinsville	Barn Door	Brown-Jordan	Casual Lamps
American Reproductions	Bassett	Broyhill	Charleston Forge
A. P. Industries	Bassett Mirror	Builtright Chair Co.	Chatham
Arbek	Bean Station	Butler Specialty	Chromcraft
Ardley Hall	Benecia Beds	Cal-Style	Claridge Manor
Artistica Metal Design	Benchcraft	Canal Dover	Clark Casual
Ashley	Berkline	Capitol Leather	Classic Leather

Phone orders accepted:	**No**
Discount:	**50%-70% off mfrs. suggested retail**
Payment methods:	**VISA, MC, Discover, personal checks**
In-house financing available:	**No**
Deposits required:	**Not applicable**
Catalog available:	**No**
Clearance center:	**Not applicable**
Delivery:	**Full service in-home delivery and set-up. Customer pays freight company directly for shipping costs.**

Directions: **From I-40, near Greensboro, NC, take Hwy. 29 north at exit #127. After about 30 miles you will come to the Reidsville area. Take the first Reidsville exit, and go west on Business 29. After about 8 miles, you will come to a major intersection where Business 29 will bear left. Stay on Business 29. About 2 miles after the intersection, you will see the A & H Wayside Clearance Center on the right side of the road across the street from a Lowes grocery store, approximately 1 1/2 miles past A & H Wayside's main store.**

A & H Wayside Clearance Center (cont.)

Lines carried (cont.):

Classic Rattan
Clayton-Marcus
Cochrane
Colonial
Comfort Designs
Conant Ball
Conover Chair
Cooper Classics
Corsican Brass
Country Concepts
Country Manor
County Seat Dinettes
Cox Furniture Mfg.
Craftique
Craftmaster
Craftwork Guild
Crawford
Crestline
Dansen Contemporary
Decorative Arts & Crafts
Designer Wicker
Designmaster
Dillon
Distinction Leather
Dobbs
Eagle Craft Desks
Elliott's Design
Executive Leather
Fairfax
Fairfield Chair Co.
Fashion Bed Group
Fashion House
Ficks-Reed
Flexsteel
Florida
Franklin
Frederick Cooper
Frederick Edwards
Friendship
HTB
Hammary
Hekman
Henry Link
Heritage Leather
Hickory Hill
Hickory House
Hickory International
Hickory Leather Co.
Hickory Tavern

Highland House
Hollywoods
Hood Furniture
Hooker
Houston House
Howard Miller
Hukla Leather
Huntington House
Hyundai Furniture
International
JDI
J. Royale
Jasper Cabinet
Johnston Benchworks
Johnston Casuals
JTB
Karpen
Keller
Kessler
Key City
Kiani-USA Inc.
Kimball
King Hickory
Kings Creek
Klaussner
Knob Creek
La Marina Oak
Laine
Lane
Lea Industries
Leathertrend
Legacy Leather
Leisters
Leonards
Lexington
Life Style California
Ligo
Link Taylor
Lloyd Flanders
Lyon-Shaw
Madison Square
Marlowe
Martinsville Novelty
Master Design
Masterfield
McKinley Leather
Meadowcraft
Mersman
Millenium

Mobel
Mohawk
Morgan Stewart
Morris Greenspan Lamps
National Of Mt. Airy
New England Clock
Nichols & Stone
North Hickory
Northwood
Null
Oak Craft
Ohio Table Pad Co.
Old Hickory Tannery
P & P Chair Co.
Pearson Co.
Pennsylvania Classics
Peoplelounger
Peters-Revington
Pine-Tique
Pinnacle
Pulaski
Reflections
Regency House
Rex
Richardson Bros.
Ridgeway Clocks
Ridgewood
Riverside
Rock City
Royal Patina
Saloom
Sam Moore
Schnadig
Sealy
Seay
Selig
Serta Mattress
Simply Southern
Skillcraft
Sleepworks
Sligh
South Sea Rattan
Southern Craftsmen's
        Guild
Southern Furniture
Southwood
Spring Air Mattress
Stakmore
Stanton-Cooper

Statesville Chair
Statton
Stiffel
Stoneville
Stratalounger
Stratford
Sumter Cabinet
Superior
Swaim
Swan Brass
Taylor-King
Taylorsville Upholstery
Telescope
Temple-Stuart
Temple Upholstery
The Chair Co.
Timberwood Trading Co.
Tradition France
Tropitone
Universal
Uttermost
Uwharrie Chair
Vanguard
Vaughn
Vaughn-Bassett
Veneman
Venture
Victorian Classics
Villageois, Inc.
Virginia House
Virginia Metalcrafters
Walton
Wambold
Waterford
Webb
Weiman
Wesley Allen
Wesley Hall
Whitaker
Wildwood
Winston
Wisconsin
Woodard
Woodmark Originals
Wright Tables
Yesteryear Wicker
Yorkshire Leather

Alan Ferguson Associates

422 South Main St.
High Point, NC 27260

Phone:	(336) 889-3866	**Hours:**	M-F 9:00-5:00, Sat 10:00-4:00
Toll Free:	None	**E-mail:**	None
Fax:	(336) 889-6271	**Web site:**	None

This is a wonderful source for high-end contemporary and traditional furnishings. The ground floor has a beautifully decorated traditional showroom. There are some lovely antiques, as well as new pieces from Wellington Hall, Thayer Coggin, Bevan-Funnell and many other lines. Most of the furniture here is 40%-50% off retail.

Alan Ferguson Associates specializes in the unusual, even among their traditional lines. If you're looking for an 8 1/2 foot tall entertainment center for a high-ceilinged room, for instance, they've got one.

The entire second floor is devoted to contemporary furnishings. They have a particularly nice selection of contemporary dining room sets, such as the one from Sirio pictured at right. This set retails for $7,720.00, but here it only costs $3,860.00, 50% off. They also have a nice assortment of contemporary occasional chairs.

If you're on the lookout for contemporary furniture and accessories, or something just a bit out of the ordinary in the traditional vein, you should definitely visit this source!

Lines carried:

Accessories International	Country Affaire-Elden	George Kovacs Lamps	Mila Glassware
Allusions	Dale Tiffany Inc.	Heirloom Upholstery	Niels Ole Hansen
Ambience	DIA Metal Furniture	Italmond	Oriental Lacquer
Andrew Pearson Design	Directional Upholstery	John Richard	Preview Upholstery
Arte De Mexico	Elements By Grapevine	Johnston Casuals	Quoizel
AXI	Ello Casegoods & Chairs	Lane	Sirio
Bevan-Funnell	Fabrica Rugs	Lee Upholstery	Speer Lamps
Cambridge Lamps	Ferguson Copeland	Leeazanne	Swaim
Casa Bique	Fine Art Lamps	Lexington	Thayer Coggin
Casa Stradivari	Fire Farm Lamps	Lorts	Van Teal
Charleston Forge	Furniture Guild Casegoods	Maitland Smith	Wasserklar
Corsican	General Store Iron Furniture	Masland	Wellington Hall

Phone orders accepted:	Yes
Discount:	40%-50% off mfrs. suggested retail
Payment methods:	VISA, MC, personal checks
Deposits required:	50% deposit when order is placed, balance due when furniture is ready to be shipped
Catalog available:	No
Clearance center:	No
Delivery:	Full service in-home delivery and set-up. Customer pays freight company directly for shipping costs.

Directions: Alan Ferguson Associates is in downtown High Point, NC. From I-85, take exit #111 (Hwy. 311), and head northwest into High Point. After several miles, when you reach downtown High Point, Hwy. 311 will become S. Main St. Alan Ferguson Associates is on the left hand side of the road, right past the Atrium furniture mall.

Alan Ferguson Associates (cont.)

Alan Ferguson Associates

Contemporary dining room set from Sirio

Retail: $7,720.00   Discounted price: $3,860.00
Savings at Alan Ferguson Associates: $3,860.00 = 50% off retail

Alman's Home Furnishings

110 E. First St.
Newton, NC 28658

Phone:	**(704) 464-3204**	**Hours:**	**M-F 9:00-5:00**
Toll Free:	**(800) 729-0422**	**E-mail:**	**almanfurn@twave.net**
Fax:	**(704) 464-3208**	**Web site:**	**www.almanfurniture.com**

Family owned and operated since 1946, Alman's is a well-established discounter for many medium to high end lines including Hooker, Bassett, Stanley, Natuzzi, and Lexington, among many others.

Their galleries occupy four large buildings in downtown Newton, NC, about ten miles southeast of Hickory, NC. Alman's is certainly worth a visit if you're in the Hickory area.

If you're ordering furniture by phone, definitely check Alman's prices. They have one of the best phone order policies I've ever seen: they accept credit cards for your final payment as well as your deposit, they have a written satisfaction guarantee, etc. Their reputation for customer service is excellent.

Lines carried:

Action Lane	Chromcraft	Klaussner	Pulaski
American Drew	Clark Casual	Lane	Rex
Ashley	Cochrane	Lea	Ridgewood
Barcolounger	Craftique	Lexington	Riverside
Bassett	Flexsteel	Lloyd Flanders	Richardson Brothers
Benchcraft	Hammary	Lyon Shaw	Singer Furniture
Berkline	Henry Link	Morgan Stewart	Southern Furniture
Berkshire	Highland House	Morganton Chair	Stanley
Broyhill	Hooker	National Mt. Airy	Universal
Clayton Marcus	J. Royale	Natuzzi	Vanguard
Classic Leather	Keller	Nichols and Stone	Vaughan
Charleston Forge	Kincaid	Palliser	Wesley Allen

Phone orders accepted:	**Yes**
Discount:	**Approximately 50% off mfrs. suggested retail**
Payment methods:	**VISA, MC, AMEX, Discover, personal checks**
In-house financing available:	**Yes**
Deposits required:	**25% deposit when order is placed, balance due when furniture is ready to be shipped**
Catalog available:	**No**
Clearance center:	**No**
Delivery:	**Full service in-home delivery and set-up. Customer pays freight company directly for shipping costs.**

Directions: **Alman's is located near Hickory, NC. From I-40, take the Hwy. 16 exit (exit #131). Go south five miles to downtown Newton. Turn left at the courthouse.**

American Accents

The Atrium
430 S. Main St.
High Point, NC 27260

Phone:	**(336) 885-7412**	**Hours:**	**M-F 9:00-6:00, Sat 9:00-5:00**
Toll Free:	**None**	**E-mail:**	**None**
Fax:	**(336) 884-4171**	**Web site:**	**None**

American Accents is definitely a great source to check out. They specialize in high-quality shaker and country reproductions, so if you want the early American look, this is the place to go.

This source also carries a nice variety of high-quality but lesser known lines that have the same look as better known brands. For instance, they had a very nice solid oak arts & crafts dining room set on display from Arts & Crafts Industries that was indistinguishable from the identical dining room set I viewed at the Stickley factory sale. The only thing that wasn't identical was the price tag. Arts & Crafts Industries was considerably less expensive than Stickley for the very same quality and appearance.

Pictured on the following page, the Arts & Crafts Industries dining room set I viewed at American Accents was priced at $7,689.00 for the table, four side chairs, two arm chairs, the hutch, and a separate buffet. I was then able to haggle the salesman down to $7,000.00 even if I made the purchase that day. Compare that to Stickley's prices on the identical products! American Accents also carries some very nice arts & crafts style furniture from Brown Street and Skillcraft.

If you're looking for the "Bob Timberlake" look, you might want to check out pieces by Chatham County at American Accents instead of the pricier, but nearly identical, authorized Bob Timberlake line by Lexington. The quality was excellent, and I seriously doubt that anyone could tell the difference without looking inside the drawers for the Bob Timberlake tag.

I was very impressed with American Accents. If you're looking for the "latest in-thing" by Stickley, Bob Timberlake, or any other line, you would be doing yourself a big favor to call American Accents and see what they have to offer. If you'll be in High Point in person, don't forget to check out their clearance center!

Lines carried:	**Please see page 18**
Phone orders accepted:	**Yes**
Discount:	**40%-55% off mfrs. suggested retail**
Payment methods:	**Cash or personal checks. No credit cards.**
In-house financing available:	**No**
Deposits required:	**1\3 deposit when order is placed, balance due when furniture is ready to be shipped**
Catalog available:	**No**
Clearance center:	**Yes - See American Accents Clearance Center**
Delivery:	**Full service in-home delivery and set-up. Customer pays freight company directly for shipping costs.**

Directions: American Accents is located inside the Atrium complex in downtown High Point. Please see The Atrium for complete directions.

American Accents (cont.)

Mission oak dining room set from Arts & Crafts Industries

Retail: $12,815.00   Discounted price: $7,000.00
Savings at American Accents: $5,815.00 = 45% off retail

Lines carried:

Ashton Pictures	Cassady	Heritage House	Orderest
Athens	Charleston Forge	Kingsley Bates	Park Place
Bassett	Chatham	Lt. Moses Willard Lamps	Penns Creek
Big Sky Carvers	Cherry Pond Designs	Masterfield	Philadelphia
Bradco	Classic Rattan	McKay Table Pad	Phillips Furniture
Brown Street	Conover Chair	Mobel	P & P Chair
Cape Craftsmen	E. R. Buck	Mohawk	Skillcraft
Carolina Choice	Edrich Mills Wood Shop	Null	The Chair Co.
Cast Classics	Friendship	Ohio Table Pad	Two Day Design

American Accents Clearance Center

1300 S. Main St.
High Point, NC 27260

Phone:	**(336) 885-1304**	**Hours:**	**M-F 9:00-6:00, Sat 9:00-5:30**
Toll Free:	**None**	**E-mail:**	**None**
Fax:	**(336) 884-4171**	**Web site:**	**None**

American Accents Clearance Center carries customer returns, discontinued items, and floor samples from the American Accents showroom in the Atrium complex in High Point. Most of their stock is early American and shaker, but there are also some other traditional styles mixed in.

The deals here are very good. Pictured on the following page is a terrific deal they had on a solid pine entertainment center. It was in perfect condition and only $549.00.

They will also sell by phone if you know what you want and they have it on the sale floor. If you're in High Point, definitely stop in here.

Lines carried:

Ashton Pictures	Cassady	Heritage House	Orderest
Athens	Charleston Forge	Kingsley Bates	Park Place
Bassett	Chatham	Lt. Moses Willard Lamps	Penns Creek
Big Sky Carvers	Cherry Pond Designs	Masterfield	Philadelphia
Bradco	Classic Rattan	McKay Table Pad	Phillips Furniture
Brown Street	Conover Chair	Mobel	P & P Chair
Cape Craftsmen	E. R. Buck	Mohawk	Skillcraft
Carolina Choice	Edrich Mills Wood Shop	Null	The Chair Co.
Cast Classics	Friendship	Ohio Table Pad	Two Day Design

Phone orders accepted:	**Yes**
Discount:	**50%-60% off mfrs. suggested retail**
Payment methods:	**Cash or personal checks. No credit cards.**
In-house financing available:	**No**
Deposits required:	**Payment in full required at time of purchase**
Catalog available:	**No**
Clearance center:	**Not applicable**
Delivery:	**Company's own trucks in some areas, otherwise a full-service delivery company. Customer pays freight company directly for shipping costs.**

Directions: **American Accents Clearance Center is in downtown High Point, NC. From I-85, take exit #111 (Hwy. 311), and head northwest into High Point. After several miles, when you reach downtown High Point, Hwy. 311 will become S. Main St. American Accents Clearance Center is on the left hand side of the road, at the intersection of S. Main St. and Kearns Ave. Turn left on Kearns Ave., and park behind the store.**

American Accents Clearance Center (cont.)

American Accents Clearance Center

Solid pine entertainment center from American Accents

Retail: $1,099.00   Discounted price: $549.00
Savings at American Accents: $550.00 = 50% off retail

American Reproductions

The Atrium
430 S. Main St.
High Point, NC 27260

Phone:	**(336) 889-8305**	**Hours:**	**M-F 9:00-6:00, Sat 9:00-5:00**
Toll Free:	**None**	**E-mail:**	**american@northstate.net**
Fax:	**(336) 889-8302**	**Web site:**	**www.americanreproductions.com**

American Reproductions has a gorgeous showroom in the Atrium furniture complex in High Point. They have a very nice selection of high end traditional reproduction furniture.

For instance, they had a very nice mahogany triple arch bookcase from Hooker (pictured on the following page) for only $1800, down from a retail of $3,360.00. I was able to haggle the salesman down to $1665.00 for this piece if I bought it that day. Most pieces are marked at about 40% off retail, but you can haggle them down to about 50% off on many brands if you try. A few lines are as much as 70% off retail.

If you are looking for something unique in high-end traditional furniture, definitely visit this showroom. This source also accepts phone orders and ships nationwide.

Lines carried:

A. A. Laun	Brady Furniture	Cottage Pine	Executive Leather
American Chair & Table	Braxton Culler	Cox Furniture Mfg.	Fairfield Chair Co.
American Of High Point	British Collector's Ed.	Craftmaster	Fine Art
American Impressions	British Traditions	Crawford Furniture Co.	General Store Inc.
Amindo	Brown-Jordan	C. R. Laine Upholstery	Green Door
Amiran Corporation	Bruce L. Robertson	Custom Shoppe	Hickory Hill Furniture
Andre' Originals Mfg.	Butler Specialty Co.	D & F Wicker & Rattan	Hooker
Artistica	Cal-Bear	Imports	JDI Group
Barcalounger	Cambridge Lamps	David Kent	John Richard Collection
Bassett	Charleston Forge	Designer Wicker	Kessler Industries
Benchcraft Rattan	Chatham County	Designmaster Furniture	Klaussner Upholstery
Benicia East Inc.	Conestoga Wood Inc.	Eagle Craft Desks	Kimball Furniture
Bevan Funnel Ltd.	Cooper Classics	El Condor	Kings Creek Inc.
Black Hawk Furniture Inc.	Corsican Brass	Elliott's Designs Inc.	Lane Co.

Phone orders accepted:	**Yes**
Discount:	**40%-70% off mfrs. suggested retail**
Payment methods:	**VISA, MC, personal checks**
In-house financing available:	**No**
Deposits required:	**50% deposit when order is placed, balance due when furniture is ready to be shipped**
Catalog available:	**No**
Clearance center:	**No**
Delivery:	**Full service in-home delivery and set-up. Customer pays freight company directly for shipping costs.**

Directions: American Reproductions is located inside the Atrium complex in downtown High Point. Please see *The Atrium* for complete directions.

American Reproductions (cont.)

Solid mahogany triple-arch bookcase from Hooker

Retail: $3,360.00   Discounted price: $1,665.00
Savings at American Reproductions: $1,695.00 = 50% off retail

Lines carried (cont.):

Legacy Leather Furniture	North Franklin Furniture	Royal Patina Inc.	Temple Inc.
Leisters Furniture	Oakwood Interiors	Sam Moore	Tom Seely Furniture
Ligo Products Inc.	Ohio Table Pad Co.	Sarreid, Ltd.	Traditional Heirlooms
Lloyd/Flanders Wicker	PAMA	Sealy Furniture	Uwharrie Chair
Lyon-Shaw Inc.	Pennsylvania Classics	Serta Mattress	Vaughan Furniture Co.
Maison Square	Peters Revington	Sleepworks. Inc.	Wall Street Designs
Master Design Furniture	Pine-Tique Furniture	Sligh Furniture Co.	Waterford Furniture
McKay Custom Products	Pulaski Furniture Corp.	Southern Furniture	William Alan, Inc.
Michaels Company	Rex Furniture Co.	Spring Air Mattress	Winners Only
Mobel, Inc.	Riverside Furniture Co.	Stylecraft	Winston Furniture Ind.
Mohawk Furniture Inc.	Rock City Furniture	Taylor King	Wisconsin

Arts By Alexander

701 Greensboro Rd.
High Point, NC 27260

Phone:	(336) 884-8062	**Hours:**	M-F 8:30-5:00, Sat 9:00-4:00
Toll Free:	None	**E-mail:**	None
Fax:	(336) 884-8064	**Web site:**	None

Arts By Alexander has a lovely high-end gallery in High Point. Most of their stock is traditional, but they do also have some contemporary and outdoor lines. They also have a nice selection of oriental furniture. There are no market samples or discontinued pieces in stock.

Lines carried:

Accentrics by Pulaski	CBK Ltd., Inc.	Garcia Imports	Pulaski Furniture
American Of High Point	Cebu Imports	Gatco	Sarreid Ltd.
Artisan House	Chapman Mfg. Co.	Hart Associates	Scullini
Artisan's Guild	Charles Sadek Imports	Hickory Leather	Stiffel Lamps
Autumn Guild	Charles Serouya	Interlude	Swan/Corsican Beds
Bassett	Charleston Forge	JDI Inc.	Tapestries Ltd.
Boling Chair	Clark Casual Furniture	Johnston Casuals	Telescope Casual Furniture
Bradburn Company	Classic Traditions	Kinder-Harris	Thayer Coggin
Bradington-Young	Comfort Designs	LaBarge Mirrors	Tropitone
Brasscrafters	Corona Decor	Lane	Tyndale Lamps
Braxton Culler	Crawford Furniture	Lloyd/Flanders	Universal Furniture
Butler Specialty Co.	Davis & Small	Lyon-Shaw Inc.	Uttermost
Cal-Bear	Decorative Crafts, Inc.	Mario Lamps	Virginia Metalcrafters
Carolina Mirror Corp.	Edward P. Paul	Miller Import Co.	Wellington Hall
Carter Furniture	Elements By Grapevine	Oriental Accents	Winston Furniture Co.
Carver's Guild	Fashion Bed Group	Oriental Lacquer	Woodard Furniture
Casa Bique	Fort Steuben	Park Place Corp.	Woodmark/Stanton Cooper
Casa Stradivari	Frederick Cooper Lamps	Passport Furniture, Inc.	

Phone orders accepted:	Yes
Discount:	**40%-50% off mfrs. suggested retail**
Payment methods:	**Cash or personal checks**
In-house financing available:	No
Deposits required:	**30% deposit when order is placed, balance due when furniture is ready to be shipped**
Catalog available:	No
Clearance center:	No
Delivery:	**Full service in-home delivery and set-up. Customer pays freight company directly for shipping costs.**

Directions: From I-85, take exit #111 (Hwy. 311), and head northwest into High Point. Go completely through downtown High Point until you come to Lexington Ave. Turn right on Lexington. Arts By Alexander will be about 3 miles down on the left.

Ashley Interiors (Braxton Culler Factory Outlet)

310 S. Elm St.
(inside the Braxton Culler Bldg.)
High Point, NC 27260

Phone:	**(336) 889-7333**	**Hours:**	**M-Sat 9:00-5:00**
Toll Free:	**None**		**Closed April and October**
Fax:	**None**	**E-mail:**	**None**
		Web site:	**None**

Ashley Interiors is a retailer of new furniture, but they also function as the Braxton Culler factory outlet. They will take orders by phone or in person for new furniture from Braxton Culler's current line at 50% off the manufacturer's suggested retail.

The showroom also has a limited selection of Braxton Culler floor samples and discontinued styles at 75% off retail. These can be purchased by phone if you know exactly what style you want and the outlet happens to have it on the sales floor.

This showroom is closed during April and October due to the bi-annual High Point International Home Furnishings Market, when retailers from all over the U. S. converge on High Point, NC, to see and purchase the latest furniture styles. However, just prior to closing for market, Ashley Interiors normally has a special sale where all items, including those from Braxton Culler's current line, are marked down to 75% off retail. These sales normally run for the entire months of March and September.

So, if you're planning a trip to the High Point area in March or September, you should definitely check out this outlet. If you specifically wish to purchase new Braxton Culler furniture, you should strongly consider waiting for the March or September sale and buying it here. I haven't seen any other source that can match Ashley Interiors' special sale prices on the Braxton Culler line.

Phone orders accepted:	Yes
Discount:	**50%-75% off mfrs. suggested retail**
Payment methods:	**VISA, MC, AMEX, personal checks**
In-house financing available:	**No**
Deposits required:	**35% deposit when order is placed, balance due when furniture is ready to be shipped**
Catalog available:	**No**
Clearance center:	**Not applicable**
Delivery:	**Full service in-home delivery and set-up. Customer pays freight company directly for shipping costs.**

Directions: **From I-85, take exit #111 (Hwy. 311), and head northwest into High Point. Go several miles into downtown High Point. Just after you pass The Atrium furniture mall and Alan Ferguson associates on your left, turn left at the next light onto Russell Ave. Ashley Interiors, inside the Braxton Culler Bldg., is one block down on your right on the corner of Russell and Elm St.**

The Atrium

430 S. Main St.
High Point, NC 27260

Phone:	(336) 882-5599	**Hours:**	M-F 9:00-6:00, Sat 9:00-5:00
Toll Free:	None	**E-mail:**	sales@theatrium.com
Fax:	(336) 882-6950	**Web site:**	www.theatrium.com

The Atrium Furniture Mall is a huge four-story building in downtown High Point which contains 22 furniture showrooms. Several of the showrooms are true factory outlets. The remainder are legitimate discounters which have good bargains on hundreds of different lines.

Please see the individual listings in this book for each gallery or outlet for details on payment, shipping, lines carried, etc:

American Accents	(336) 885-7412
American Reproductions	(336) 889-8305
Decorators Choice	(336) 889-6115
FEFCO Fine Furniture	(336) 882-0180
French Heritage Outlet	(336) 884-0022
Hickory Park	(336) 883-3800
Home Focus	(336) 882-7031
Kagan's American Drew	(336) 885-8568
Kagan's Gallery	(336) 885-1333
Kagan's Gallery	(336) 885-8300
Kincaid Galleries	(800) 527-2570
Leather Unlimited	(336) 885-4386
Medallion Furniture	(336) 889-3432
Pennsylvania House	(336) 886-5200
Robert Bergelin Co.	(800) 296-7977
Wood-Armfield	(336) 889-6522
World Of Leather	(336) 887-2060
Zagaroli Classics	(336) 882-7385

The Atrium has some good bargains on airfares and trip packages to the High Point area, so definitely call their main office above when making your travel plans.

They also have two very good mall-wide sales in May and November, right after the bi-annual High Point International Home Furnishings Market. Many other factory outlets and showrooms in the High Point area have special sales during these months, too, so you may wish to plan any trips to High Point to take advantage of these extra discounts.

Directions:	**The Atrium Furniture Mall is in downtown High Point, NC. From I-85, take exit #111 (Hwy. 311), and head northwest into High Point. After several miles, when you reach downtown High Point, Hwy. 311 will become S. Main St. The Atrium Furniture Mall is on the left hand side of the road, right next to Alan Ferguson Associates.**

The Atrium (cont.)

The Atrium Furniture Mall

Baker Factory Outlet

146 West Ave.
Kannapolis, NC 28081

Phone:	(704) 938-9191	**Hours:**	M-Sat 9:00-6:00
Toll Free:	None	**E-mail:**	None
Fax:	(704) 932-2503	**Web site:**	None

The Baker Factory Outlet is located inside the Village Furniture House in Cannon Village. This is Baker's original North Carolina factory outlet, and they do have some great deals.

Most of the stock here are floor samples and discontinued styles in new first-quality condition. Of course, Baker is a very high-end line, so the furniture here is gorgeous. There's a nice selection of case goods and some upholstery.

On my most recent visit here, I found a Baker Hepplewhite desk (pictured on the following page) that normally retails for $3,416.00 marked down to only $1,499.00. It was a floor sample in first-quality condition.

If you are traveling to North Carolina to buy furniture, you really should consider taking one extra day to visit Cannon Village in Kannapolis. In addition to the Baker outlet, there are also true factory outlets for Century and Maitland-Smith here that are well worth a visit. Kannapolis is about one half hour's drive north of Charlotte, one hour's drive south of High Point, and one hour's drive east of Hickory.

Phone orders accepted:	**No**
Discount:	**60%-75% off mfrs. suggested retail**
Payment methods:	**Personal checks. No credit cards.**
In-house financing available:	**No**
Deposits required:	**Not applicable**
Catalog available:	**Not applicable**
Clearance center:	**Not applicable**
Delivery:	**Full service in-home delivery and set-up. Customer pays freight company directly for shipping costs.**

Directions: **From I-85, take exit #63, and follow the signs to Cannon Village. The Baker Factory Outlet is accessible through the Village Furniture House on West Ave. inside Cannon Village.**

Baker Factory Outlet (cont.)

Baker Furniture Factory Outlet in Kannapolis, NC

Hepplewhite desk from Baker Furniture

Retail: $3,416.00   Discounted price: $1,499.00
Savings at the Baker Furniture Factory Outlet: $1,917.00 = 56% off retail

Baker Odds & Ends (Factory Outlet)

765-J Woodlake Rd.
Kohler, WI 53044

Phone:	**(920) 458-2033**	**Hours:**	**M-F 10:00-6:00, Sat 10:00-5:00**
Toll Free:	**None**		**Sun 12:00-5:00**
Fax:	**None**	**E-mail:**	**None**
		Web site:	**None**

Baker Odds & Ends in Kohler, WI, is the first of Baker Furniture's new outlets direct to the public. Baker is owned by the Kohler Co., which is based here. Kohler, WI, is a suburb of Sheboygan, WI, about one hour's drive north of Milwaukee on Interstate 43. The store is a bit small compared to most furniture factory outlets, but it does have some very good bargains.

On my last visit here, I found a very nice mahogany dining room set from Baker's Williamsburg Reproduction Collection (pictured on the following page). The table normally retails for $6,286.00, but the outlet price was only $2,995.00. The chairs normally retail for $2,091.00 each, but the outlet had them for only $795.00 apiece. The total discount was about 55% off Baker's normal retail price on this set. The set I found at the outlet was a floor sample in new first-quality condition.

The outlet has a good variety of upholstered pieces, beds, desks, armoires, chests, etc. Most pieces are floor samples from the various Baker wholesale showrooms in design centers around the U. S. Some are overruns from their manufacturing plants in nearby Holland, MI, and Grand Rapids, MI. There are a few seconds, but the vast majority of the stock here is in new first-quality condition. New pieces arrive every Wednesday. If you're going to be in the Milwaukee or Madison area, you should definitely consider taking a side trip to this outlet.

Baker is rumored to be opening more Odds & Ends stores around the U. S. in the near future. I will post announcements at www.smartdecorating.com of each new Baker factory outlet as they open.

Phone orders accepted:	**No**
Discount:	**60%-75% off mfrs. suggested retail**
Payment methods:	**VISA, MC, AMEX, Discover, personal checks**
In-house financing available:	**No**
Deposits required:	**Not applicable**
Catalog available:	**No**
Clearance center:	**Not applicable**
Delivery:	**A separate company, Jim's Delivery, makes deliveries from this outlet to Chicago and various points in Indiana and Michigan. Please call (920) 565-3738 for more information. Other customers must make their own arrangements to take purchases home.**

Directions: **From I-43, take exit #126 (Hwy. 23) and head west into Kohler, WI. After about 2/3 of a mile, take the "Y" exit into the village of Kohler. You will see the Shops at Woodlake on your left. Baker Odds & Ends is near the center of the Shops at Woodlake strip mall.**

Baker Odds & Ends (Factory Outlet) (cont.)

Inside Baker Odds & Ends in Kohler, WI

Williamsburg Reproduction mahogany dining room set from Baker Furniture

Retail: $14,650.00   Discounted price: $6,175.00
Savings at Baker Odds & Ends: $8,475.00 = 58% off retail

Baker Odds & Ends (Factory Outlet)

10027 Manchester Rd.
Warson Woods, MO 63122

Phone:	(314) 909-7902	**Hours:**	M-F 10:00-8:00, Sat 10:00-5:00
Toll Free:	None		Sun 12:00-5:00
Fax:	None	**E-mail:**	None
		Web site:	None

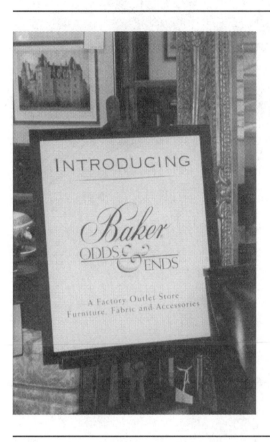

Baker Odds & Ends in the St. Louis area is the newest of Baker Furniture's direct outlets to the public. Like the first Baker Odds & Ends store in Kohler, WI, the outlet is fairly small, but it has some terrific bargains.

On my most recent visit here, I found a beautiful mahogany highboy from Baker's Williamsburg Reproduction Collection (pictured on the following page) for 62% off retail. This piece normally retails for $26,140.00, but the outlet had one available for $9,995.00. It was a floor sample in new first-quality condition.

This outlet has a nice variety of upholstered pieces, beds, desks, armoires, chests, etc. Most pieces are floor samples from the various Baker wholesale showrooms in design centers all over the U. S. There are a few seconds, but the vast majority of the stock here is in new first-quality condition. New pieces arrive every week. If you're going to be in the St. Louis area, you should definitely check out this outlet.

Baker is rumored to be opening more Odds & Ends stores around the U. S. in the near future. I will post announcements at www.smartdecorating.com of each new Baker factory outlet as they open.

Phone orders accepted:	No
Discount:	**60%-75% off mfrs. suggested retail**
Payment methods:	**VISA, MC, AMEX, Discover, personal checks**
In-house financing available:	No
Deposits required:	**Not applicable**
Catalog available:	No
Clearance center:	**Not applicable**
Delivery:	**Delivery in St. Louis area for a flat $75 fee per trip, regardless of the amount of furniture purchased. Out-of-town customers must make their own arrangements to take purchases home.**

Directions: **From the I-270 perimeter around St. Louis, take exit #9 (Manchester Rd.) and head east into St. Louis. Baker Odds & Ends is about 3 miles down on the right side of Manchester Rd.**

Baker Odds & Ends (Factory Outlet) (cont.)

Baker Odds & Ends in St. Louis, MO (Warson Woods)

Williamsburg Reproduction mahogany highboy from Baker Furniture

Retail: $26,140.00   Discounted price: $9,995.00
Savings at Baker Odds & Ends: $16,145.00 = 62% off retail

Bassett Furniture Direct

121 North Coley
Tupelo, MS 38801

Phone:	**(601) 841-0222**	**Hours:**	**M-Sat 9:00-7:00, Sun 1:00-5:00**
Toll Free:	**None**	**E-mail:**	**None**
Fax:	**(601) 841-2814**	**Web site:**	**www.bassettfurniture.com**

Bassett Furniture Direct in Tupelo is part of Bassett Furniture's new chain of outlets direct to the public. They also have stores in Springdale, AR; Augusta, GA; Wilmington, DE; Baton Rouge, LA; and Jackson, MS; with more opening soon. I will post announcements at www.smartdecorating.com of each new Bassett Furniture Direct store as they open.

Bassett Furniture Direct isn't a true factory outlet in the sense of being a place to liquidate floor samples, seconds, irregulars, and returns. Bassett has no factory owned outlet for that purpose. Bassett Furniture Direct is exactly like a traditional furniture store except that it's owned by the manufacturer itself, much as Ethan Allen has done for years.

Bassett does significantly discount its furniture here. Most pieces are about 30% off retail. Designers and decorators receive an extra 10% off everything. However, I have found better discounts on Bassett furniture from various order-by-phone furniture discounters who still carry the line. By all means, check Bassett's prices at their own stores, but don't assume that they are the lowest prices out there on this brand.

On my most recent trip to their Tupelo store, I found a good deal on a Mission Oak bedroom set from their Grove Park Collection (pictured on the following page). The bed, entertainment center, nightstand, chest, and mirror normally retail separately for $4,843.00, but you can order the same set through Bassett Furniture Direct for only $2,996.00, or about 38% off.

Be sure to pick up a catalog at the service counter when you visit the store or request one when you call. They generally have a $25.00 off gift certificate in the back which can be used on any purchase of $50.00 or more.

Phone orders accepted:	**Yes**
Discount:	**Approximately 30% off mfrs. suggested retail (Decorators and designers receive 40% off)**
Payment methods:	**VISA, MC, or personal check**
In-house financing available:	**Yes**
Deposits required:	**20% deposit when order is placed, balance due when furniture is ready to be shipped**
Catalog available:	**Yes**
Clearance center:	**No**
Delivery:	**Full service in-home delivery and set-up. Customer pays freight company directly for shipping costs.**

Directions: **From Hwy. 78, take the Belden exit. You don't have a choice of which way to turn. The exit will automatically put you in the right direction. Go to the 2nd traffic light and turn right (you'll see a Shell station on the corner) onto Coley Rd. Basset Furniture Direct is on the right side of the road, about a mile past the Tupelo Furniture Market.**

Bassett Furniture Direct (cont.)

Bassett Furniture Direct

Mission Oak bedroom set from Bassett Furniture

Retail: $4,843.00   Discounted price: $2,996.00
Savings at Bassett Furniture Direct: $1,847.00 = 38% off retail

Beacon Hill Factory Outlet

Inside the Henredon/Drexel Heritage Factory Outlet
3004-A Parquet Dr.
Dalton, GA 30720

I'm sorry to have to report that this terrific outlet closed on February 1, 1999. I was told that the outlet was closed at the request of certain furniture retailers in the Atlanta area who objected to having this outlet located 75 miles away from their stores.

It is an unfortunate fact of life in the home furnishings industry that manufacturers who sell directly to the public are often subjected to extreme pressure from the retailers whose profit margins shrink as a result. Every time this kind of bullying from retailers results in the closure of another factory outlet or deep discounter, you and I all pay higher prices for furniture as a result.

The best way to combat this problem is for all consumers to pressure manufacturers to keep selling through factory outlets and deep discounters. Vote with your checkbook. Pressure manufacturers to sell in a way that is in YOUR best interests, rather than in the middlemen's best interests.

Fortunately, there are still two terrific Beacon Hill factory outlets in Hickory, NC, and this line is sold over the phone by a number of deep discounters.

Beacon Hill Factory Outlet
Levels 1 & 2
Hickory Furniture Mart
U. S. Hwy. 70 SE
Hickory, NC 28602

Phone:	**(828) 324-2220**	**Hours:**	**M-Sat 9:00-6:00**
Toll Free:	**None**	**E-mail:**	**info@hickoryfurniture.com**
Fax:	**(828) 323-8445**	**Web site:**	**www.hickoryfurniture.com**

   The Drexel-Heritage/Beacon Hill Factory Outlet at the Hickory Furniture Mart is huge, covering over one-eighth of the entire square footage of the Mart between its two levels. This outlet also serves as a factory-owned factory outlet for Drexel-Heritage, La Barge, Baldwin Brass, and Maitland Smith.

   Most of the stock here is in new first-quality condition: floor samples, customer returns, discontinued items, and stock overruns. There is a fairly even mix of case goods and upholstery.

   Their normal discount runs between 50% to 80%. In January, the outlet runs a month-long sale with even bigger discounts. During the sale, all items are 75% to 80% off retail. The outlet also runs shorter sales in May and September with the same discounts.

   The outlet will not take phone orders for new furniture from Beacon Hill's current lines, but if you know exactly which item you want, they will see if they have that particular style in stock at the outlet and allow you to order it by phone. They do accept credit cards for payment, and they will arrange shipping. They do require you to pay in full for the item when your order is placed, but they also ship almost immediately.

   This outlet, along with the Hickory Furniture Mart in general, is a "must-visit" on any trip to Hickory, NC. If you don't find exactly what you want at this outlet, Drexel Heritage/Beacon Hill does have another outlet nearby in Hickory that is also very impressive.

   Please also see the listings under Hickory Furniture Mart for more information on travel bargains to the Mart and ways of saving money on shipping.

Phone orders accepted:	**Yes**
Discount:	**50%-80% off mfrs. suggested retail**
Payment methods:	**VISA, MC, AMEX, personal checks**
In-house financing available:	**No**
Deposits required:	**Full payment due with order**
Catalog available:	**No**
Clearance center:	**Not applicable**
Delivery:	**Full service in-home delivery and set-up. Customer pays freight company directly for shipping costs.**

Directions: Please see *Hickory Furniture Mart* for complete directions.

Benchcraft Factory Outlet

703 Coley Rd.
Tupelo, MS 38803

Phone:	**(601) 841-1329**	**Hours:**	**M-Sat 9:30-5:30**
Toll Free:	**None**	**E-mail:**	**None**
Fax:	**(601) 844-9063**	**Web site:**	**None**

This is Benchcraft's only true factory outlet, near their factory in Tupelo. They have a good selection of upholstered furniture, primarily recliners and leather sofas. The quality is medium-end, and most of the items in stock are in new first-quality condition. There are a few seconds in-stock, but they were very well marked and kept in a separate room in the back of the outlet.

On my last visit here, I found a very nice first-quality leather sofa (pictured on the following page). The retail on this sofa is normally $1,172.00, but the outlet had several for only $384.00.

If you're looking for good deals on medium-quality upholstery, this outlet is definitely worth a visit.

Phone orders accepted:	**No**
Discount:	**50%-75% off mfrs. suggested retail**
Payment methods:	**Personal checks. No credit cards.**
In-house financing available:	**Yes**
Deposits required:	**Not applicable**
Catalog available:	**No**
Clearance center:	**Not applicable**
Delivery:	**No delivery available. Customer's must make their own arrangements to take furniture home.**

Directions: **From Hwy. 78, take the Belden exit. You don't have a choice of which way to turn. The exit will automatically put you in the right direction. Go to the 2nd traffic light and turn right (you'll see a Shell station on the corner) onto Coley Rd. The Benchcraft Factory Outlet is on the right side of the road, just past the Tupelo Furniture Market.**

Benchcraft Factory Outlet (cont.)

Benchcraft Factory Outlet

Leather sofa from Benchcraft

Retail: $1,172.00   Discounted price: $384.00
Savings at the Benchcraft Factory Outlet: $788.00 = 67% off retail

Bernhardt Factory Outlet

Manufacturer-Owned Factory Outlets (Lenoir Mall)
1031 Morganton Blvd.
Lenoir, NC 28645

Phone:	(828) 758-0532	**Hours:**	M-Sat 10:00-7:00, Sun 1:00-5:00
Toll Free:	None	**E-mail:**	None
Fax:	None	**Web site:**	www.bernhardtfurniture.com

This is Bernhardt's only factory outlet nationwide. It's located in the Lenoir Mall, near their factory in Hickory, NC. The outlet itself is fairly large and has a good selection of upholstery and case goods. Virtually all of the furniture in stock is first-quality, although there are a few seconds and irregulars. Make sure you look each piece over very carefully because, unlike most outlets, Bernhardt does not use special coded tags to mark pieces that have flaws or damage.

Don't forget to check Bernhardt's other space right across the hall from the main outlet. They have a nice selection of occasional tables and chairs there.

This is a particularly good outlet to visit if you're looking for high-end contemporary furniture, which can be hard to find at U. S. factory outlets. They had a nice selection of contemporary upholstery and case goods, in addition to many more traditional styles.

Bernhardt has made arrangements with a local refinisher to correct any flaws or damage for $50.00-$150.00, depending on the specific job that needs to be done. They guarantee a 7 day turnaround on this service.

On my most recent visit here, I found a great bargain on an armoire (pictured on the following page). It was a discontinued style in first-quality condition. This item normally retailed for $6,225.00, but the outlet had this one in stock for only $2,490.00.

If you're in the Hickory area, this outlet should definitely be on your "must-visit" list.

Phone orders accepted:	**No**
Discount:	**65%-75% off mfrs. suggested retail**
Payment methods:	**Personal checks. No credit cards.**
In-house financing available:	**No**
Deposits required:	**Not applicable**
Catalog available:	**Not applicable**
Clearance center:	**Not applicable**
Delivery:	**Full service in-home delivery and set-up. Customer pays freight company directly for shipping costs.**

Directions: From I-40, take exit #123 (Hwy. 321) and head north through Hickory toward Lenoir. Turn left on Hwy. 64, then turn left again on the Hwy. 18S Bypass. The outlet is on the left inside Lenoir Mall.

Bernhardt Factory Outlet (cont.)

Bernhardt Factory Outlet at the Manufacturer Owned Furniture Outlets in Lenoir, NC

Armoire by Bernhardt Furniture

Retail: $6,225.00   Discounted price: $2,490.00
Savings at the Bernhardt Factory Outlet: $3,735.00 = 60% off retail

Better Homes Discount Furniture

248 1st Ave. NW
Hickory, NC 28601

Phone:	**(828) 328-8302**	**Hours:**	**M-F 9:00-5:30, Sat 9:00-5:00**
Toll Free:	**None**	**E-mail:**	**julie@interpath.com**
Fax:	**(828) 327-6088**	**Web site:**	**www.bhdf.com**

Better Homes Discount Furniture has been in business since 1917 and has an excellent reputation for selling furniture by phone. They are bonded and insured, and they back up all manufacturers' warranties.

They have some of the best discounts I've seen among North Carolina discounters, and they advertise that they will beat any other discounter's prices, so take them up on it! I've also found that they can order just about any brand of furniture, so don't take their list of advertised lines below to be the full extent of their stock. If you're ordering any brand of furniture by phone, you should definitely check this source's prices.

Lines carried:

American Drew	Clayton Marcus	Howard Miller Clocks	Pulaski
American Of Martinsville	Cochrane	J/B Ross	Richardson Bros.
Athens	Craftique	Keller	Ridgewood
Barclay	Dresher	Kincaid	Riverside
Bassett	England Corsair	Kingsdown Bedding	Rock City
Berkline	Fairfield	Kroehler	Rowe
Berkshire	Fashion Bed	Lane	Stoneville
Best Chair	Flexsteel	Lea	Universal
Blacksmith Shop	Florida Furniture	Ligo	U. S. Furniture
Broyhill	Hammary	Millennium	Vaughn
Catnapper	Hekman	Morgan Stewart	Vaughan-Bassett
Chatham County	Hickory Hill	National Mt. Airy	Winners Only
Chromecraft	Hooker	Ohio Table Pad	

Phone orders accepted:	**Yes**
Discount:	**40%-70% off mfrs. suggested retail**
Payment methods:	**Personal checks and cash**
In-house financing available:	**Yes, but only for NC residents**
Deposits required:	**25% deposit when order is placed, balance due when furniture is ready to be shipped**
Catalog available:	**No**
Clearance center:	**No**
Delivery:	**Full service in-home delivery and set-up. Customer pays freight company directly for shipping costs.**

Directions: **Better Homes Discount Furniture is in downtown Hickory, NC. From I-40, take exit #125 (Lenoir-Rhyne Rd.), and head north for one and a half miles. Turn left onto Tate Blvd. SE. Go to the first red light, and turn right onto Hwy. 127 SE. Go to the first red light, and turn left onto 1st Ave. NE. Go to the second red light, and you'll see Better Homes on your right.**

Black's Furniture Company

2800 Westchester Dr.
High Point, NC 27262

Phone:	**(336) 886-5011**	**Hours:**	**M-F 8:00-5:00, Sat 9:00-5:00**
Toll Free:	**None**	**E-mail:**	**None**
Fax:	**(336) 886-4734**	**Web site:**	**None**

Black's Furniture in High Point has a very nice store with a good selection of very high-end furniture from brands such as Hickory White, Baker, Century, Thomasville, Hooker, Lexington, and others.

Most of the furniture in-stock is new first-quality, and they charge the same price whether you buy in person or over the phone. Most brands are discounted 40%-55% off retail.

They advertise that their clearance center in the back basement is only open on the last Saturday of every month, but I've always found that you can pretty much waltz right in whenever you want. Just look for the brick-walled stairs in the far right rear corner of the store. I've never found the clearance center door locked. Unfortunately, the clearance center rarely has much in stock.

If you're planning to visit High Point in person, your time would be better spent at other factory outlets and clearance centers in the area that have a better selection of floor samples and discontinued styles at bigger discounts. However, if you plan to order your furniture over the phone, you should definitely give this source a call. They have excellent bargains on many lines.

Lines carried:	**Please see page 44**
Phone orders accepted:	**Yes**
Discount:	**40%-55% off mfrs. suggested retail**
Payment methods:	**Personal checks. No credit cards.**
In-house financing available:	**No**
Deposits required:	**1/3 deposit when order is placed, balance due when furniture is ready to be shipped**
Catalog available:	**No**
Clearance center:	**Yes**
Delivery:	**Full service in-home delivery and set-up. Customer pays freight company directly for shipping costs.**

Directions: **From I-85, take exit #111 (Hwy. 311), and head northwest into High Point. After several miles, when you reach downtown High Point, Hwy. 311 will become S. Main St. Go through High Point until you come to Westchester Ave. on the north side of town. Turn left on Westchester. Black's Furniture is a few miles down on the right side of the road.**

Black's Furniture Company (cont.)

Black's Furniture Company

Black's Furniture Company (cont.)

Lines carried (cont.):

American Drew
As You Like It Lamps
Arte de Mexico
Artistica
Baldwin Brass Beds
Barcalounger
Baker
Bassett Mirror Co.
Benicia Foundry Beds
Berkline
Bevan Funnell
Blacksmith Shop
Bradington Young
Braxton Culler
Brown Jordan
Bucks County Collection
C. R. Laine
Cal-Style
Carlton McLendon
Carsons
Casa Bique
Cebu
Century
Chapman
Charleston Forge
Chatham County
Christian Mosso
Chromecraft
Classic Gallery
Classic Leather
Classic Rattan
Clayton Marcus
Cochrane
Colgate Baby Mattress
Cooper Classics
Corsican Brass Co.
Cox
Craftique
Craftwork Guild
Crawford
Creative Metal
Crystal Clear
CTH-Carolina Tables
Daystrom
Decorative Arts
Decorative Crafts
Denny Lamps
Ducks Unlimited
Elliotts Design

Emerson et Cie
Entree
Fairfield Chair
Fashion Bed Group
Ficks Reed
Fine Arts Lamps
Flexsteel
Founders
Frederick Cooper
Fremarc
Friedman Mirrors
Garcia Imports
George Kovacs
Glass Arts
Glober
Grace Mfg.
Grandeur Beds
Great City Traders
Guildmaster
Hammary
Hart Industries
Hekman
Henry Link Wicker
Heritage Haus
Hickory Hill
Hickory Leather
Hickory-White
High Point Furniture
Hood
Hooker
Howard Miller Clocks
Hyundai
Impressions by
            Thomasville
International Images
            by Salterini
International
            Carolina Glass
Jasper Cabinet
Johnston Casuals
Kingsdown Bedding
La Barge
La-Z-Boy
Lam Lee Group
Lane
Lea
Leda
Leathercraft
Leeazanne

Lexington
Library Lamps
Link Taylor
Lloyd/Flanders
Lyon Shaw
Mario
McKay Table Pads
McKinley Leather
Madison Square
Marbro Lamps
Meadowcraft
Mikhail Darafeev
Moosehead
Nichols & Stone
Nora Fenton
Null
Ohio Table Pads
Old Hickory Tannery
OLF Oriental Lacquer
Passport
Pearson
Pennsylvania Classics
Peters Revington
Plant Plant
Pulaski
Quoizel
Rex Furniture
Riverside
Royal Patina
Sam Moore
Sarreid
Sedgefield
Sedgewick Rattan
Serta Mattress
Shady Lady
Sherrill Occasional
Swan Brass Beds
Swaim
Southern Reproductions
Stakmore
Stanton Cooper
Statesville Chair
Stiffel Lamps
Style
Superior Furniture
Telescope
Thayer Coggin
Thomasville
Tim Houting

Tropitone
Universal
Uttermost
Uwharrie Chair
Valco
Vanguard
Vaughan
Vaughan Bassett
Victorian Classics
Virginia Metalcrafters
Wesley Hall
Wesley Allen
Westwood Lamps
Wildwood
Winston
Woodard
Woodmark

Blackwelders

294 Turnersburg Hwy.
Statesville, NC 28625

Phone:	(704) 872-8921	**Hours:**	24 hours/7 days a week
Toll Free:	(800) 438-0201	**E-mail:**	jblackwelder@i-america.net
Fax:	(704) 872-4491	**Web site:**	www.homefurnish.com/blackwelders

Blackwelder's is a phone-order-only service from Statesville, NC, right between Hickory and High Point. They've been in the furniture business for over 60 years, and they have an excellent reputation for customer service.

They have no showroom, which allows them to keep costs even lower. They do have a beautiful catalog, which you can request at the "800" number above.

Blackwelder's has some terrific bargains. If you plan to order furniture by phone, you should absolutely call them to compare prices.

Lines carried:	Please see page 46
Phone orders accepted:	Yes
Discount:	40%-60% off mfrs. suggested retail
Payment methods:	VISA, MC, Discover, personal checks
In-house financing available:	No
Deposits required:	50% deposit when order is placed, balance due when furniture is ready to be shipped
Catalog available:	Yes
Clearance center:	No
Delivery:	Full service in-home delivery and set-up. Customer pays freight company directly for shipping costs.

Directions: Blackwelder's has no showroom open to the public.

Blackwelders (cont.)

Lines carried:

Action By Lane
Alexvale
American Drew
American Of Martinsville
American Victorian
Artistic Leather
Athens Furniture
Baker Furniture
Barcalounger
Bassett
Bassett Mirror
Benchcraft
Bentley Designs of CA
Berkeley Upholstery
Bernhardt
Blacksmith Shop
Boling Chair
Bradington Young
Brady
Brass Beds Of America
Braxton Culler
Brown Jordan
Broyhill
Burlington
Burris Chair
Butler Specialty
Capel Mills
Caro-Craft
Carolina Collection
Carolina Mirror
Carson's Of High Point
Casa Bique
Cebu Imports
Century
Chadwick Leather
Chaircraft
Charleston Forge
Chatham County
Chromecraft
Classic Leather
Classic Rattan
Clayton Marcus
Clyde Pearson
Cochrane
Colonial Mills
Conant Ball
Corsican Iron Beds
Councill Craftsmen
Cox

C. R. Laine
Craftique
Craftmaster
Crawford
Crestline
DMI
Dansen
Davis Cabinet
Designmaster
Dillingham
Dillon
Distinction Leather
Dixie
Dresher
Drexel Heritage
Duo-Sofa
Ello
Emerson Leather
Fairchild
Fairfield
Fancher
Fashioncraft
Ficks Reed
Flair
Fogle
Frederick Cooper
Frederick Edwards
Friedman Bros.
Gilliam
Gordon Tables
Habersham Plantation
Hammary
Harden
Hekman
Henkel-Harris
Henry Link
Henredon
Hickory Chair
Hickory Hill
Highland House
Hill
Hood
Hooker
HTB
Howard Miller Clocks
Huntington House
Hyundai Furniture
Jasper Cabinet
J. B. Ross Brass Beds

Jeffco
Johnston Casuals
Keller
Kessler
Kimball
Kittinger
La Barge
Lane
Lea
Leathercraft
Lexington
Link Taylor
Lyon Shaw
Madison Square
Marlow
Mastercraft
Masterfield
Mersman
Miller Desk
Mobilia
Montgomery Chair
Myrtle Desk
Nathan Hale
National Mt. Airy
Null
Old Hickory Tannery
Pande Cameron Rugs
Paul Robert Chair
Peoplelounger
Perfection
Pulaski
Richardson Bros.
Ridgeway
Riverside
Schweiger
Sealy
Sedgefield Lamp
Selig
Sherrill
Shuford
Singer
Sligh
Southwood Reproductions
Stanley
Statesville Chair
Stiffel Lamps
Style
Sunset Lamps
Swan Brass Beds

Taylor Woodcraft
Taylorsville
Temple Stuart
Tell City Chair
Temple Upholstery
Thayer Coggin
Thomasville
Tropitone
Union National
Unique
Universal
Vaughan
Vanguard
Venture
Virginia House
Virginia Metalcrafters
Vogue Rattan
Weiman
Wells
Wellington Hall
White Of Mebane
Whitaker
Wildwood Lamps
Woodlee
Woodmark
Woodard
Young Hinkle

Blowing Rock Furniture Company

3428 Hickory Blvd. N.
Hwy. 321
Hudson, NC 28638

Phone:	**(828) 396-3186**	**Hours:**	**M-Sat 8:30-5:00**
Toll Free:	**None**	**E-mail:**	**info@blowingrockfurniture.com**
Fax:	**(828) 396-6031**	**Web site:**	**www.blowingrockfurniture.com**

Blowing Rock Furniture Co. has an extensive high-end gallery on Hwy. 321 just north of Hickory, NC. The store has large galleries for Thomasville, Broyhill, Cochrane, Lexington (including Bob Timberlake and the Palmer Home Collection), Stanley, and Universal (including Alexander Julian).

The discounts here range from 40%-70% off retail on new first-quality special-order furniture, depending on the particular brand. There are no floor samples or discontinued styles sold here, and there is no clearance center.

There isn't much reason to go in person. You'll get an equivalent discount if you order from home. However, the deals here are quite good, and the staff is very helpful. They do a booming special order business here. If you plan to order furniture by phone, definitely check prices here before you buy.

Lines carried:	**Please see page 48**
Phone orders accepted:	**Yes**
Discount:	**40%-70% off mfrs. suggested retail**
Payment methods:	**VISA, MC, personal checks**
In-house financing available:	**No**
Deposits required:	**50% deposit when order is placed, balance due when furniture is ready to be shipped**
Catalog available:	**No**
Clearance center:	**No**
Delivery:	**Full service in-home delivery and set-up. Customer pays freight company directly for shipping costs.**

Directions: From I-40, take exit #123 and head north on Hwy. 321. After about fifteen miles, you'll enter the town of Hudson. Blowing Rock Furniture is on the right side of the highway about two miles beyond the bridge.

Blowing Rock Furniture Company

Lines carried:

Action By Lane
American Drew
American Of Martinsville
Ardley Hall
Ashton Prints
Austin Sculpture
Barcalounger
Bassett
Bassett Mirror
Berkline
Blacksmith Shop
Bradington Young
Broyhill
Built Right Chairs
Butler
Cambridge Chair Co.
Capel Rugs
Carolina Mirror
Carsons
Carter
Casa Bique
Century
Charleston Forge
Chatham County
Chromecraft
Clark Casual
Classic Rattan
Cochrane
Comfort Designs
Cox
Crawford
C. R. Laine
Crystal Clear
Denny Lamps
Dillon
Dinaire
Fairfield
Fashion Bed Group
Ficks Reed
Flexsteel
Frederick Cooper
Guardsman
Habersham Plantation
Hammary
Hart Lamps & Accessories
Hekman
Henry Link
Hickory Hill
High Point Desk

Hitchcock Chair
Hooker
Howard Miller Clocks
International
Jasper Cabinet
John Richards Lamps
          & Accessories
Kaiser Kuhn
Karpen
Kimball Reproductions
King Hickory
Lane
Lea
Lexington
Leister Tables
Lloyd/Flanders
Lyon Shaw
Madison Square
Masland Rugs
McKay Table Pads
Millender
National Mt. Airy
Nichols & Stone
Ohio Table Pads
Passport
Peters-Revington
Plant Plant
Pulaski
Quoizel
Regency House
Richardson Bros.
Ridgeway Clocks
Ridgewood
Riverside
Sadek
Saloom
Sarreid
Schnadig
Serta
Shelby-Williams
Simmons
Skillcraft
Southern Furniture
Speer
Stakmore
Stanley
Stanton Cooper
Stiffel
Stylecraft

Thomasville
Tropitone
Universal
Vaughan-Bassett
Venture
Virginia Metalcrafters
Weiman
Wellington Hall
Wesley Allen
Wildwood Lamps
Winston
Woodmark

Bonita Furniture Galleries

210 13th St. SW and Hwy. 321
Hickory, NC 28603

Phone:	**(704) 324-1992**	**Hours:**	**M-Sat 9:00-5:00**	
Toll Free:	**(800) 438-0201**	**E-mail:**	**None**	
Fax:	**(704) 872-4491**	**Web site:**	**www.hfnet.com/bonita.html**	

Bonita Furniture Galleries has a very high-end store in Hickory with large galleries for Thomasville, Bernhardt, and Century. Discounts here generally run about 40%-50% off the manufacturer's retail price, with the exception of Thomasville and Bernhardt which have lesser discounts mandated by the manufacturer.

There are a very few floor samples and discontinued items on the sales floor, marked down to about 65%-75% off retail, but these are few and far between. This is primarily a special order source, so it's generally more efficient to order by phone from this source instead of making a personal visit.

They do have good deals on many lines. Anyone ordering furniture by phone should call this source to compare prices.

Lines carried:	**Please see page 50**
Phone orders accepted:	**Yes**
Discount:	**40%-50% off mfrs. suggested retail**
Payment methods:	**Personal checks. No credit cards.**
In-house financing available:	**No**
Deposits required:	**50% deposit when order is placed, balance due when furniture is ready to be shipped**
Catalog available:	**No**
Clearance center:	**No**
Delivery:	**Full service in-home delivery and set-up. Customer pays freight company directly for shipping costs.**

Directions: From I-40, take exit #123 and go one mile north on Hwy. 321. Bonita Furniture Galleries is on the right side of the road.

Bonita Furniture Galleries (cont.)

Lines carried:

American Drew
American Of Martinsville
Athol
Baldwin Brass
Barcalounger
Bassett
Bernhardt
Blacksmith Shop
Bradington Young
Carson's
Casa Bique
Century
Charleston Forge
Chatham County
Clayton Marcus
Clyde Pearson
Cochrane
Cox
Craftique
C. R. Laine
Dixie
Elliott's Designs
Fairfield
Fine Art Lamps
Fitz & Floyd
Flexsteel
Frederick Cooper
Great City Traders
Guildmaster
Hammary
Hekman
Henry Link
Highland House
Hooker
Howard Miller Clocks
Jasper Cabinet
Johnston Casuals
Keller
Kimball
Kincaid
King Hickory
Knob Creek
Lane
La-Z-Boy
Leathercraft
Lexington
Link-Taylor
Madison Square
Masland Rugs

Nichols & Stone
Null
Pennsylvania House
Pulaski
Rex
S. Bent
Sadek
Sam Moore
Sarreid
Sedgefield Collection
Serta
Shuford
Skillcraft
Southwood Reproductions
Stanley
Statton
Stiffel
Sumter Cabinet
Superior
Thayer Coggin
Toyo
Universal
Velco Bedspreads
Virginia Metalcrafters
Waterford Furniture
Weiman
Wellington Hall
Wesley Allen
Wildwood
Woodard
Woodcraft Lamps
Young Hinkle

Boyles Clearance Center

739 Old Lenoir Rd.
Hickory, NC 28601

Phone:	**(828) 326-1700**	**Hours:**	**M-F 9:00-6:00, Sat 9:00-5:00**
Toll Free:	**(888) 316-3351**	**E-mail:**	**None**
Fax:	**None**	**Web site:**	**www.boyles.com**

This is the combined clearance center for all 12 Boyles stores, including Hendrick's in Mocksville, plus Boyles' huge telephone sales operation.

Most of the furniture in stock is very high-end and in new first-quality condition. Most are floor samples, discontinued styles, and a few customer returns. The clearance center itself is huge, one of the largest clearance centers of its type in North Carolina. There's an even mix of upholstery and case goods here.

They have some terrific deals. On my most recent visit here, I found a Councill-Craftsmen mahogany drum table (pictured on the following page) that normally retails for $3,830.00 marked down to $1,474.00, over 60% off. This particular piece was a floor sample in new first-quality condition.

If you're traveling to the Hickory, NC, area in person to shop for high-end furniture, you should definitely check out Boyles' clearance center. This one is a "must-visit".

Lines carried:

American Drew	Hekman	La Barge	Shuford
Baker	Henkel-Harris	Lane	Sligh
Bernhardt	Henkel-Moore	Leathercraft	Southwood Reproductions
Bevan Funnell	Henredon	Lexington	Stanley
Bob Timberlake	Hickory Chair	Madison Square	Thomasville
Bradington Young	Hickory White	Maitland Smith	Tradition House
Casa Bique	Hooker	Marge Carson	Universal
Century	Jasper Cabinet	Pennsylvania House	Weiman
Charleston Forge	Jeffco	Precedent	Wellington Hall
Councill Craftsmen	Karges	Riverside	Wesley Allen
Hancock & Moore	Kincaid	Sam Moore	Whittemore-Sherrrill
Harden	Kingsdown	Sherrill	

Phone orders accepted:	**No**
Discount:	**40%-60% off mfrs. suggested retail**
Payment methods:	**VISA, MC, personal checks**
In-house financing available:	**No**
Deposits required:	**Not applicable**
Catalog available:	**Not applicable**
Clearance center:	**Not applicable**
Delivery:	**Full service in-home delivery and set-up. Customer pays freight company directly for shipping costs.**

Directions: From I-40, take exit #123 and head north on Hwy. 321. After about ten miles, turn right onto Old Lenoir Rd. The clearance center is on the right, behind Boyles Country Shop.

Boyles Clearance Center (cont.)

Boyles Clearance Center

Councill-Craftsmen mahogany drum table

Retail: $3,830.00   Discounted price: $1,474.00
Savings at Boyles Clearance Center: $2,356.00 = 62% off retail

Boyles Country Shop

739 Old Lenoir Rd.
Hickory, NC 28601

Phone:	(828) 326-1700	**Hours:**	M-F 9:00-6:00, Sat 9:00-5:00
Toll Free:	(888) 316-3351	**E-mail:**	None
Fax:	None	**Web site:**	www.boyles.com

The "Country Shop" is Boyles' original furniture store in Hickory, NC. Of course, now Boyles has 11 more locations, and they've become one of the biggest furniture discounters in North Carolina.

Like the other Boyles locations, this store has an extensive high-end gallery. All of the furniture in stock is new first-quality. The discounts range from 30%-50% off retail depending on the brand. All of Boyles' floor samples and discontinued items are sent to their clearance center, located right behind the "Country Shop".

One significant advantage to buying from Boyles is that, unlike most discounters, they will allow you to make your final payment for your furniture on delivery instead of requiring that you pay the rest of your bill before the furniture is shipped to your home. This is some extra security, and it's worth taking into account when you're deciding where to shop. They are also very well established, and they have a good reputation with their customers.

If you're buying furniture by phone, you should compare prices with this source. If you're traveling to the Hickory, NC, area in person to shop, you should definitely check out Boyles' clearance center.

Lines carried:

American Drew	Guy Chaddock	Hickory White	Sam Moore
Baker	Habersham Plantation	Hooker	Sherrill
Bernhardt	Hancock & Moore	Jeffco	Southampton
Bradington Young	Harden	Karges	Southwood Reproductions
Brown Jordan	Hekman	Kingsdown	Stanley
Casa Bique	Henkel-Harris	Lane	Whittemore-Sherrill
Century	Henkel-Moore	Lexington	
Charleston Forge	Henredon	Maitland-Smith	
Councill Craftsmen	Hickory Chair	Marge Carson	

Phone orders accepted:	Yes
Discount:	30%-50% off mfrs. suggested retail
Payment methods:	VISA, MC, personal checks
In-house financing available:	No
Deposits required:	1/3 deposit when order is placed, balance due when furniture is delivered to your home
Catalog available:	No
Clearance center:	Yes -- See *Boyles Clearance Center*
Delivery:	Full service in-home delivery and set-up. Customer pays freight company directly for shipping costs.

Directions: From I-40, take exit #123 and head north on Hwy. 321. After about ten miles, turn right onto Old Lenoir Rd. The Country Shop is on the right.

Boyles Distinctive Furniture

616 Greensboro Rd.
High Point, NC 27261

Phone:	**(336) 884-8088**	**Hours:**	**M-W 8:30-5:30, Sat 8:30-5:30**
Toll Free:	**(888) 316-3351**		**Th-F 8:30-8:30**
Fax:	**None**	**E-mail:**	**None**
		Web site:	**www.boyles.com**

Boyles Distinctive Furniture is the only Boyles location in High Point proper. There is also a much bigger Boyles store a few miles away in Jamestown, NC.

Like the other Boyles locations, this store has an extensive high-end gallery. All of the furniture in stock is new first-quality. The discounts range from 30%-50% off retail depending on the brand. All of Boyles' floor samples and discontinued items are sent to their clearance center, located right behind the "Country Shop" in Hickory, NC.

One significant advantage to buying from Boyles is that, unlike most discounters, they will allow you to make your final payment for your furniture on delivery instead of requiring that you pay the rest of your bill before the furniture is shipped to your home. This is some extra security, and it's worth taking into account when you're deciding where to shop. They are also very well established, and they have a good reputation with their customers.

If you're buying furniture by phone, you should compare prices with this source. If you're traveling to the Hickory, NC, area in person to shop, you should definitely check out Boyles' clearance center.

Lines carried:

Baker	Hancock & Moore	Karges	Sealy
Classic Oriental Rugs	Harden	Kingsdown	Sherrill
Councill Craftsmen	Henkel-Harris	Lloyd/Flanders	Southampton
Fine Arts	Henredon	Maitland-Smith	Southwood Reproductions
Frederick Cooper	Hickory Chair	Marge Carson	Thomasville
Garcia	Hooker	Motioncraft	Whittemore-Sherrill
Guy Chaddock	Jeffco	Precedent	Wildwood
Habersham Plantation	John Richard	Sam Moore	

Phone orders accepted:	**Yes**
Discount:	**30%-50% off mfrs. suggested retail**
Payment methods:	**VISA, MC, personal checks**
In-house financing available:	**No**
Deposits required:	**1/3 deposit when order is placed, balance due when furniture is delivered to your home**
Catalog available:	**No**
Clearance center:	**Yes -- See *Boyles Clearance Center***
Delivery:	**Full service in-home delivery and set-up. Customer pays freight company directly for shipping costs.**

Directions: From I-85, take exit #111, and head north on Hwy. 311 into High Point. Turn right on Greensboro Rd. Boyles is a few miles down on the right.

Boyles Distinctive Furniture

5700 Riverdale Dr.
Jamestown, NC 27282

Phone:	(336) 812-2200	**Hours:**	M-W 8:30-5:30, Sat 8:30-5:30
Toll Free:	None		Th-F 8:30-8:30
Fax:	None	**E-mail:**	None
		Web site:	www.boyles.com

This is Boyles' flagship store, perched on a hill right above I-85 on the outskirts of High Point, NC. Boyles also has 11 more locations, and they've become one of the biggest furniture discounters in North Carolina.

Like the other Boyles locations, this store has an extensive high-end gallery. All of the furniture in stock is new first-quality. The discounts range from 30%-50% off retail depending on the brand. All of Boyles' floor samples and discontinued items are sent to their clearance center, located right behind the "Country Shop".

One significant advantage to buying from Boyles is that, unlike most discounters, they will allow you to make your final payment for your furniture on delivery instead of requiring that you pay the rest of your bill before the furniture is shipped to your home. This is some extra security, and it's worth taking into account when you're deciding where to shop. They are also very well established, and they have a good reputation with their customers.

If you're buying furniture by phone, you should compare prices with this source. If you're traveling to the Hickory, NC, area in person to shop, you should definitely check out Boyles' clearance center.

Lines carried:

Baker	Drexel Studio	Hickory Chair	Sealy Mattress
Bernhardt	Gentleman's Home	Hickory White	Sherrill
Century	Hancock & Moore	Kingsdown	Thomasville
Classic Oriental Rugs	Harden	Lexington	
Councill Craftsmen	Henkel-Harris	Lillian August	
Drexel Heritage	Henredon	Marge Carson	

Phone orders accepted:	Yes
Discount:	**30%-50% off mfrs. suggested retail**
Payment methods:	**VISA, MC, personal checks**
In-house financing available:	No
Deposits required:	**1/3 deposit when order is placed, balance due when furniture is delivered to your home**
Catalog available:	No
Clearance center:	**Yes -- See *Boyles Clearance Center***
Delivery:	**Full service in-home delivery and set-up. Customer pays freight company directly for shipping costs.**

Directions: **From I-85, take exit #118, and go west on Riverdale Rd. You'll see Boyles right in front of you. It's easily visible from the interstate.**

Boyles Distinctive Furniture (cont.)

Boyles Distinctive Furniture in Jamestown, NC

Boyles Drexel Heritage

Level 1
Hickory Furniture Mart
2220 Hwy. 70 SE
Hickory, NC 28602

Phone:	**(828) 326-1060**	**Hours:**	**M-Sat 9:00-6:00**
Toll Free:	**(888) 316-3351**	**E-mail:**	**None**
Fax:	**None**	**Web site:**	**www.boyles.com**

This is Boyles' main Drexel-Heritage gallery, taking up about one-third of the first level of the Hickory Furniture Mart. Boyles also has 11 more locations, and they've become one of the biggest furniture discounters in North Carolina.

Like the other Boyles locations, this store is high-end. All of the furniture in stock is new first-quality. The discount runs about 50% off retail. All of Boyles' floor samples and discontinued items are sent to their clearance center, located right behind the "Country Shop".

One significant advantage to buying from Boyles is that, unlike most discounters, they will allow you to make your final payment for your furniture on delivery instead of requiring that you pay the rest of your bill before the furniture is shipped to your home. This is some extra security, and it's worth taking into account when you're deciding where to shop. They are also very well established, and they have a good reputation with their customers.

If you're buying Drexel-Heritage by phone, you should compare prices with this source. If you're traveling to the Hickory, NC, area in person to shop, you should definitely check out Boyles' clearance center.

Phone orders accepted:	**Yes**
Discount:	**50% off mfrs. suggested retail**
Payment methods:	**VISA, MC, personal checks**
In-house financing available:	**No**
Deposits required:	**1/3 deposit when order is placed, balance due when furniture is delivered to your home**
Catalog available:	**No**
Clearance center:	**Yes -- See *Boyles Clearance Center***
Delivery:	**Full service in-home delivery and set-up. Customer pays freight company directly for shipping costs.**

Directions: Please see *Hickory Furniture Mart* for complete directions.

Boyles Galleries

Level 4
Hickory Furniture Mart
2220 Hwy. 70 SE
Hickory, NC 28602

Phone:	**(828) 326-1740**	**Hours:**	**M-Sat 9:00-6:00**
Toll Free:	**(888) 316-3351**	**E-mail:**	**None**
Fax:	**None**	**Web site:**	**www.boyles.com**

This Boyles' gallery takes up about one-fourth of the fourth level of the Hickory Furniture Mart. Boyles also has 11 more locations, and they've become one of the biggest furniture discounters in North Carolina.

Like the other Boyles locations, this store has extensive galleries for many very high-end brands such as Baker and Councill-Craftsmen. All of the furniture in stock is new first-quality. The discounts run about 30%-50% off retail, depending on the particular brand. All of Boyles' floor samples and discontinued items are sent to their clearance center, located right behind the "Country Shop".

One significant advantage to buying from Boyles is that, unlike most discounters, they will allow you to make your final payment for your furniture on delivery instead of requiring that you pay the rest of your bill before the furniture is shipped to your home. This is some extra security, and it's worth taking into account when you're deciding where to shop. They are also very well established, and they have a good reputation with their customers.

If you're buying furniture by phone, you should compare prices with this source. If you're traveling to the Hickory, NC, area in person to shop, you should definitely check out Boyles' clearance center.

Lines carried:

Baker	Hickory Chair	Mastercraft	Thomasville
Bob Timberlake	Hickory White	Nichols & Stone	Wesley Allen
Brown Jordan	Jessica Charles	Palmer Home Collection	
Councill Craftsmen	Karges	Sligh	
Designmaster	Kingsdown	Southampton	
Henkel-Harris	Lexington	Southwood Reproductions	

Phone orders accepted:	**Yes**
Discount:	**30%-50% off mfrs. suggested retail**
Payment methods:	**VISA, MC, personal checks**
In-house financing available:	**No**
Deposits required:	**1/3 deposit when order is placed, balance due when furniture is delivered to your home**
Catalog available:	**No**
Clearance center:	**Yes -- See *Boyles Clearance Center***
Delivery:	**Full service in-home delivery and set-up. Customer pays freight company directly for shipping costs.**

Directions: Please see *Hickory Furniture Mart* for complete directions.

Boyles Lexington Gallery

Level 4
Hickory Furniture Mart
2220 Hwy. 70 SE
Hickory, NC 28602

Phone:	**(828) 326-1709**	**Hours:**	**M-Sat 9:00-6:00**
Toll Free:	**(888) 316-3351**	**E-mail:**	**None**
Fax:	**None**	**Web site:**	**www.boyles.com**

This is Boyles' main Lexington gallery. Boyles also has 11 more locations, and they've become one of the biggest furniture discounters in North Carolina.

Like the other Boyles locations, this store is high-end. All of the furniture in stock is new first-quality. The discount runs about 50% off retail. All of Boyles' floor samples and discontinued items are sent to their clearance center, located right behind the "Country Shop".

One significant advantage to buying from Boyles is that, unlike most discounters, they will allow you to make your final payment for your furniture on delivery instead of requiring that you pay the rest of your bill before the furniture is shipped to your home. This is some extra security, and it's worth taking into account when you're deciding where to shop. They are also very well established, and they have a good reputation with their customers.

If you're buying Lexington by phone, you should compare prices with this source. They have a nice selection of all of Lexington's lines, including the very popular Bob Timberlake and Palmer Home Collection (Arnold Palmer) signature lines. If you're traveling to the Hickory, NC, area in person to shop, you should definitely check out Boyles' clearance center.

Phone orders accepted:	**Yes**
Discount:	**50% off mfrs. suggested retail**
Payment methods:	**VISA, MC, personal checks**
In-house financing available:	**No**
Deposits required:	**1/3 deposit when order is placed, balance due when furniture is delivered to your home**
Catalog available:	**No**
Clearance center:	**Yes -- See *Boyles Clearance Center***
Delivery:	**Full service in-home delivery and set-up. Customer pays freight company directly for shipping costs.**

Directions: Please see *Hickory Furniture Mart* for complete directions.

Boyles Showcase

Level 2 & 3
Hickory Furniture Mart
2220 Hwy. 70 SE
Hickory, NC 28602

Phone:	**(828) 326-1735**	**Hours:**	**M-Sat 9:00-6:00**
Toll Free:	**(888) 316-3351**	**E-mail:**	**None**
Fax:	**None**	**Web site:**	**www.boyles.com**

   Boyles' Showcase Gallery is huge, taking up about one-fourth of the second and third floors of the Hickory Furniture Mart. Boyles also has 11 more locations, and they've become one of the biggest furniture discounters in North Carolina.

   Like the other Boyles locations, this store has extensive galleries for many very high-end brands such as Maitland-Smith and Bernhardt. All of the furniture in stock is new first-quality. The discounts run about 30%-50% off retail, depending on the particular brand. All of Boyles' floor samples and discontinued items are sent to their clearance center, located right behind the "Country Shop".

   One significant advantage to buying from Boyles is that, unlike most discounters, they will allow you to make your final payment for your furniture on delivery instead of requiring that you pay the rest of your bill before the furniture is shipped to your home. This is some extra security, and it's worth taking into account when you're deciding where to shop. They are also very well established, and they have a good reputation with their customers.

   If you're buying furniture by phone, you should compare prices with this source. If you're traveling to the Hickory, NC, area in person to shop, you should definitely check out Boyles' clearance center.

Lines carried:

Bernhardt	Garcia	Kingsdown	Raymond Waites
Bradington Young	Guy Chaddock	La Barge	Sam Moore
Brown Jordan	Habersham Plantation	Lane	Sherrill
Casa Bique	Hancock & Moore	Maitland Smith	Southern Of Conover
Casa Stradivari	Harden	Marge Carson	Stanley
Classic Oriental Rugs	Henredon	Motioncraft	Whittemore-Sherrill
Drexel Studio	Hooker	Platt	
Entree	Jeffco	Precedent	

Phone orders accepted:	**Yes**
Discount:	**30%-50% off mfrs. suggested retail**
Payment methods:	**VISA, MC, personal checks**
In-house financing available:	**No**
Deposits required:	**1/3 deposit when order is placed, balance due when furniture is delivered to your home**
Catalog available:	**No**
Clearance center:	**Yes -- See *Boyles Clearance Center***
Delivery:	**Full service in-home delivery and set-up. Customer pays freight company directly for shipping costs.**

Directions: Please see *Hickory Furniture Mart* for complete directions.

Bradington Young Gallery

Level 3
Hickory Furniture Mart
U. S. Hwy. 70 SE
Hickory, NC 28602

Phone:	(828) 328-5257	**Hours:**	M-Sat 9:00-6:00
Toll Free:	None	**E-mail:**	info@blowingrockfurniture.com
Fax:	(828) 324-4219	**Web site:**	www.blowingrockfurniture.com

The Bradington Young Gallery at the Hickory Furniture Mart is owned by Blowing Rock Furniture Co., which has an extensive high-end gallery on Hwy. 321 just north of Hickory, NC.

The discounts here run about 50% off retail on new first-quality furniture, from Bradington Young's current line. There are no floor samples or discontinued styles sold here, and there is no clearance center.

There isn't much reason to go in person. You'll get an equivalent discount if you order from home. If you plan to order Bradington Young by phone, definitely check prices here before you buy.

Phone orders accepted:	Yes
Discount:	50% off mfrs. suggested retail
Payment methods:	VISA, MC, personal checks
In-house financing available:	No
Deposits required:	50% deposit when order is placed, balance due when furniture is ready to be shipped
Catalog available:	No
Clearance center:	No
Delivery:	Full service in-home delivery and set-up. Customer pays freight company directly for shipping costs.

Directions: Please see *Hickory Furniture Mart* for complete directions.

Brass Bed Shoppe

12421 Cedar Rd.
Cleveland Heights, OH 44106

Phone:	**(216) 371-0400**	**Hours:**	**M-Sat 10:00-6:00**
Toll Free:	**None**	**E-mail:**	**None**
Fax:	**(216) 292-0026**	**Web site:**	**None**

The Brass Bed Shoppe is a true factory outlet. They manufacture their own line of brass and iron beds and sell them at about 50% off retail. The quality is very good, and they have a nice selection of traditional styles. If you're interested in a brass or iron bed, you should definitely order their catalog.

They also have a written "quality guarantee". Unlike most furniture discounters and factory outlets, Brass Bed Shoppe accepts returns for exchange or refund for any reason and without any restocking fees.

Unlike most furniture discounters, Brass Bed Shoppe does not use a full service delivery company. They ship all beds via common carrier (trucking companies, UPS, etc.). All beds arrive disassembled and must be put together by the customer. This is very simple, and shouldn't pose a problem for the average person.

They are also able to special order brass and iron beds from "any national manufacturer". They don't publish a list, but they will tell you over the phone if they can get you the brand and model you want and at what price. They also have a written "lowest price guarantee", so hold them to it! If you're considering buying a brass or iron bed from any manufacturer, definitely give these people a call.

Lines carried:	**All major national brands. Please call for product information.**
Phone orders accepted:	**Yes**
Discount:	**50% off mfrs. suggested retail**
Payment methods:	**VISA, MC, personal checks**
In-house financing available:	**Layaway program available**
Deposits required:	**50% deposit when order is placed, balance due when furniture is ready to be shipped**
Catalog available:	**Yes**
Clearance center:	**No**
Delivery:	**All orders are shipped by common carrier. Customer must unpack and assemble beds. Customer pays freight charges directly to driver.**

Directions: From I-271, take exit #32, and go west 6 miles on Cedar Rd. The Brass Bed Shoppe is on the right side of the road across from Firestone Tire.

Brentwood Manor

317 Virginia Ave.
Clarksville, VA 23927

Phone:	**(804) 374-4297**	**Hours:**	**M-F 9:00-5:00**
Toll Free:	**(800) 225-6105**	**E-mail:**	**None**
Fax:	**(804) 374-9420**	**Web site:**	**None**

Brentwood Manor has a well furnished store with a nice selection of medium to high-end furniture from brands such as Stanley, Jasper Cabinet, Lexington, Hekman, Hooker, Universal, and others. They don't have a clearance center or any discounted floor samples or discontinued styles on the sales floor, though.

For this reason, it really isn't necessary to visit the store in person. However, they do have good deals on many brands sold by phone. So, if you plan to order your furniture over the phone, do give this source a call to compare their prices.

Lines carried:	**Please see page 64**
Phone orders accepted:	**Yes**
Discount:	**40% to 50% off mfrs. suggested retail**
Payment methods:	**VISA, MC, personal checks**
In-house financing available:	**No**
Deposits required:	**25% deposit when order is placed. If order is delivered by common carrier, balance must be paid before order is shipped. If order is to be delivered by Brentwood Manor's own in-house delivery service, balance can be paid to the driver when the order is delivered to your home.**
Catalog available:	**No**
Clearance center:	**No**
Delivery:	**Small items (lamps, etc.) are typically shipped by common carrier. Most furniture is shipped via Brentwood Manor's in-home delivery service with full unpacking and set up.**

Directions: From I-85, take exit #15 (Hwy. 1), and head west on Hwy. 1. After about 5 miles, turn left on Business 58 and continue on about 20 miles into downtown Clarksville. You will see signs for Brentwood Manor when you get into downtown Clarksville.

Brentwood Manor (cont.)

Lines carried:

American Drew
American Of Martinsville
Barcalounger
Bassett
Benchcraft
Bob Timberlake
Bradington Young
Broyhill
Butler Specialty
Classic Leather
Clayton Marcus
Clyde Pearson
Cochrane
Collingwood
Colonial
Conover Chair
Councill Craftsman
Couristan Rugs
Craftique
D-Scan
Davis Cabinet
Decorative Crafts
D&F Wicker and Rattan
Distinction Leather
Dixie
Elliott's
Emerson Leather
Fairfield
Fairmont Designs
Flexsteel
Georgian Reproductions
Glenncraft
Hearthside Chair
Hekman
Henry Link
Hickory White
Highland House
Hitchcock Chair
Hooker
Jasper Cabinet
Keller
Kimball
Kingsdown
Kirsch
Lane
Lexington
Link Taylor
Lloyd/Flanders
Lyon Shaw

Markel
Moosehead
Nathan Hale
National Mt. Airy
Nichols & Stone
North Hickory
Northwood
Null
Ohio Table Pads
Peters Revington
Pine-tique
Pulaski
Restonic Mattress
Ridgewood
Richardson Bros.
Robinson
Sealy
Sedgefield
Shermag
Skillcraft
Sligh
Somma Mattress
Southern Craftsman Guild
Southern Reproductions
Stakmore
Stanley
Stanton-Cooper
Statesville Chair
Stiffel
Sumter
Superior
Taylor Woodcrafters
Taylorsville
Therapedic
Universal
Vaughan Bassett
Victorius
Virginia House
Virginia Metalcrafters
Wesley Allen
Winston
Woodfield Ltd.
Woodmark
Young Hinkle

Broyhill Factory Outlet

Manufacturer-Owned Factory Outlets (Lenoir Mall)
1031 Morganton Blvd.
Lenoir, NC 28645

Phone:	**(828) 758-8899**	**Hours:**	**M-Sat 10:00-7:00, Sun 1:00-5:00**
Toll Free:	**None**	**E-mail:**	**None**
Fax:	**(828) 754-5038**	**Web site:**	**None**

This is Broyhill's only true factory outlet. It's a fairly large warehouse-style outlet occupying three large spaces in the Manufacturer-Owned Factory Outlets at Lenoir Mall, just north of Hickory, NC.

Most of the stock here is upholstery, although they do have some armoires, china cabinets, beds, dining room sets, and other case goods. Most of the furniture in stock are floor samples and discontinued items, although they do have a few well-marked seconds. The quality is generally about medium.

On my most recent visit here, I found a good deal on a solid oak dining room set from Broyhill's "Watermark" collection (pictured at right). The retail on this set is $3,536.00, but this floor sample at the outlet was marked down to only $615.00, over 82% off the original retail. The only signs of wear were two small scratches on the table surface which were barely visible and could be very easily and inexpensively fixed. Most of the items in the outlet were marked down about 65% to 75% off retail.

Don't forget to check their "Value Center". It's a small room through a little door in the very back of the outlet, and it's easy to miss if you aren't looking out for it. This is where they keep most of the seconds and samples with significant flaws. Most of these pieces are over 80% off, though, and they did have some very good bargains here. The best deals in the "Value Center" were on occasional chairs.

This outlet is supposed to also be a factory outlet for Highland House, but I saw very few Highland House items on display.

If you're in the Lenoir area, and you're looking for medium-end furniture, this is an outlet you should definitely check out.

Phone orders accepted:	**No**
Discount:	**65%-85% off mfrs. suggested retail**
Payment methods:	**VISA, MC, personal checks**
In-house financing available:	**No**
Deposits required:	**Not applicable**
Catalog available:	**Not applicable**
Clearance center:	**Not applicable**
Delivery:	**Full service in-home delivery and set-up. Customer pays freight company directly for shipping costs.**

Directions:	**From I-40, take exit #123 (Hwy. 321) and head north through Hickory toward Lenoir. Turn left on Hwy. 64, then turn left again on the Hwy. 18S Bypass. The outlet is on the left inside Lenoir Mall.**

Broyhill Factory Outlet (cont.)

Broyhill Factory Outlet at the Manufacturer Owned Furniture Outlets in Lenoir, NC

Watermark solid oak dining room set from Broyhill

Retail: $3,536.00   Discounted price: $615.00
Savings at the Broyhill Factory Outlet: $2,921.00 = 82% off retail

Broyhill Showcase Gallery

Level 4
Hickory Furniture Mart
U. S. Hwy. 70 SE
Hickory, NC 28602

Phone:	(828) 324-9467	**Hours:**	M-Sat 9:00-6:00
Toll Free:	None	**E-mail:**	info@hickoryfurniture.com
Fax:	(828) 324-4219	**Web site:**	www.hickoryfurniture.com

The Broyhill Showcase Gallery in the Hickory Furniture Mart is not a true factory outlet, but they are a legitimate deep discounter for this brand.

Their showroom in the Hickory Furniture Mart carries all kinds of traditional styles: bedroom furniture, living room furniture, upholstery, etc. However, they don't sell off the floor. All furniture must be special ordered. Broyhill is the only brand carried by this source. They will special order any Broyhill piece you find at a local furniture retailer. They also have a nice full-color catalog.

Their discounts are very good, about 40% to 60% off of retail. Most of the pieces on the floor were priced at about 50% off retail. For example, on my last visit here, I found a living room group that normally retailed for $2,729.00 marked down to $1,330.00 (pictured on the next page). Like all of the other furniture here, this price was for brand new furniture in first quality condition.

This is certainly a good source to check out for new Broyhill products from their current lines. For better bargains on floor samples and discontinued styles, check out Broyhill's factory-owned factory outlet in Lenoir, NC.

Phone orders accepted:	Yes
Discount:	40%-60% off mfrs. suggested retail
Payment methods:	VISA, MC, personal checks
In-house financing available:	No
Deposits required:	50% deposit when order is placed, balance due when furniture is ready to be shipped
Catalog available:	Yes
Clearance center:	Yes -- please see *Broyhill Factory Outlet*
Delivery:	Full service in-home delivery and set-up. Customer pays freight company directly for shipping costs.

Directions: Please see *Hickory Furniture Mart* for complete directions.

Broyhill Showcase Gallery (cont.)

Living room group from Broyhill

Retail: $2,729.00   Discounted price: $1,330.00
Savings at the Broyhill Showcase Gallery: $1,399.00 = 51% off retail

Bryant's Furniture Manufacturing

629 Coley Rd.
Tupelo, MS 38801

Phone:	**(601) 841-0026**	**Hours:**	**M-F 9:00-5:00**
Toll Free:	**(800) 2-BRYANT**	**E-mail:**	**None**
Fax:	**(601) 841-0708**	**Web site:**	**None**

Bryant's Furniture Manufacturing is a true factory outlet located in the front of the Tupelo Furniture Mart, a major wholesale trade center for low to medium-end furniture.

Bryant's own line of upholstered furniture is medium quality, and the sofas and chairs they have in stock are priced at 50%-70% off. The main attraction about this outlet though is the fact that they buy up market samples from the Tupelo Mart wholesale furniture shows and resell them to the public. They have some terrific bargains on these.

On my most recent visit here, I found a Lexington Palmer Home Collection bedroom set (pictured on the following page) priced to move. It was a market sample set in new first-quality condition. Normally, the queen bed, mirror, chest, entertainment center, and two end tables retail for $9,006.00 as a group. Bryant's had this set marked down to $4,399.00, and I was able to haggle the salesman down to $4,000.00 even.

If you're in Tupelo, definitely check this source out. They do have some terrific deals.

Phone orders accepted:	**No**
Discount:	**50%-75% off mfrs. suggested retail**
Payment methods:	**Personal checks. No credit cards.**
In-house financing available:	**No**
Deposits required:	**Not applicable**
Catalog available:	**Not applicable**
Clearance center:	**Not applicable**
Delivery:	**Customers must make own arrangements to take furniture home**

Directions: From Hwy. 78, take the Belden exit. You don't have a choice of which way to turn. The exit will automatically put you in the right direction. Go to the 2nd traffic light and turn right (you'll see a Shell station on the corner) onto Coley Rd. Bryant's is on the right, inside the Tupelo Furniture Market.

Bryant's Furniture Manufacturing (cont.)

Bryant Furniture Manufacturing

Palmer Home Collection bedroom set from Lexington Furniture

Retail: $9,006.00   Discounted price: $4,000.00
Savings at Bryant Furniture Manufacturing: $5,006.00 = 56% off retail

Bulluck Furniture Company

124 S. Church St.
Rocky Mount, NC 27804

Phone:	**(252) 446-1138**	**Hours:**	**M-F 9:00-5:30, Sat 9:00-5:00**
Toll Free:	**None**	**E-mail:**	**None**
Fax:	**(252) 977-7870**	**Web site:**	**None**

Bulluck Furniture has been in business since 1900, and they have a lovely showroom in Rocky Mount, NC, about an hour's drive east of Raleigh on Hwy. 64. They have good deals by phone. Check them out!

Lines carried:

Allibert	Gregson	Link Taylor	Statton
Amotek/USA	Habersham Plantation	Lloyd/Flanders	Statesville Chair
Barcalounger	Hale Of Vermont	Lone Star Leather	Stewart
Bevan Funnell	Hancock & Moore	Madison Square	Telescope
Bradington Young	Henkel-Harris	Maitland Smith	Tomlin
Carolina Mirror	Henry Link	McGuire	Tradition House
Carvers Guild	Hickory Chair	Meadowcraft	Tramswall
Casa Bique	High Point Furniture	Michael Thomas	Trosby
CEO	Hooker	National Mt. Airy	Vogue Rattan
Colonial Traditions	Howard Miller Clocks	Nichols & Stone	Wellington Hall
Councill Craftsmen	Hyundai Furniture	O'Asian	Wesley Hall
Craftique	Jamestown Sterling	Pleion	Wicker World by
Cramer	Jasper Cabinet	Pompeii	Henry Link
Creative Metal	Jasper Desk	Ridgeway Clocks	Wildwood Lamps &
Dixie	J. B. Ross	Royal Patina	Accessories
Ello	Jeffco	Schott	Winston
Fairington	Jofco	Shelby Williams	Woodfield
Ficks Reed	John Boos	Southampton	Woodmark Chair
Finkel	John Richard	Southwood Reproductions	Wright Table
Fremarc	Lane	St. Timothy	Young Hinkle
Friedman Bros. Mirrors	Lane/Venture	Stanley	
Garcia	Lexington	Stanton-Cooper	

Phone orders accepted:	**Yes**
Discount:	**30%-50% off mfrs. suggested retail**
Payment methods:	**VISA, MC, personal checks**
In-house financing available:	**No**
Deposits required:	**50% deposit when order is placed, balance due when furniture is ready to be shipped**
Catalog available:	**No**
Clearance center:	**No**
Delivery:	**Full service in-home delivery and set-up. Customer pays freight company directly for shipping costs.**

Directions: From I-85, take exit #138, and head a few miles east into Rocky Mount, NC. You'll see signs for Bulluck Furniture as you enter town.

Carolina Discount Furniture

4382 Hickory Blvd.
Granite Falls, NC 28630

Phone:	(828) 396-2347	**Hours:**	M-Sat 9:00-6:00
Toll Free:	None	**E-mail:**	None
Fax:	(828) 396-6746	**Web site:**	None

Carolina Discount Furniture is a large warehouse type store with a good selection of the brands listed below in stock. Their discounts run around 30%-50% off retail. There are no discontinued items or floor samples in stock. All in stock furniture is new and is sold at exactly the same price whether you shop in person or by phone.

Unlike many other furniture discounters, this source is not able to order any lines other than those listed below. They say that by concentrating on only a few brands, they can buy in sufficient volume to get the very best price and service for their customers.

So, if you're interested in any of the brands listed below, definitely give this source a call.

Lines carried:

American Drew	England Corsair	Lane	Vaughan
Athens	Jetton	Null	Webb
Broyhill	Kingsdown	Riverside	

Phone orders accepted:	**Yes**
Discount:	**30%-50% off mfrs. suggested retail**
Payment methods:	**VISA, MC, personal checks**
In-house financing available:	**No**
Deposits required:	**50% deposit when order is placed, balance due when furniture is ready to be shipped**
Catalog available:	**No**
Clearance center:	**No**
Delivery:	**Full service in-home delivery and set-up. Customer pays freight company directly for shipping costs.**

Directions: From I-40, take exit #123 and drive north on Hwy. 321 to Granite Falls. Carolina Discount Furniture is on the right side of the road.

Carolina Furniture Of Williamsburg

5425 Richmond Rd.
Williamsburg, VA 23188

Phone:	**(757) 565-3000**	**Hours:**	**M-Thurs & Sat 9:00-5:00**
Toll Free:	**(800) 582-8916 (VA only)**		**Fri 9:00-9:00, Sun 1:00-6:00**
Fax:	**(757) 565-4476**	**E-mail:**	**furnish@carolina-furniture.com**
		Web site:	**www.carolina-furniture.com**

Carolina Furniture Of Williamsburg is located only 3 miles from Colonial Williamsburg, just 30 miles north of Norfolk, VA. They have a very nice selection of high end lines, including a large Pennsylvania House gallery.

They don't have a clearance center or any floor samples or discontinued pieces on display. For this reason, there is no monetary advantage to visiting in person. They do have great deals on many lines sold over the phone, though. So, if you're planning to order your furniture by phone, definitely give this source a call to compare their prices.

Lines carried:	**Please see page 74**
Phone orders accepted:	**Yes**
Discount:	**35%-60% off mfrs. suggested retail**
Payment methods:	**VISA, MC, AMEX, Discover, personal checks**
In-house financing available:	**No**
Deposits required:	**50% deposit when order is placed, balance due when furniture is ready to be shipped**
Catalog available:	**No**
Clearance center:	**No**
Delivery:	**Full service in-home delivery and set-up. Customer pays freight company directly for shipping costs.**

Directions: **Carolina Furniture Of Williamsburg is located 3 miles west of Colonial Williamsburg on State Route 60.**

Carolina Furniture Of Williamsburg (cont.)

Lines carried:

American Drew
American Of Martinsville
Ardley Hall
Artistica
Athol
Bailey & Griffin
Baker
Baldwin Brass
Banks, Coldstone Co.
Barcalounger
Bausman
Bernhardt
Blacksmith Shop
Bevan Funnell
Brown Jordan
Brunschwig & Fils
Casa Stradivari
Century
Chapman
Chelsea House
Clarence House
Clark Casual
Classic Leather
Conover
Councill Craftsmen
Craftique
Custom Comfort
Duralee
Eldred Wheeler
E. J. Victor
Ello
Ficks Reed
Flexsteel
Frederick Cooper
Frederick Edward
Friedman Mirrors
Furniture Guild
George Kovacs
Georgian Lighting
Giemme
Hale Of Vermont
Hancock & Moore
Heirloom
Hekman
Henkel-Harris
Henkel-Moore
Henredon
Henry Link
Hickory Chair

Hickory White
Hitchcock
Hooker
Jasper Cabinet
John Boos
John Widdicomb
Johnston Casuals
Karges
Kimball
Kingsdown
Kingsley Bates
Kreiss
La Barge
Lane
Lane/Venture
Lee Jofa
Lineage
Lexington
Lloyd/Flanders
Lyon Shaw
Madison Square
Maitland-Smith
Marge Carson
Meadowcraft
Melinda Trent
Michael Thomas
Miles Talbot
Motion Only
Motioncraft
National Mt. Airy
Nichols & Stone
Payne
Pearson
Pennsylvania Classics
Pennsylvania House
Pine-tique
Platt
Precedent
Robert Allen
Romweber
Salterini
Sarreid
S. Bent
Scalamandre
Schumacher
Sealy
Sedgefield
Sherrill
Shuford

Simmons
Sligh
Southampton
Southwood Reproductions
Speer
Stanley
Statton
Stiffel
Superior
Swaim
Tell City Chair
Thayer Coggin
Thomasville
Tradition House
Tropitone
Trosby
Union National
Virginia Galleries
Virginia House
Virginia Metalcrafters
Waverly
Weiman
Wellington Hall
Wesley Allen
Westgate
Whitecraft
Wildwood Lamps
Winston
Wood & Hogan
Wright Table Co.

Carolina Furniture World

I-77, Exit #82-A
Rock Hill, SC 29731

Phone:	(803) 328-3005	**Hours:**	M-Sat 9:00-5:30
Toll Free:	None	**E-mail:**	None
Fax:	(803) 328-3906	**Web site:**	None

Carolina Furniture World has a very nice 12,000 square foot store with galleries for high-end lines such as Broyhill, Hooker, American Drew, and Lane. They also do a big business in phone sales.

They don't have a clearance center or any floor samples or discontinued styles on the sales floor, so there's really no advantage to visiting in person. However, they do have good deals on some brands sold over the phone, anywhere from 30%-50% off retail.

If you plan to order furniture by phone, this source is worth calling to compare prices.

Lines carried:

American Drew	Cochrane	Lane
Broyhill	Hooker	Stanley
Charleston Forge	Kingsdown Bedding	Temple Upholstery

Phone orders accepted:	**Yes**
Discount:	**30%-50% off mfrs. suggested retail**
Payment methods:	**Personal checks. No credit cards.**
In-house financing available:	**No**
Deposits required:	**50% deposit when order is placed, balance due when furniture is ready to be shipped**
Catalog available:	**No**
Clearance center:	**No**
Delivery:	**Full service in-home delivery and set-up. Customer pays freight company directly for shipping costs.**

Directions: From I-77, take exit #82-A. Carolina Furniture World is right off the expressway.

Carolina Interiors

100 Oak Ave.
Kannapolis, NC 28081

Phone:	(704) 933-2261	**Hours:**	M-Sat 9:00-6:00
Toll Free:	None	**E-mail:**	None
Fax:	(704) 932-0434	**Web site:**	None

Carolina Interiors in Cannon Village has a very nice store with a good selection of high-end furniture. Most of the furniture in stock is new first-quality, and priced at about 40%-50% off retail. There are a few floor samples and discontinued styles scattered around priced at 50%-70% off retail. They will also sell by phone, and they claim to save you 30%-60% off retail on special order furniture. Also, the staff here tends to announce very quickly that all prices are negotiable, so be sure to haggle.

On my last visit here, I found a very good deal on a Hekman triple-arch bookcase (pictured on the following page). The retail on this piece is normally $7,518.00, but this one was marked down to only $3,799.00. This piece was brand-new and in first-quality condition.

If you are traveling to North Carolina to buy furniture, you really should consider taking one extra day to visit Cannon Village in Kannapolis. In addition to the Carolina Interiors, there are also true factory outlets for Baker, Century, and Maitland-Smith here that are well worth a visit. Kannapolis is about one half hour's drive north of Charlotte, one hour's drive south of High Point, and one hour's drive east of Hickory.

If you are ordering furniture by phone, definitely give this source a call. They have a very good reputation for customer service, and they will haggle. I have found that they will try hard to outdo any competitor's prices. Let them!

Lines carried:	**Please see page 78**
Phone orders accepted:	**Yes**
Discount:	**30%-60% off mfrs. suggested retail**
Payment methods:	**Personal checks. No credit cards.**
In-house financing available:	**No**
Deposits required:	**1/3 deposit when order is placed, balance due when furniture is ready to be shipped**
Catalog available:	**No**
Clearance center:	**No**
Delivery:	**Full service in-home delivery and set-up. Customer pays freight company directly for shipping costs.**

Directions: From I-85, take exit #63, and follow the signs to Cannon Village.

Carolina Interiors (cont.)

Carolina Interiors

Triple-arch bookcase from Hekman

Retail: $7,518.00   Discounted price: $3,799.00
Savings at Carolina Interiors: $3,719.00 = 50% off retail

Carolina Interiors (cont.)

Lines carried:

Accentrics By Pulaski
Action By Lane
Alexvale
American Drew
Artistica
As You Like It
Athol
Austin
Baker
Baldwin Brass
Barcalounger
Bashian Carpets
Bassett
Berkline
Bevan Funnell
Blacksmith Shop
Bradington Young
Braxton Culler
Broyhill
Butler Specialty
Cal-Style
Carolina Mirror
CTH/Sherrill
Carsons
Casa Bique
Casa Stradivari
Century
Chapman Lamps
Charleston Forge
Chelsea House/Port Royal
Chromecraft
Clark Casual
Clayton Marcus
Colonial
Councill Craftsmen
Couristan
Cox
Craftique
Craftwork Guild
C. R. Laine Upholstery
Davis & Davis Carpets
Decorative Crafts
Designmaster
Dillon
Dinaire
Distinction Leather
Ello
Fairfield
Fashion Bed Group

Flexsteel
Frederick Cooper
Friedman Bros.
Georgian Home Furnishings
Glass Arts
Great City Traders
Guildmaster
Habersham Plantation
Hammary
Hancock & Moore
Hart Lamps
Heirloom
Hekman
Henry Link Wicker
Hickory Chair
Hickory Frye
Hickory Leather
Hickory White
High Point Desk
Highland House
Hitchcock Chair
Hooker
House Parts
Howard Miller Clocks
HTB Lane
Hyundai Furniture
J. Royale
Jasper Cabinet
John Boos
John Richard
John Widdicomb
Johnston Casuals
Karges
Keller
Key City
Kimball
Kincaid
King Hickory
Kingsdown
Kingsley-Bate
Klaussner
La Barge
Lane
Lea
Lexington
Lloyd/Flanders
Lyon Shaw
Madison Square
Maitland-Smith

Marbro Lamps
Masland Carpet
McGuire
McKinley Leather
Michael Thomas
Moosehead
Motioncraft
Nichols & Stone
Old Hickory Tannery
Pande Cameron
Paoli
Park Place
Paul Robert
Pearson
Pennsylvania Classics
Pennsylvania House
Pine-tique
Pompeii
Preview
Pulaski
Richardson Bros.
Ridgeway Clocks
Riverside
Rowe
Royal Patina
S. Bent
Salem Square
Saloom
Sarreid
Sedgefield Lamps
Shuford
Sligh Desk/Clocks
Southampton
Southern Furniture
        Reproductions
Southern Of Conover
Southwood Reproductions
Speer Lamps
Stanford
Stanley
Stanton Cooper
Statesville Chair
Statton
Stein World
Stiffel
Stoneleigh
Swaim
Taylorsville
Thayer Coggin

Tianjin Philadelphia
        Carpets
Tradition House
Tropitone
Universal
Vanguard
Vaughan
Vaughan Bassett
Venture/Lane
Vermont Tubbs
Virginia House
Virginia Metalcrafters
Waterford Furniture
Wellington Hall
Wesley Allen
Wesley Hall
Wildwood Lamps
Winston
Woodard
Woodmark
Yorkshire House

Carolina Patio Warehouse

58 Largo Dr.
Stamford, CT 06907

Phone:	(203) 975-9939	**Hours:**	M-F 8:30-6:00, Sat 9:00-4:00
Toll Free:	(800) 672-8466	**E-mail:**	None
Fax:	(203) 975-7897	**Web site:**	www.carolinapatio.com

Carolina Patio Warehouse isn't actually based in North Carolina. It's operated by R & R Pool & Patio in Stamford, CT. Nevertheless, they do have a written guarantee promising to beat any competitors prices on wicker, rattan, and outdoor furniture. They also carry poolside furniture and umbrellas.

Their prices are generally about 30%-50% below the manufacturer's suggested retail. The store has no discontinued styles or floor samples available at added discounts, so there's not much reason to shop in person. If you plan to buy patio furniture over the phone, though, do give this source a call. They promise to beat any competitor's prices, so hold them to it!

Lines carried:

Atlantic Bench	Galtech	Pawley's Island	Triconfort
Basta Sole	Homecrest	Polywood	Tropitone
Beka	Kettler	Prairie Leisure	Tye-Sil Patio
Casual Creations	Kingsley Bate	Samsonite Aluminum	Veneman
Colonial Castings	Lane Venture	Scanply	Windsor Design
Coppa	Lyon Shaw	Summer Classics	Windward Classics
Cushion Factory	Outdoor Classics	Telescope	Zip

Phone orders accepted:	Yes
Discount:	30%-50% off mfrs. suggested retail
Payment methods:	VISA, MC, personal checks
In-house financing available:	No
Deposits required:	50% deposit when order is placed, balance due when furniture is ready to be shipped
Catalog available:	Yes
Clearance center:	No
Delivery:	Full service in-home delivery and set-up. Customer pays freight company directly for shipping costs.

Directions: From I-95 just north of Stamford, CT, take the Hwy. 106 exit and head north. After you go about 2 miles, turn left on Largo Dr. You'll see R & R Pool and Patio right after you turn onto Largo Dr.

Carrington Court Factory Outlet

Furniture Clearance Center
66 Hwy. 321 NW
Hickory, NC 28601

Phone:	**(828) 323-1558**	**Hours:**	**M-F 9:00-6:00, Sat 9:00-5:00**
Toll Free:	**None**	**E-mail:**	**None**
Fax:	**(828) 326-9846**	**Web site:**	**None**

The Furniture Clearance Center in Hickory, NC, is a combined factory-owned factory outlet for Drexel-Heritage, La Barge, Maitland-Smith, Sedgewick Rattan, Carrington Court, and Craftique. It occupies a huge warehouse building.

The stock consists of floor samples, customer returns, photography samples, and discontinued styles. Virtually all of the furniture here is in new first-quality condition. The discounts run from 50%-70% off retail, with most pieces around 60% off. They usually have a big sale every January and May when they mark most pieces an extra 10%-20% off.

If you travel to Hickory to shop for high-end traditional furniture, this outlet is a "must visit"!

Phone orders accepted:	**No**
Discount:	**50%-70% off mfrs. suggested retail**
Payment methods:	**VISA, MC, personal checks**
In-house financing available:	**No**
Deposits required:	**Not applicable**
Catalog available:	**Not applicable**
Clearance center:	**Not applicable**
Delivery:	**Full service in-home delivery and set-up. Customer pays freight company directly for shipping costs.**

Directions: From I-40, take exit #123 and drive north on Hwy. 321 into Hickory.

Cayton Furniture

4525 Hwy. 264 W.
Washington, NC 27889

Phone:	**(252) 946-4121**	**Hours:**	**M-F 9:00-5:00**
Toll Free:	**(800) 849-8286**	**E-mail:**	**caytonfurniture@coastalnet.com**
Fax:	**(252) 975-6225**	**Web site:**	**www.caytonfurniture.com**

Cayton Furniture has been discounting furniture by phone for over 40 years. They have an established reputation for reliable delivery and fairly good prices. They can special order nearly any line, with the exception of some of the most high-end manufacturers.

They have plenty of new first-quality furniture on the sales floor at their showroom, but virtually no floor samples or discontinued styles. This is frequently the case with discounters who are so far removed from the main furniture manufacturing centers and wholesale showrooms around Hickory and High Point, NC. There isn't much reason to shop here in person, but they are certainly worth considering as an order-by-phone source.

Cayton Furniture is in Washington, NC, about three hours drive east of High Point. As there are no other factory outlets or discounters within a three hour radius, it really isn't practical to plan a visit to this source if you're traveling to North Carolina from out-of-state to shop. However, if you're considering ordering your furniture by phone, it is certainly worth comparing prices here.

Lines carried:	**Please see page 82**
Phone orders accepted:	**Yes**
Discount:	**40%-50% off mfrs. suggested retail**
Payment methods:	**VISA, MC, personal checks**
In-house financing available:	**Yes**
Deposits required:	**50% deposit when order is placed, balance due when furniture is ready to be shipped**
Catalog available:	**No**
Clearance center:	**No**
Delivery:	**Full service in-home delivery and set-up. Customer pays freight company directly for shipping costs.**

Directions: From I-95, take exit #121 (Hwy. 264), and take Hwy. 264 east about one hour to Washington, NC. Cayton Furniture is on Hwy. 264 in downtown Washington.

Cayton Furniture (cont.)

Lines carried:

Accentrics
Action Industries
Alexander Julian
Alliance Art
American Chair & Table
American Country West
American Drew
Amindo Inc.
Amiran Corporation
Arnold Palmer
Art Master Pictures
Ashley Furniture Industry
Ashton Art
Athol
Atlantic Overtures
Austin Originals
Barcalounger
Barn Door
Bassett
Bassett Mirror
Beaulieu
Benchcraft
Berkline
Berkshire Furniture
Bob Timberlake
Brasscrafters
Broyhill
Builtrite Chair Co.
Butler Specialty
Cabin Craft Carpets
Caldwell Chair
Cambridge Chair
Cambridge Lamps
Canadel
Carolina Furniture Works
Carolina Mirror
Carter Contemporary
Chapel Hill Collections
China Trader
Classic Leather
Classic Rattan
Clayton House
Clayton Marcus
Colonial Mills Inc.
Cooper Classics
Coulbourn Lumber
Craftique
Craftmaster Furniture Co.
Craftsman Unlimited

Craftwood
Crawford Furniture Mfg.
Dalyn Oriental Rugs
Decorative Crafts Inc.
Design Horizons
Dillon
Distinction Leather
Distinctive Designs
Dixie Furniture Co.
Eddie Bauer
Ekornes
Embassy Furniture Co.
Fairfield Chair Co.
Fashion Bed Group
Fashion House
Fine Art Lamps
Flexsteel
Floral Art
Franklin Recliner
GMS
Hammary
Hancock & Moore
Heirloom Enterprises
Hekman
Henry Link Wicker
Heritage Picture Co.
Hickory Hill
Hickory Leather Co.
Highland House
High Point Furniture Co.
High Point Woodworking
Holiday Lamp & Lighting
Hood
Hooker
International Tables
J. H. Craver
Jasper Cabinet
Jetton Upholstery
Johnston Benchworks
JSF Industries
Kaiser-Kuhn Lamps
Keller Manufacturing Co.
Kennebunk Weavers
Keystone Lamp Mfg. Co.
Kimball International
Kincaid Furniture
Kingcraft Dining Room
Kingsdown Bedding
King Hickory

Koch
Lampcrafters
Lane
Lea
Leisters Furniture
Lexington
Lloyd/Flanders
Lyndon Shaker Furniture
Madison Square
Mar-Clay Manor
Martinsville Novelty Co.
Meadowcraft
Mer Rugs
Metal Arts
Michael Arts
Mobel
Morgan Stewart
Morganton Chair
Napp Deady Accessories
Nathan Hale
Natural Light Inc.
Nichols & Stone
Null Manufacturing Corp.
Olde Salem Collection
Ohio Table Pad Co.
Omega Rugs
Orderest Inc.
Oriental Lacquer
Oriental Weavers Rugs
Pande Cameron Rugs
Park Place
Pee Gee Lamps
Pennsylvania Classics
Pennsylvania House
Peoplelounger
Peters-Revington
Phillip-Reinich Curio
    Cabinets
Pulaski
Regency House
Reliance Lamps
Rembrandt Lamps
Rex Furniture
Richardson Bros.
Ridgewood Furniture
Riverside
Robert Abbey Lamps
Royola Pacific Ltd.
Rug Hold

Sam Moore Chair
S. K. Products
Saloom
Sarreid Ltd.
Sauder Woodworking
Schnadig International
Seay Furniture
Sedgefield Lamps
Serta
Shaw Rugs
Sherrill
Sherwood
Shoal Creek Lighting
Sidex International
Simmons Bedding
Somerset Studios
Something Different
Southern Craftsmen
Southern Manor
Spring Air Bedding
Stakmore
Stanley
Statesville Chair
Statton
Stratolounger
Studio One Accessories
Stylecraft Lamps
Superior Furniture
The Chair Co.
The Uttermost Co.
Timmerman
Towne Square
Toyo Trading Co.
Traders League
Triad Butcher Block
Tropitone
Universal
U. S. Furniture
Uttermost Mirrors
V. B. Williams Furn.
Vaughan Furniture
Victorian Classics
Villa Rey
Vintage Furniture
Virginia House
Virginia Metal
Waverly
Whitaker
Whitewood

Cedar Rock Home Furnishings

3483 Hickory Blvd., Hwy. 321 S.
Hudson, NC 28638

Phone:	(828) 396-2361	**Hours:**	M-Sat 9:00-5:00
Toll Free:	None	**E-mail:**	None
Fax:	(828) 396-7800	**Web site:**	None

Cedar Rock Home Furnishings is located just a few miles north of Hickory, NC. They have a very nice selection of high end lines, including Lexington, Broyhill, Stanley, and Hooker.

They don't have a clearance center or any floor samples or discontinued pieces on display. For this reason, there is no monetary advantage to visiting in person. They do have great deals on many lines sold over the phone, though. So, if you're planning to order your furniture by phone, definitely give this source a call to compare their prices.

Lines carried:	Please see page 84
Phone orders accepted:	Yes
Discount:	30%-50% off mfrs. suggested retail
Payment methods:	VISA, MC, personal checks
In-house financing available:	No
Deposits required:	50% deposit when order is placed, balance due when furniture is ready to be shipped
Catalog available:	No
Clearance center:	No
Delivery:	Full service in-home delivery and set-up. Customer pays freight company directly for shipping costs.

Directions: From I-40, take exit #123 and drive north on Hwy. 321 to Hudson, NC. Cedar Rock Home Furnishings is on the right side of the road.

Cedar Rock Home Furnishings (cont.)

Lines carried:

Action Lane
American Drew
American Of High Point
American Of Martinsville
Arnold Palmer
Art Gallery
As You Like It
Athens
Athol
Barcalounger
Bard
Bassett
Bassett Mirror
Berkline
Bevan Funnell
Bob Timberlake
Bradington Young
Brady Furniture
Brandon Manor
Brasscrafters
Braxton Culler
Brown Street
Broyhill
Broyhill Premiere
Builtright Chair
Cambridge Chair
Carolina Furniture Works
Carolina Mirror
Carolina Tables
Carter
Charleston Forge
Chromecraft
Classic Leather
Clayton Marcus
Clyde Pearson
Coaster Co.
Cochrane
Colonial Braided Rugs
Colonial Furniture
Conover Chair
Cosco Baby Furniture
Councill Craftsmen
Craftique
Craftmaster
Crawford
Crescent
C. R. Laine
Crown Arts
Denny Lamps

Design Horizons
Dillon
Dinaire
Distinction Leather
Edward Art
Emerson Leather
Excel. Office-Contract
Fairfield Chair
Fairmont Designs
Fashion Bed Group
Ficks Reed
Flexsteel
Froelich
H. A. DeNunzio
        Oil Paintings
Hammary
Hampton Hall
Hanover Heirlooms
Hekman
Henry Link
Hickory Classics
Hickory Hill
Hickory Leather
Hickory Tavern
Highland House
Hitchcock Chair
Hooker
Howard Miller
Huntington House
Hyundai Furniture
International-Karpen
Jasper Cabinet
Johnston Casuals
J. Royale
Keller
Key City
Kimball Upholstery
King Hickory
Lane
Lane/Venture
Lea
Leather Classics
Leathercraft
Leisters
Lexington
Link Taylor
Lyn Hollyn-Lexington
Lyon Shaw
Madison Square

Master Design
Masterfield
Mobel
Morgan Stewart
Morganton Chair
Nathan Hale
National Mt. Airy
Nichols & Stone
North Hickory
Null
Oakland Furniture
Ohio Table Pads
Old Hickory Tannery
Palliser
Paragon Pictures
Park Place
Paul Roberts
Pennsylvania Classics
Peters-Revington
Pinnacle
Polcor Bedding
Pulaski
Quoizel
Reprocrafters
Rex Furniture
Richardson Bros.
Ridgeway Clocks
Riverside
Rosalco
Rowe
Salem Square
Sam Moore
Sarreid
Schweiger
Sealy Bedding
Serta Bedding
Signature Lamps
Simmons Baby/Juvenile
Skillcraft
Southern Graphics
Southern Of Conover
Southwood Reproductions
Spring Wall Bedding
Stanley
Stanton-Cooper
Statesville Chair
Stiffel Lamps
Sumter Cabinet
Superior Furniture

Symbol Bedding
Taylorsville Upholstery
Temple
Temple-Stewart
Timeless Bedding
Town Square
Uwharrie Chair
Universal
Vanguard
Vaughan
Vaughan-Bassett
Venture
Virginia House
Virginia Metalcrafters
Weiman Tables
Wellington Hall
Wesley Allen
Winston
Woodmark
Yorkshire Leather

Central Furniture Outlet

2352 English Rd.
High Point, NC 27262

Phone:	(336) 882-9511	**Hours:**	M-Sat 9:00-6:00, Sun 12:00-5:00
Toll Free:	None	**E-mail:**	None
Fax:	(336) 882-0212	**Web site:**	None

Central Furniture Outlet buys market samples at the various wholesale shows in the area and resells them to the public. The deals here range from pretty good to not great.

Most of the stock here was Bassett and Natuzzi on my most recent visit here, but the brands they have in stock change constantly. They typically have a "winter blowout sale" every January when they discount everything an extra 30%.

This can be a confusing place for an amateur furniture shopper. If you have a good understanding of what furniture is worth, you can get some good deals here. Otherwise, it would be better to stick with the true factory outlets in the area which have clearer and more consistent pricing.

Phone orders accepted:	No
Discount:	40%-50% off mfrs. suggested retail
Payment methods:	VISA, MC, personal checks
In-house financing available:	No
Deposits required:	Not applicable
Catalog available:	Not applicable
Clearance center:	Not applicable
Delivery:	Full service in-home delivery and set-up. Customer pays freight company directly for shipping costs.

Directions: From I-85, take exit #111 (Hwy. 311), and head northwest into High Point. After several miles, when you reach downtown High Point, Hwy. 311 will become S. Main St. As you get into downtown High Point, turn left on College Dr., and go about five miles. Turn right on English Rd. Central Furniture Outlet is about two miles down on the left.

Century Factory Outlet

1120 Hwy. 16 N.
Conover, NC 28613

Phone:	**(828) 464-9940**	**Hours:**	**M-Sat 9:00-6:00**
Toll Free:	**None**	**E-mail:**	**None**
Fax:	**(828) 464-9964**	**Web site:**	**None**

The Century Factory Outlet is a part of Factory Direct Furniture in Conover, NC. This showroom also serves as the factory outlet for Councill Craftsmen and Hickory Chair. This location and their other showroom in the Hickory Furniture Mart, operated by the same company, are the only two factory-owned factory outlets for these three brands.

The discounts on the outlet furniture generally runs a straight 60% off across the board. Virtually all of the furniture here is in new first-quality condition.

At both locations, the sales staff immediately volunteers to customers that they can come down even further from the price marked, so be sure to haggle. Factory Direct Furniture also runs periodic sales, usually giving another 10%-20% off the marked discount. These sales normally run in January, March, May, and September.

Both locations have an excellent selection. Most of the pieces are traditional, but there are usually a few contemporary styles. On my most recent visit here, I found a Century writing desk (pictured on the following page) that normally retails for $4,410.00 marked down to $1,764.00, a discount of 60% off the normal retail price. This particular piece was a floor sample in first-quality condition.

If you're traveling to the Hickory area, this outlet is a "must-visit". If you don't find what you're looking for here, be sure to check their other location about ten minutes away at the Hickory Furniture Mart.

Phone orders accepted:	**No**
Discount:	**60% off mfrs. suggested retail**
Payment methods:	**VISA, MC, personal checks**
In-house financing available:	**No**
Deposits required:	**Not applicable**
Catalog available:	**Not applicable**
Clearance center:	**Not applicable**
Delivery:	**Full service in-home delivery and set-up. Customer pays freight company directly for shipping costs.**

Directions: From I-40, take exit #131, and go one-quarter mile north on Hwy. 16 North. Factory Direct Furniture will be on the right side of the highway.

Century Factory Outlet (cont.)

Century Factory Outlet at FactoryDirect Furniture in Conover, NC

Writing desk from Century Furniture

Retail: $4,410.00   Discounted price: $1,764.00
Savings at the Century Factory Outlet: $2,646.00 = 60% off retail

Century Factory Outlet

Level 4
Hickory Furniture Mart
U. S. Hwy. 70 SE
Hickory, NC 28602

Phone:	**(828) 324-9400**	**Hours:**	**M-Sat 9:00-6:00**
Toll Free:	**None**	**E-mail:**	**info@hickoryfurniture.com**
Fax:	**(828) 464-9964**	**Web site:**	**www.hickoryfurniture.com**

The Century Factory Outlet is a part of the National Furniture Outlets space at the Hickory Furniture Mart. This showroom also serves as the factory outlet for Councill Craftsmen and Hickory Chair. This location and one more warehouse in nearby Conover, NC, operated by the same company are the only two factory-owned factory outlets for these three brands.

This location is about half-stocked with antiques and accessories, with the other half of the showroom devoted to discontinued styles and floor samples from the above-mentioned three brands. The discounts on the outlet furniture generally runs a straight 60% off across the board. Virtually all of the furniture here is in new first-quality condition.

At both locations, the sales staff immediately volunteers to customers that they can come down even further from the price marked, so be sure to haggle. National Furniture Outlets also runs periodic sales, usually giving another 10%-20% off the marked discount. These sales normally run in January, March, May, and September.

Both locations have an excellent selection. Most of the pieces are traditional, but there are usually a few contemporary styles. On my most recent visit here, I found a Century leather sofa (pictured on the following page) that normally retails for $5,040.00 marked down to $2,016.00, a discount of 60% off the normal retail price. This particular piece was a floor sample in first-quality condition.

If you're traveling to Hickory, this outlet is a "must-visit". If you don't find what you're looking for here, be sure to check their other location about ten minutes away in Conover, NC.

Phone orders accepted:	**No**
Discount:	**60% off mfrs. suggested retail**
Payment methods:	**VISA, MC, personal checks**
In-house financing available:	**No**
Deposits required:	**Not applicable**
Catalog available:	**Not applicable**
Clearance center:	**Not applicable**
Delivery:	**Full service in-home delivery and set-up. Customer pays freight company directly for shipping costs.**

Directions: Please see *Hickory Furniture Mart* for complete directions.

Century Factory Outlet (cont.)

Leather sofa from Century Furniture

Retail: $5,040.00   Discounted price: $2,016.00
Savings at the Century Factory Outlet: $3,024.00 = 60% off retail

Century Factory Outlet

146 West Ave.
Kannapolis, NC 28081

Phone:	**(704) 938-9191**	**Hours:**	**M-Sat 9:00-6:00**
Toll Free:	**None**	**E-mail:**	**None**
Fax:	**(704) 932-2503**	**Web site:**	**None**

The Century Factory Outlet is located inside the Village Furniture House in Cannon Village. This is the smallest of Century's three North Carolina factory outlets, but they do have some terrific deals here.

Most of the stock here are floor samples and discontinued styles in new first-quality condition. There's a nice selection of case goods: dining room sets, desks, armoires, beds, etc.

On my most recent visit here, I found a discontinued Century mahogany dining room set (pictured on the following page). The table normally retails for $3,824.00, but it was marked down to $1,199.00. The chairs normally retail for $2,262.00 each, but they were marked down to $699.00 apiece. The set was in brand-new first-quality condition.

If you are traveling to North Carolina to buy furniture, you really should consider taking one extra day to visit Cannon Village in Kannapolis. In addition to the Century outlet, there are also true factory outlets for Baker and Maitland-Smith here that are well worth a visit. Kannapolis is about one half hour's drive north of Charlotte, one hour's drive south of High Point, and one hour's drive east of Hickory.

Phone orders accepted:	**No**
Discount:	**60%-75% off mfrs. suggested retail**
Payment methods:	**Personal checks. No credit cards.**
In-house financing available:	**No**
Deposits required:	**Not applicable**
Catalog available:	**Not applicable**
Clearance center:	**Not applicable**
Delivery:	**Full service in-home delivery and set-up. Customer pays freight company directly for shipping costs.**

Directions: From I-85, take exit #63, and follow the signs to Cannon Village. The Century Factory Outlet is accessible through the Village Furniture House on West Ave. inside Cannon Village.

Century Factory Outlet (cont.)

Century Factory Outlet in Kannapolis, NC

Mahogany dining room set from Century Furniture

Retail: $12,872.00   Discounted price: $3,995.00
Savings at the Century Factory Outlet: $8,877.00 = 69% off retail

Cherry Hill Furniture & Interiors

P. O. Box 7405
Furnitureland Station
High Point, NC 27264

Phone:	**(336) 882-0933**	**Hours:**	**M-F 9:00-6:00, Sat 10:00-6:00**
Toll Free:	**(800) 328-0933**	**E-mail:**	**None**
	(800) 888-0933	**Web site:**	**None**
Fax:	**(336) 882-0900**		

Cherry Hill Furniture & Interiors is an order-by-phone service only. They have a huge distribution center in High Point, but there is no facility for customers to visit in person.

In most cases, customers should avoid ordering by phone from companies that don't have a showroom open to the public, but Cherry Hill Furniture is an exception. They've been in business for over sixty-five years, and they have an excellent reputation. In fact, they were one of the very first North Carolina furniture discounters to begin taking phone orders nationwide.

Cherry Hill Furniture does not publish a list of the lines they carry. However, I have found that they can order almost any brand. If you're considering ordering any brand of furniture or accessories by phone, definitely call this source to compare their price first.

Lines carried:	**Please call for more information**
Phone orders accepted:	**Yes**
Discount:	**40% to 50% off mfrs. suggested retail**
Payment methods:	**VISA, MC, personal checks**
In-house financing available:	**No**
Deposits required:	**50% deposit when order is placed, balance due when furniture is ready to be shipped**
Catalog available:	**No**
Clearance center:	**No**
Delivery:	**Full service in-home delivery and set-up. Customer pays freight company directly for shipping costs.**

Directions: Not applicable. This source has no showroom open to the public.

Classic Leather Factory Outlet (Alamance Furniture Outlet)

2631 Ramada Rd.
Burlington, NC 27215

Phone:	**(336) 570-0444**	**Hours:**	**M-F 10:00-5:30, Sat 10:00-5:00**
Toll Free:	**(800) 328-0933**	**E-mail:**	**None**
Fax:	**(336) 570-0473**	**Web site:**	**None**

This is the only factory-owned factory outlet for Classic Leather. They have a terrific selection of leather sofas and chairs, including executive office chairs. If you're ever decorating a law office, this is the place to shop!

Virtually all of the stock here is discontinued styles and colors and floor samples. The prices run 40%-60% off retail. The vast majority of the stock here is Classic Leather, but they also have a small area with case goods from Pennsylvania Classics and Statesville Chair. There are also some pieces from Kaiser Kuhn Lighting.

On my last visit here, I found a beautiful burgundy leather sofa (pictured on the next page) that retailed for $4,050.00, marked down to $2,321.00. It was a discontinued color in new first-quality condition.

The outlet won't allow customers to special order from Classic Leather's current line, but if you know what style and color you want, you can call the outlet to see if they have that style and color (or something similar) on the sales floor. If they do, you can order it over the phone at the outlet price and have it shipped to you.

Also, Classic Leather uses this outlet to get rid of their remaining stock of discontinued leathers. If you see a Classic Leather style that you like in a retail store, you can call the outlet and tell them the particular style and color you're interested in. They won't special order that particular color for you because it's part of their current line which is restricted to retailers only. However, they will search their stock of discontinued leathers for the closest color they can find to the one you want, and send you a swatch for approval. If you decide to order, they will custom make your sofa or chair in any style you like upholstered in the discontinued leather. All of this is still at the outlet price of 40%-60% off retail.

The staff here is amazingly friendly and helpful. If you're in the Burlington area, about an hour's drive east of High Point, you really should consider stopping in. This outlet, along with the Pennsylvania House and Hickory White outlets next door, is a "must visit" if you're looking for leather furniture.

If you plan to special order leather furniture, give these folks a chance to find you the color and style you want first before you order new furniture elsewhere. Assuming they have the color leather you want in their discontinued stock, and they had a very wide selection to choose from, you'll get your best deal here.

Phone orders accepted:	**Yes**
Discount:	**40% to 60% off mfrs. suggested retail**
Payment methods:	**VISA, MC, personal checks**
In-house financing available:	**No**
Deposits required:	**Full payment due with order**
Catalog available:	**Not applicable**
Clearance center:	**Not applicable**
Delivery:	**Full service in-home delivery and set-up. Customer pays freight company directly for shipping costs.**

Directions: From I-40, take exit #143. The outlet is just off the interstate.

Classic Leather Factory Outlet (cont.)

Classic Leather Factory Outlet

Leather sofa from Classic Leather

Retail: $4,050.00   Discounted price: $2,321.00
Savings at the Classic Leather Factory Outlet: $1,729.00 = 43% off retail

Clayton-Marcus Factory Outlet

Triplett's Furniture Fashions
2084 Hickory Blvd. SW
Lenoir, NC 28645

Phone:	**(828) 728-8211**	**Hours:**	**M-Sat 8:30-5:00**
Toll Free:	**None**	**E-mail:**	**None**
Fax:	**(828) 726-0171**	**Web site:**	**None**

Triplett's Furniture Fashions houses a brand-new factory outlet for Clayton-Marcus. This is Clayton Marcus' only factory outlet anywhere.

The stock is made up of floor samples, discontinued styles, and customer returns. All of the furniture here is upholstery: sofas and occasional chairs. The discounts run from 65%-75% off retail. Virtually all of the furniture here is in new first-quality condition.

On my most recent visit here, I found a great deal on a Clayton-Marcus armchair (pictured on the following page). It normally retails for $401.00, but this one was only $145.00. It was in new first-quality condition, but the fabric had been discontinued.

If you're in the Lenoir/Hickory area, and you're looking for high-end upholstery, you may wish to stop by here. Clayton-Marcus produces very fine quality upholstery, and the prices at the outlet here are very good.

Phone orders accepted:	**No**
Discount:	**65%-75% off mfrs. suggested retail**
Payment methods:	**VISA, MC, personal checks**
In-house financing available:	**No**
Deposits required:	**Not applicable**
Catalog available:	**Not applicable**
Clearance center:	**Not applicable**
Delivery:	**Full service in-home delivery and set-up. Customer pays freight company directly for shipping costs.**

Directions: **From I-40, take exit #123 and drive north on Hwy. 321 to Lenoir. Triplett's Furniture Fashions is on the left side of the road.**

Clayton-Marcus Factory Outlet (cont.)

Armchair from Clayton-Marcus

Retail: $401.00   Discounted price: $145.00
Savings at the Clayton Marcus Factory Outlet: $256.00 = 65% off retail

Coffey Furniture

Hwy. 321, Poovey Dr.
Granite Falls, NC 28630

Phone:	(828) 396-2900	**Hours:**	M-F 9:00-5:00
Toll Free:	None	**E-mail:**	None
Fax:	(828) 396-3050	**Web site:**	None

Coffey Furniture specializes in purchasing market samples from the various wholesale trade shows and reselling them to the public. They have three huge warehouses filled with all kinds of case goods and upholstery. They will also special order new furniture from many lines.

Nothing is marked at a discount; everything is just one flat price. This can make it confusing for an amateur furniture shopper to make sure their getting the best deal without the original manufacturer's retail as a reference point. The prices I have observed here seem to run approximately 30% to 60% off retail. There are some very good deals here mixed in with some other not-so-good deals.

This is a good place for an experienced furniture shopper to visit. Others may find it confusing. Those who don't have a good basic knowledge of what furniture is worth should stick with other sources.

Lines carried:

Action by Lane	Crawford	J. B. Ross	Pulaski
American Drew	Denny Lamps	Kimball Victorian	Ridgeway Clocks
Athens	Dining Ala Carte	Lane	Royale Komfort
Bassett	Dresher	Lane/Venture	Bedding
Bassett Baby/Juvenile	Fairfield Chair	Lea	Seay
Berkshire	Fashion Bed Group	Liberty	Spring Air Bedding
Blacksmith Shop	Flexsteel	Link Taylor	Temple Upholstery
Cal-Style	Goodwin Weavers	Lloyd/Flanders	U. S. Furniture Industry
Century Rugs	Hickory Hill	Morganton Chair	Universal
Chatham County	Hickory Mark	Ohio Table Pad	Vanguard Pictures
Chromecraft	Holiday House Sleepers	Parker Southern	Wesley Allen
Clayton Marcus	Howard Miller Clocks	Peters Revington	
Cochrane	Hyundai Furniture	Philip Reinisch Co.	

Phone orders accepted:	Yes
Discount:	30%-60% off mfrs. suggested retail
Payment methods:	Personal checks. No credit cards.
In-house financing available:	No
Deposits required:	50% deposit when order is placed, balance due when furniture is ready to be shipped
Catalog available:	No
Clearance center:	No
Delivery:	Full service in-home delivery and set-up. Customer pays freight company directly for shipping costs.

Directions: From I-40, take exit #123 and drive north on Hwy. 321 to Granite Falls. Coffey Furniture is off the highway on the left at the end of Poovey Dr.

Coffey Furniture (cont.)

Coffey Furniture

Colfax Furniture

3501 McCuiston Ct.
I-85 at Holden Rd.
Greensboro, NC 27407

Phone:	**(336) 855-0498**	**Hours:**	**M-F 10:00-9:00, Sat 10:00-6:00,**
Toll Free:	**None**		**Sun 1:00-6:00**
Fax:	**None**	**E-mail:**	**None**
		Web site:	**None**

Colfax Furniture specializes in purchasing market samples from the various wholesale trade shows and reselling them to the public. They have an enormous warehouse filled with all kinds of case goods and upholstery, including a wide selection of recliners. Most of the furniture here is medium-quality. I saw very few high-end brands.

Nothing is marked at a discount; everything is just one flat price. This can make it confusing for an amateur furniture shopper to make sure their getting the best deal without the original manufacturer's retail as a reference point. The prices I have observed here seem to run approximately 30% to 70% off retail. There are some very good deals here mixed in with some other not-so-good deals.

This is a good place for an experienced furniture shopper to visit. Others may find it confusing. Those who don't have a good basic knowledge of what furniture is worth should stick with other sources.

Phone orders accepted:	**No**
Discount:	**30%-70% off mfrs. suggested retail**
Payment methods:	**VISA, MC, AMEX, personal checks**
In-house financing available:	**Yes**
Deposits required:	**Not applicable**
Catalog available:	**Not applicable**
Clearance center:	**Not applicable**
Delivery:	**Full service in-home delivery and set-up. Customer pays freight company directly for shipping costs.**

Directions: From I-85, take exit #121 (Holden Rd.). Colfax Furniture is right off the interstate on the frontage road.

Collector's Furniture Gallery

1300 N. Main St.
High Point, NC 27262

Phone:	**(336) 887-3000**	**Hours:**	**M-F 9:00-6:00, Sat 9:00-5:00**
Toll Free:	**None**	**E-mail:**	**collgall@northstate.net**
Fax:	**(336) 887-0329**	**Web site:**	**www.acollectorsgallery.com**

Collector's Furniture Gallery has a very impressive store in downtown High Point, NC, with a good selection of high end furniture from Pennsylvania House, Hekman, Flexsteel, and others. Most lines are priced at 50% off retail, with a few lines discounted as much as 60% off retail.

There are a few floor samples and discontinued styles on the sales floor as well, marked at even higher discounts. On my most recent visit here, I found a wonderful bargain on a Hekman solid mahogany entertainment center (pictured on the following page). The normal retail on this piece is $6,223.00, but this one at Collector's was marked down to $2,495.00, a discount of 60% off retail. This piece was in perfect condition.

I was also very impressed with the helpfulness of the staff here. If you plan to be in High Point anyway, you should definitely stop by to check out the bargains on discontinued styles and floor samples. If you plan to order your furniture by phone (particularly Pennsylvania House), you should call Collector's to compare their prices.

Lines carried:

American Drew	Hammary	Pennsylvania Classics	Statesville Chair
Craftique	Hekman	Pennsylvania House	Woodmark
Crawford	Howard Miller Clocks	Sealy Mattress	
Flexsteel	La Barge	Serta Mattress	

Phone orders accepted:	**Yes**
Discount:	**50%-60% off mfrs. suggested retail**
Payment methods:	**VISA, MC, personal checks**
In-house financing available:	**No**
Deposits required:	**50% deposit when order is placed, balance due when furniture is ready to be shipped**
Catalog available:	**No**
Clearance center:	**No**
Delivery:	**Full service in-home delivery and set-up. Customer pays freight company directly for shipping costs.**

Directions: **From I-85, take exit #111 (Hwy. 311), and head northwest into High Point. After several miles, when you reach downtown High Point, Hwy. 311 will become Main St. Collector's Furniture Gallery is beyond the downtown area on the right side of Main St.**

Collector's Furniture Gallery (cont.)

Collector's Furniture Gallery

Solid mahogany entertainment center from Hekman

Retail: $6,223.00   Discounted price: $2,495.00
Savings at Collector's Furniture Gallery: $3,728.00 = 60% off retail

Corner Hutch Furniture

210 Signal Hill Dr.
Statesville, NC 28687

Phone:	(704) 873-1773	**Hours:**	M-F 9:00-5:30, Sat 10:00-5:30
Toll Free:	None	**E-mail:**	None
Fax:	(704) 873-1637	**Web site:**	None

Corner Hutch Furniture located just a few miles north of Hickory, NC. They have a good selection of high end lines, including galleries for Hickory Chair, Statton, Century, and Councill Craftsmen.

They don't have a clearance center or any floor samples or discontinued pieces on display, so there's no reason to go in person. They do have great deals on many lines sold over the phone, though.

Lines carried:

American Drew	Distinction Leather	Kingsdown Bedding	Sarreid
Baldwin Brass	Fashion Bed Group	La Barge	Sedgefield
Barcalounger	Frederick Cooper Lamps	Lane	Serta
Boling Chair	Hancock & Moore	Lane/Venture	Southampton
Bradington Young	Friedman Bros. Mirrors	Lea	Southwood Reproductions
Brown Jordan	Habersham Plantation	Lexington	
Broyhill	Hale Of Vermont	Lloyd/Flanders	Stanley
Builtright Chair	Hammary	Lyon Shaw	Stiffel Lamps
Carolina Mirror	Hekman	Madison Square	Superior
Cebu Imports	Henry Link Wicker	Maryland Classics	S. Bent
Chapman Lamps	Hickory Tavern	McKay Table Pads	Tradition House
Charleston Forge	Hickory White	Nichols & Stone	Tropitone
Chelsea House	Highland House	North Hickory Upholstery	Universal
Clark Casual	Hitchcock Chair	Ohio Table Pads	Virginia House
Cochrane	Hooker	Old Hickory Tannery	Virginia Metalcrafters
Colonial	Howard Miller Clocks	Pande Cameron Rugs	Wellington Hall
Conover Upholstery	Jasper Cabinet	Park Place Upholstery	Wildwood Lamps
Corsican Beds	Kaiser Kuhn Lamps	Pulaski	Winston
Cox Upholstery	Keller	Richardson Bros.	Woodmark Chairs
Craftique	King Hickory Upholstery	Salem Square	

Phone orders accepted:	Yes
Discount:	**40%-50% off mfrs. suggested retail**
Payment methods:	**VISA, MC, personal checks**
In-house financing available:	No
Deposits required:	**50% deposit when order is placed, balance due when furniture is ready to be shipped**
Catalog available:	No
Clearance center:	No
Delivery:	**Full service in-home delivery and set-up. Customer pays freight company directly for shipping costs.**

Directions: **From I-40, take exit #123 and drive north on Hwy. 321 to Granite Falls. Thomas Home Furnishings is on the right side of the road.**

Councill-Craftsmen Factory Outlet

1120 Hwy. 16 N.
Conover, NC 28613

Phone:	**(828) 464-9940**	**Hours:**	**M-Sat 9:00-6:00**
Toll Free:	**None**	**E-mail:**	**None**
Fax:	**(828) 464-9964**	**Web site:**	**None**

The Councill-Craftsmen Factory Outlet is a part of Factory Direct Furniture in Conover, NC. This showroom also serves as the factory outlet for Century and Hickory Chair. This location and their other showroom in the Hickory Furniture Mart, operated by the same company, are the only two factory-owned factory outlets for these three brands.

The discounts on the outlet furniture generally runs a straight 60% off across the board. Virtually all of the furniture here is in new first-quality condition.

At both locations, the sales staff immediately volunteers to customers that they can come down even further from the price marked, so be sure to haggle. Factory Direct Furniture also runs periodic sales, usually giving another 10%-20% off the marked discount. These sales normally run in January, March, May, and September.

Both locations have an excellent selection. Most of the pieces are traditional, but there are usually a few contemporary styles.

If you're traveling to the Hickory area, this outlet is a "must-visit". If you don't find what you're looking for here, be sure to check their other location about ten minutes away at the Hickory Furniture Mart.

Phone orders accepted:	**No**
Discount:	**60% off mfrs. suggested retail**
Payment methods:	**VISA, MC, personal checks**
In-house financing available:	**No**
Deposits required:	**Not applicable**
Catalog available:	**Not applicable**
Clearance center:	**Not applicable**
Delivery:	**Full service in-home delivery and set-up. Customer pays freight company directly for shipping costs.**

Directions: **From I-40, take exit #131, and go one-quarter mile north on Hwy. 16 North. Factory Direct Furniture will be on the right side of the highway.**

Councill-Craftsmen Factory Outlet

Level 4
Hickory Furniture Mart
U. S. Hwy. 70 SE
Hickory, NC 28602

Phone:	**(828) 324-9400**	**Hours:**	**M-Sat 9:00-6:00**
Toll Free:	**None**	**E-mail:**	**info@hickoryfurniture.com**
Fax:	**(828) 464-9964**	**Web site:**	**www.hickoryfurniture.com**

The Councill-Craftsmen Factory Outlet is a part of the National Furniture Outlets space at the Hickory Furniture Mart. This showroom also serves as the factory outlet for Century and Hickory Chair. This location and one more warehouse in nearby Conover, NC, operated by the same company are the only two factory-owned factory outlets for these three brands.

This location is about half-stocked with antiques and accessories, with the other half of the showroom devoted to discontinued styles and floor samples from the above-mentioned three brands. The discounts on the outlet furniture generally runs a straight 60% off across the board. Virtually all of the furniture here is in new first-quality condition.

At both locations, the sales staff immediately volunteers to customers that they can come down even further from the price marked, so be sure to haggle. National Furniture Outlets also runs periodic sales, usually giving another 10%-20% off the marked discount. These sales normally run in January, March, May, and September.

Both locations have an excellent selection. Most of the pieces are traditional, but there are usually a few contemporary styles.

If you're traveling to Hickory, this outlet is a "must-visit". If you don't find what you're looking for here, be sure to check their other location about ten minutes away in Conover, NC.

Phone orders accepted:	**No**
Discount:	**60% off mfrs. suggested retail**
Payment methods:	**VISA, MC, personal checks**
In-house financing available:	**No**
Deposits required:	**Not applicable**
Catalog available:	**Not applicable**
Clearance center:	**Not applicable**
Delivery:	**Full service in-home delivery and set-up. Customer pays freight company directly for shipping costs.**

Directions: Please see *Hickory Furniture Mart* for complete directions.

Craftique Factory Outlet

Furniture Clearance Center
66 Hwy. 321 NW
Hickory, NC 28601

Phone:	**(828) 323-1558**	**Hours:**	**M-F 9:00-6:00, Sat 9:00-5:00**
Toll Free:	**None**	**E-mail:**	**None**
Fax:	**(828) 326-9846**	**Web site:**	**None**

The Furniture Clearance Center in Hickory, NC, is a combined factory-owned factory outlet for Drexel-Heritage, La Barge, Maitland-Smith, Sedgewick Rattan, Carrington Court, and Craftique. It occupies a huge warehouse building.

The stock consists of floor samples, customer returns, photography samples, and discontinued styles. Virtually all of the furniture here is in new first-quality condition. The discounts run from 50%-70% off retail, with most pieces around 60% off. They usually have a big sale every January and May when they mark most pieces an extra 10%-20% off.

If you travel to Hickory to shop for high-end traditional furniture, this outlet is a "must visit"!

Phone orders accepted:	**No**
Discount:	**50%-70% off mfrs. suggested retail**
Payment methods:	**VISA, MC, personal checks**
In-house financing available:	**No**
Deposits required:	**Not applicable**
Catalog available:	**Not applicable**
Clearance center:	**Not applicable**
Delivery:	**Full service in-home delivery and set-up. Customer pays freight company directly for shipping costs.**

Directions: **From I-40, take exit #123 and drive north on Hwy. 321 into Hickory. Furniture Clearance Center is about two miles down on the right.**

Dallas Furniture

215 N. Centennial St.
High Point, NC 27261

Phone:	(336) 884-5759	**Hours:**	M-Sat 9:00-5:30
Toll Free:	None	**E-mail:**	None
Fax:	(336) 884-8830	**Web site:**	None

Dallas Furniture is located near downtown High Point, NC. They have a good selection of medium to high-end lines, including Lexington, Broyhill, Wellington Hall, and Hooker.

They don't have a clearance center or any floor samples or discontinued pieces on display. For this reason, there is no monetary advantage to visiting in person.

Dallas Furniture sometimes has good deals on furniture purchases over the phone, though. If you're planning to buy your furniture over the phone, it's worth your time to call this source and compare prices.

Phone orders accepted:	Yes
Discount:	30%-50% off mfrs. suggested retail
Payment methods:	VISA, MC, personal checks
In-house financing available:	No
Deposits required:	50% deposit when order is placed, balance due when furniture is ready to be shipped
Catalog available:	No
Clearance center:	No
Delivery:	Full service in-home delivery and set-up. Customer pays freight company directly for shipping costs.

Directions: From I-85, take exit #111 (Hwy. 311), and head northwest into High Point. After several miles, when you reach downtown High Point, Hwy. 311 will become S. Main St. Just after you go past Business 85 heading into downtown High Point, turn right on Centennial St. Dallas Furniture is a few miles down on the left side of the road.

Dallas Furniture (cont.)

Lines carried:

Alexander Julian
American Drew
American Mirror
American Of Martinsville
Andrea Sadek
Art Gallery
Arte de Mexico
As You Like It
Ashley Manor
Athens
Bassett
Berkline
Bernards
Best Chairs
Brasscrafters
Braxton Culler
Brett Austin
British Traditions
Broyhill
Capel Rugs
Capitol Leather
Carolina Furniture
Carolina Mirror
Carver's Guild
CBK
Charles Sadek
Chatham County
Classic Georgian
Claude Gable
Colonial
Comfort Designs
Corolla Classics
Craftique
Crawford
Crystal Clear
D & F Wicker & Rattan
Dauphine Mirror
Decorative Crafts
DeNunzio
Design Guild Lamps
Distinctive Designs
Dowell Craft
Erwin Lambeth
Fairfield Chair
Fashion Bed Group
Flair
Flexsteel
Florida Furniture
Franklin

Froelich
Futuristic
Games
Glass Arts
Harden
Harris Marcus
Hekman
Henry Link
Hickory Hill
Hooker
Howard Miller Clocks
Hyundai Furniture
Interline Leather
Jay Willfred
Kimball
Kincaid
Koch
Lane
Lea
Leisters
Lexington
Lyon Shaw
Madison Square
Mario
Martinsville Novelty
Master Design
Millennium
Mobel
Nora Fenton
Norman Perry Lamps
Northern Harvest
Null
Old Hickory Tannery
Pama
Paper White
Passport
Pilliod
Progressive
Pulaski
Rex
Riverside
Rowe
Salem Square
Sam Moore
Samuel Lawrence
SEE Imports
Sedgefield
Select
Sentry Rugs

Stakmore
Stein World
Stylecraft
Tafco
Taylorsville
Terrycraft
Timmerman
Tomlin
Universal
U. S. Furniture
Uttermost
Uwharrie Chair
Vaughan
Vaughan Bassett
Virginia Metalcrafters
Webb
Weiman
Wellington Hall
Wildwood
William Alan
Winston

Don Lamor

Level 4
Hickory Furniture Mart
U. S. Hwy. 70 SE
Hickory, NC 28602

Phone:	**(828) 324-1776**	**Hours:**	**M-Sat 9:00-6:00**
Toll Free:	**None**	**E-mail:**	**sales@donlamor.com**
Fax:	**(828) 324-1676**	**Web site:**	**www.donlamor.com**

The Don Lamor gallery in the Hickory Furniture Mart has a good selection of contemporary and traditional furniture, case goods and upholstery. They have a huge Pennsylvania House gallery, as well as a smaller galleries for Classic Leather, Weiman, and Vanguard. They also have a huge rug room.

Don Lamor only sells new furniture. There aren't any floor samples or discontinued pieces on the sales floor, and they have no clearance center. Their discounts are pretty good, though: 40%-50% off retail. All of their Pennsylvania House furniture is 50% off retail, which is a very good discount for this line.

They also have several nice lines that sell "knock-offs" of better known brands. Michaels Furniture, for instance, has very nice quality knock-offs of Stickley's most popular pieces. Tom Seely Furniture has high quality duplicates of many Lexington pieces, including some styles that are virtually identical to Lexington's very popular Bob Timberlake designs.

If you're ordering furniture by phone, you should definitely call this source for a price comparison. They've been in business for many, many years, and they have an excellent reputation.

If you're interested in Stickley, Lexington, or any other high-priced brand, it would be a good idea to check with this source to see if they may have identical or similar furniture available from a lesser-known brand. You aren't sacrificing quality when you do this; you are just declining to pay a higher price for the name recognition of a more broadly advertised brand.

Lines carried:

Classic Leather	Lorts	Royal Patina	Vanguard
Craftique	Michaels	Statesville Chair	Weiman
Freemarc Designs	Pennsylvania Classics	Taylor King	
Lee Industries	Pennsylvania House	Tom Seely Furniture	

Phone orders accepted:	**Yes**
Discount:	**40%-50% off mfrs. suggested retail**
Payment methods:	**VISA, MC, personal checks**
In-house financing available:	**No**
Deposits required:	**50% deposit when order is placed, balance due when furniture is ready to be shipped**
Catalog available:	**No**
Clearance center:	**No**
Delivery:	**Full service in-home delivery and set-up. Customer pays freight company directly for shipping costs.**

Directions: Please see *Hickory Furniture Mart* for complete directions.

Drexel Heritage Factory Outlet

3004-A Parquet Dr.
Dalton, GA 30720

I'm sorry to have to report that this terrific outlet closed on February 1, 1999. I was told that the outlet was closed at the request of several furniture retailers in the Atlanta area who objected to having this outlet located 75 miles away from their stores.

It is an unfortunate fact of life in the home furnishings industry that manufacturers who sell directly to the public are often subjected to extreme pressure from the retailers whose profit margins shrink as a result. Every time this kind of bullying from retailers results in the closure of another factory outlet or deep discounter, you and I all pay higher prices for furniture as a result.

The best way to combat this problem is for all consumers to pressure manufacturers to keep selling through factory outlets and deep discounters. Vote with your checkbook. Pressure manufacturers to sell in a way that is in YOUR best interests, rather than in the middlemen's best interests.

Fortunately, there are still two terrific Drexel Heritage factory outlets in Hickory, NC, and this line is sold over the phone by a number of deep discounters.

Drexel Heritage Factory Outlet

Level 1 & 2
Hickory Furniture Mart
U. S. Hwy. 70 SE
Hickory, NC 28602

Phone:	**(828) 324-2220**	**Hours:**	**M-Sat 9:00-6:00**	
Toll Free:	**None**	**E-mail:**	**info@hickoryfurniture.com**	
Fax:	**(828) 323-8445**	**Web site:**	**www.hickoryfurniture.com**	

The Drexel Heritage Factory Outlet at the Hickory Furniture Mart is huge, covering over one-eighth of the entire square footage of the Mart between its two levels. This outlet also serves as a factory-owned factory outlet for La Barge, Baldwin Brass, Beacon Hill and Maitland Smith.

Most of the stock here is in new first-quality condition: floor samples, customer returns, discontinued items, and stock overruns. There is a fairly even mix of case goods and upholstery.

Their normal discount runs between 50% to 80%. In January, the outlet runs a month long sale with even bigger discounts. During the sale, all items are 75% to 80% off retail. The outlet also runs shorter sales in May and September with the same discounts.

On my most recent visit to the outlet, during their January 1999 sale, I found a great deal on a solid cherry entertainment center (pictured on the following page). The retail on this 3 piece set is normally $12,154.00. The outlet's normal price was $5,147.00. Their January sale price was only $2,999.00, for a total discount of over 75% off retail. This particular piece was a floor sample with one very small scuff, the kind that can normally be invisibly repaired for about $100.00.

The outlet will not take phone orders for new furniture from Drexel-Heritage's current lines, but if you know exactly which item you want, they will see if they have that particular style in stock at the outlet and allow you to order it by phone. They do accept credit cards for payment, and they will arrange shipping.
They do require you to pay in full for the item when your order is placed, but they also ship almost immediately.

This outlet, along with the Hickory Furniture Mart in general, is a "must-visit" on any trip to Hickory, NC. If you don't find exactly what you want at this outlet, Drexel Heritage does have another outlet nearby in Hickory that is also very impressive.

Please also see the listings under Hickory Furniture Mart for more information on travel bargains to the Mart and ways of saving money on shipping.

Phone orders accepted:	**Yes**
Discount:	**50%-80% off mfrs. suggested retail**
Payment methods:	**VISA, MC, AMEX, personal checks**
In-house financing available:	**No**
Deposits required:	**Full payment due with order**
Catalog available:	**No**
Clearance center:	**Not applicable**
Delivery:	**Full service in-home delivery and set-up. Customer pays freight company directly for shipping costs.**

Directions: Please see *Hickory Furniture Mart* for complete directions.

Drexel Heritage Factory Outlet (cont.)

Solid cherry entertainment center from Drexel Heritage

Retail: $12,154.00   Discounted price: $2,999.00
Savings at the Drexel Heritage Factory Outlet: $9,155.00 = 76% off retail

Drexel Heritage Factory Outlet

Furniture Clearance Center
66 Hwy. 321 NW
Hickory, NC 28601

Phone:	**(828) 323-1558**	**Hours:**	**M-F 9:00-6:00, Sat 9:00-5:00**
Toll Free:	**None**	**E-mail:**	**None**
Fax:	**(828) 326-9846**	**Web site:**	**None**

The Furniture Clearance Center in Hickory, NC, is a combined factory-owned factory outlet for Drexel Heritage, La Barge, Maitland-Smith, Sedgewick Rattan, Carrington Court, and Craftique. It occupies a huge warehouse building.

The stock consists of floor samples, customer returns, photography samples, and discontinued styles. Virtually all of the furniture here is in new first-quality condition. The discounts run from 50%-70% off retail, with most pieces around 60% off.   They usually have a big sale every January and May when they mark most pieces an extra 10%-20% off.

On my most recent visit here, I found a great deal on a Drexel Heritage chest on chest from their Royal Country Retreats collection (pictured on the following page). This piece retails for $2,689.00, but this market sample was only $1,094.00. It was in perfect condition.

If you travel to Hickory to shop for high-end traditional furniture, this outlet is a "must visit"!

Phone orders accepted:	**No**
Discount:	**50%-70% off mfrs. suggested retail**
Payment methods:	**VISA, MC, personal checks**
In-house financing available:	**No**
Deposits required:	**Not applicable**
Catalog available:	**Not applicable**
Clearance center:	**Not applicable**
Delivery:	**Full service in-home delivery and set-up. Customer pays freight company directly for shipping costs.**

Directions: **From I-40, take exit #123 and drive north on Hwy. 321 into Hickory. Furniture Clearance Center is about two miles down on the right.**

Drexel Heritage Factory Outlet (cont.)

Drexel Heritage Factory Outlet at the Furniture Clearance Center in Hickory, NC

Royal Country Retreats chest-on-chest from Drexel-Heritage

Retail: $2,689.00   Discounted price: $1,094.00
Savings at the Drexel Heritage Factory Outlet: $1,595.00 = 60% off retail

Drexel Heritage Factory Outlet

Furnitureland South
4th Floor
5635 Riverdale Dr.
Jamestown, NC 27282

Phone:	**(336) 841-4328**	**Hours:**	**M-W & Sat 8:30-5:30, Th-F 8:30-8:30**
Toll Free:	**None**	**E-mail:**	**Dick_Cottam@furniturelandsouth.com**
Fax:	**(336) 841-7026**	**Web site:**	**www.furniturelandsouth.com**

This Drexel Heritage Factory Outlet occupies the entire fourth floor of the new Furnitureland South building.

It's huge, and it has an enormous selection of overstocks, floor samples, discontinued styles, etc., at 60%-70% off retail. Virtually all of the furniture here is in new first-quality condition. There's an even mix of upholstery and case goods.

On my most recent visit here, I found a terrific deal on a Drexel Heritage floral sofa (pictured on the following page). This sofa normally retails for $3,510.00, but this one was marked down to $1,625.00 because the fabric had been discontinued. The sofa was new and in perfect, first-quality condition.

This is a terrific source to visit if you plan to be in High Point personally to shop for furniture.

Phone orders accepted:	**Yes**
Discount:	**60%-70% off mfrs. suggested retail**
Payment methods:	**Personal checks. No credit cards.**
In-house financing available:	**No**
Deposits required:	**Not applicable**
Catalog available:	**Not applicable**
Clearance center:	**Not applicable**
Delivery:	**Full service in-home delivery and set-up. Customer pays freight company directly for shipping costs.**

Directions: **From I-85, take exit #118, and turn west on Business 85. Furnitureland South will be about one mile down on your right at the Riverdale Rd. exit.**

Drexel Heritage Factory Outlet (cont.)

Drexel Heritage Factory Outlet at Furnitureland South in Jamestown, NC

Floral sofa from Drexel Heritage

Retail: $3,510.00   Discounted price: $1,625.00
Savings at the Drexel Heritage Factory Outlet: $1,885.00 = 54% off retail

:tor Factory Outlet

.say St.

NC 27260

Phone:	(336) 889-5500	**Hours:**	**M-F 9:00-5:00**
Toll Free:	None		**Closed April & October**
Fax:	(336) 889-5705	**E-mail:**	None
		Web site:	None

This is E. J. Victor's only factory outlet. This line is so high-end and exclusive that most people have never even heard of it. It's usually only carried by one or two very high-end stores in each state. They specialize in 18th and 19th century English reproductions. The furniture is very high-end, very high-quality, and frequently very ornate.

For what you get, however, the prices are actually quite good. As uptown as this furniture is, it won't break your bank account.

On my last visit here, I found a great deal on a solid mahogany 18th century English reproduction king bed with walnut veneer (pictured on the following page). This bed normally retails for $6,500.00, but the floor sample I found at the outlet was priced at $1,995.00 -- 70% off retail! It was in perfect condition.

Like a few other High Point outlets, this showroom is closed during the months of April and October due to the High Point wholesale furniture markets.

The furniture here is so beautiful that it will absolutely knock you out. And it's affordable! Amazing! Run, don't walk, to this outlet if you plan to do any shopping in the High Point, NC, area.

Phone orders accepted:	No
Discount:	65%-75% off mfrs. suggested retail
Payment methods:	Personal checks. No credit cards.
In-house financing available:	No
Deposits required:	Not applicable
Catalog available:	Not applicable
Clearance center:	Not applicable
Delivery:	Customers must make own arrangements to take furniture home.

Directions: From I-85, take exit #111 (Hwy. 311), and head northwest into High Point. After several miles, when you reach downtown High Point, Hwy. 311 will become Main St. After you get through downtown High Point, turn left on English Rd. Two blocks down, turn left on Lindsay St. The E. J. Victor Factory Outlet is one-half mile down on the left.

E. J. Victor Factory Outlet (cont.)

E. J. Victor Factory Outlet

Solid mahogany 18th century reproduction bed from E. J. Victor

Retail: $6,500.00   Discounted price: $1,995.00
Savings at the E. J. Victor Factory Outlet: $4,505.00 = 70% off retail

Ellenburg's Furniture

I-40 & Stamey Farm Rd.
Statesville, NC 28687

Phone:	**(704) 873-2900**	**Hours:**	**M-F 8:30-5:30, Sat 9:30-5:00**
Toll Free:	**None**	**E-mail:**	**ellenburgs@worldnet.att.net**
Fax:	**(704) 873-6002**	**Web site:**	**www.ellenburgs.com**

Ellenburg's Furniture is located in Statesville, about 30 miles east of Hickory, NC, on I-40. They have a good selection of medium to high-end lines, including Lexington, Harden, Universal, and Wellington Hall.

They don't have a clearance center or any floor samples or discontinued pieces on display. For this reason, there is no monetary advantage to visiting in person. They do have great deals on many lines sold over the phone, though. So, if you're planning to order your furniture by phone, definitely give this source a call to compare their prices.

Lines carried:

Allibert	Classic Rattan	Lloyd Flanders	Samsonite
American Heritage	Dutailier	Lo Brothers	Sedgefield Lamps
Athol	Eddie Bauer	Lyon Shaw	South Sea Rattan
Badger Bassinets	Ello	Michael Thomas	Stein World
Barn Door	Fashion Bed Group	Upholstery	Symbol Mattress
Bassett	Ficks Reed	Mirage Rugs	Tracers
Benchcraft	Harden	Jasper Cabinet	Tradition France
Bevan Funnell	Henry Link	Oklahomer Smith	Tropitone
Bob Timberlake	Highland House	Pace-Stone Rugs	Universal
Braxton Culler	Keller	Pawley's Isle Hammocks	Wellington Hall
Cane & Reed	Kingsley Bate	Pearson Upholstery	Whitney Rugs
Cebu Rattan	Lane	Pulaski	Winston Furniture
Charleston Forge	Lane/Venture	Robert Abbey Lamps	Woodard
Clark Casual	Lexington	3K Furniture	Yesteryear Wicker
Classic Georgian	Link Taylor	Salterini/Meadowcraft	

Phone orders accepted:	**Yes**
Discount:	**40%-60% off mfrs. suggested retail**
Payment methods:	**VISA, MC, personal checks**
In-house financing available:	**No**
Deposits required:	**50% deposit when order is placed, balance due when furniture is ready to be shipped**
Catalog available:	**No**
Clearance center:	**No**
Delivery:	**Full service in-home delivery and set-up. Customer pays freight company directly for shipping costs.**

Directions: From I-40, take the Stamey Farm Rd. exit and head south into Statesville. Ellenburg's Furniture is just off the interstate.

European Furniture Importers

2145 W. Grand Ave.
Chicago, IL 60612

Phone:	**(312) 243-1955**	**Hours:**	**M-F 9:00-5:00, Sat & Sun 10:00-5:00**
Toll Free:	**(800) 283-1955**	**E-mail:**	**None**
Fax:	**(312) 633-9308**	**Web site:**	**None**

European Furniture Importers has a very good selection of imported contemporary Italian furniture, including their versions of designs by Mies Van Der Rohe, Eileen Gray, Mart Stam, Marcel Breuer, and C. R. MacIntosh. They also import hand-carved Bombe' chests and wooden chairs.

Their prices are quite good, 20%-60% off retail. They do require full payment at the time your order is placed, but unlike most other furniture discounters, they stock most of the pieces they sell. Most orders are shipped within two weeks.

They've been in business for many years, and they have a very good reputation for customer service. If you're looking for good deals on contemporary furniture, this is one of the best sources you can call.

Phone orders accepted:	**Yes**
Discount:	**20%-60% off mfrs. suggested retail**
Payment methods:	**VISA, MC, Discover, personal checks**
In-house financing available:	**No**
Deposits required:	**Full payment due with order**
Catalog available:	**Yes**
Clearance center:	**No**
Delivery:	**Most furniture is shipped by UPS, the rest by common carrier. No in-home set up is available.**

Directions: **From I-290, take the Damen Ave exit, and go north to Grand Ave. Turn left, and go west on Grand Ave. European Furniture Importers is one block west on the left side of the street.**

ry Direct Furniture

y. 16 N.
Conover, NC 28613

Phone:	**(828) 464-9940**	**Hours:**	**M-Sat 9:00-6:00**
Toll Free:	**None**	**E-mail:**	**None**
Fax:	**(828) 464-9964**	**Web site:**	**None**

Factory Direct Furniture in Conover, NC, is a factory-owned factory outlet for Century, Councill-Crafsmen, and Hickory Chair. This location and their other showroom in the Hickory Furniture Mart, operated by the same company, are the only two factory-owned factory outlets for these three brands.

The discounts on the outlet furniture generally runs a straight 60% off across the board. Virtually all of the furniture here is in new first-quality condition.

At both locations, the sales staff immediately volunteers to customers that they can come down even further from the price marked, so be sure to haggle. Factory Direct Furniture also runs periodic sales, usually giving another 10%-20% off the marked discount. These sales normally run in January, March, May, and September.

Both locations have an excellent selection. Most of the pieces are traditional, but there are usually a few contemporary styles.

If you're traveling to the Hickory area, this outlet is a "must-visit". If you don't find what you're looking for here, be sure to check their other location about ten minutes away at the Hickory Furniture Mart.

Phone orders accepted:	**No**
Discount:	**60% off mfrs. suggested retail**
Payment methods:	**VISA, MC, personal checks**
In-house financing available:	**No**
Deposits required:	**Not applicable**
Catalog available:	**Not applicable**
Clearance center:	**Not applicable**
Delivery:	**Full service in-home delivery and set-up. Customer pays freight company directly for shipping costs.**

Directions: From I-40, take exit #131, and go one-quarter mile north on Hwy. 16 North. Factory Direct Furniture will be on the right side of the highway.

Farm House Furnishings ("The Red House")

1432 First Ave. SW & Hwy. 321 N
Hickory, NC 28602

Phone:	**(828) 324-4595**	**Hours:**	**M-Sat 9:00-6:00**
Toll Free:	**None**	**E-mail:**	**None**
Fax:	**None**	**Web site:**	**None**

Farm House Furnishings is located in a tiny red house in Hickory, NC. They have very little furniture on display due to space constraints, and it isn't discounted much, so there's no reason to go here in person.

They do have fairly good prices on the lines they carry, but not the best I've seen in the area. Still, if you plan to order furniture by phone, it's worth giving them a call to compare their prices.

Lines carried:

Amyx	Country Reproductions	Lea	SK Products
Athol	Fashion Bed Group	Martinsville Novelty	Southern Craftsmen's
Barfield Recliners	Heritage Haus	Murphy	Guild
Beechbrook	Hickory Leather	Oxford Leather	Timmerman
Black Forest Clocks	Hooker	Pine-tique	Top Notch Woodwork
Boling Chair	Howard Miller Clocks	Regency House	Universal
Builtright Chair	J. H. Carver	Relax-a-Cliner	Vaughan
Carolina Country	Johnston Benchworks	Riverside Bedding	Wesley Allen
Carolina Rockers	Kennedy Rockers	Rug Barn	
Carson Wind Chimes	Kevin-Christian	Sidex	

Phone orders accepted:	**Yes**
Discount:	**30%-50% off mfrs. suggested retail**
Payment methods:	**VISA, MC, personal checks**
In-house financing available:	**No**
Deposits required:	**50% deposit when order is placed, balance due when furniture is ready to be shipped**
Catalog available:	**No**
Clearance center:	**No**
Delivery:	**Full service in-home delivery and set-up. Customer pays freight company directly for shipping costs.**

Directions: **From I-40, take exit #123 and drive north on Hwy. 321 to Hickory, NC. Farm House Furnishings is on the right side of the road, one block after you pass Hwy. 70.**

Fields Furniture Company

2700 Randleman Rd.
Greensboro, NC 27406

Phone:	(336) 273-7629	**Hours:**	M-F 10:00-6:00, Sat 9:00-5:00
Toll Free:	None	**E-mail:**	jcinc@fieldsfurniture.com
Fax:	None	**Web site:**	None

Fields Furniture Co. is located in Greensboro, just north of High Point, NC. They have a good selection of medium to high-end lines, including Flexsteel, Bassett, and American Drew.

They don't have any floor samples or discontinued pieces on display, so there's no reason to shop in person. It is worth checking their prices if you plan to order your furniture by phone, though.

Lines carried:

American Drew	Craftique	Lane/Venture	Serta
American Of Martinsville	Crawford	Lank	Stanton Cooper
Athol	C. R. Laine	Lea	Statton
Barcalounger	Dixie	Lenoir House	Stratford
Bassett	Dobbs	Lexington	Stuart
Bemco	Flexsteel	Link Taylor	Taylorsville
Blacksmith Shop	Friendship	Lyon Shaw	Tell City
Boling Chair	Futuristic	Madison Square	Temple
Brady	Henry Link	Mobel	Terrycraft
Broyhill	Hickory White	National Mt. Airy	Vanguard
Carolina Furniture	High Point Woodworking	Nichols & Stone	Vaughan
Carson	Highland House	Pearson	Vaughan Bassett
Chaircraft	Hitchcock Chair	Pulaski	Virginia House
Chatham County	Hood	Reliable	Webb
Chatham Novelties	HTB Lane	Riverside	Woodmark
Classic Rattan	Hyundai Furniture	San-Don Simmons	Young Hinkle
Cochrane	Jasper Cabinet	Schweiger	
Colonial	Lane	Sealy	

Phone orders accepted:	Yes
Discount:	**30%-48% off mfrs. suggested retail**
Payment methods:	**VISA, MC, personal checks**
In-house financing available:	No
Deposits required:	**20% deposit when order is placed, balance due when furniture is ready to be shipped**
Catalog available:	No
Clearance center:	No
Delivery:	**Full service in-home delivery and set-up. Customer pays freight company directly for shipping costs.**

Directions: **From I-85, take exit #124, and go south on Randleman Rd. Fields Furniture Co. is at the top of the first hill on the right side of the road.**

Fran's Wicker & Rattan Furniture

295 Route 10 East
Succasunna, NJ 07876

Phone:	(973) 584-2230	**Hours:**	Mon, Tues, & Fri 9:00-5:30
Toll Free:	(800) 372-6799		Wed & Thurs 9:00-8:30
Fax:	(973) 584-7446		Sat 9:30-6:00, Sun 12:00-5:00
		E-mail:	None
		Web site:	www.franswicker.com

Fran's Wicker & Rattan has been disocunting wicker for over 35 years. Most of their furniture and accessories are made in their own factories in China, Indonesia, and the Philippines. They have a huge catalog. They also have an enormous showroom just to the west of Newark -- over 100,000 square feet.

Fran's can also order many other brands of wicker and rattan at significant discounts. They will not give out a list of the specific brands they have access to, but they will give you a comparison price over the phone if you call with a specific brand and item number. I have found that they can order most national brands.

Fran's has a written "lowest price" guarantee, and (unlike most order-by-phone companies) they will accept credit card payment for your entire order. For this reason, any customer thinking of buying wicker or rattan by phone should check with other sources first, and then call Fran's and ask them to match the price.

As long as Fran's does match the best price available on the product plus shipping, you should strongly consider making your actual purchase here. The fact that they will accept credit card payment for your entire order is a major advantage over their competitors.

Lines carried:	Please call for more information
Phone orders accepted:	Yes
Discount:	50% off mfrs. suggested retail
Payment methods:	VISA, MC, AMEX, Discover, checks
In-house financing available:	No
Deposits required:	Full amount due with order. Credit cards are not charged until merchandise is actually shipped.
Catalog available:	Yes
Clearance center:	No
Delivery:	Shipping costs are paid to Fran's with your order. Curbside delivery only by UPS or truck. No in-home delivery and setup available.

Directions: From I-80, take exit #28. Follow the signs to Route 10. Take Route 10 east to the first red light. Fran's is on the corner.

Franklin Furniture

3650 Hickory Blvd., Hwy. 321
Hudson, NC 28638

Phone:	**(828) 396-5214**	**Hours:**	**M-Sat 9:00-5:00**
Toll Free:	**None**	**E-mail:**	**None**
Fax:	**(828) 396-5781**	**Web site:**	**None**

Franklin Furniture is located in Hudson, just a few miles north of Hickory, NC. They have a fairly good selection of medium quality brands such as Bassett, Broyhill, and American Drew.

They do have a small clearance center out back, but the prices there aren't very good. Even on discontinued styles and floor samples, the discounts only run 20%-40% off. You can do far better than that at the many factory outlets all over the Hickory area.

Their prices on furniture sold over the phone range from 30%-40% off retail. Unfortunately, they just aren't competitive on price with other discounters in the area who carry the same lines.

Lines carried:

American Drew	Eagle Craft Desks	Masterfield	Sealy
American Pacific	Edward Art	Mobel	Stylecraft Lamps
Austin Sculptures	Henry Link Wicker	Morgan Stewart	Ther-A-Pedic Bedding
Bassett	Impact	Nora Fenton	Tree Factory
Bob Timberlake	King Hickory	Palecek	Universal
Broyhill	Kroehler	Paragon	V. B. Williams
Craftmaster Furniture	Leisters Tables	Peoplelounger	Vaughan
Crawford	Lexington	Pulaski	Vaughan-Bassett
Currey and Company	Link Taylor	Ridgeway Clocks	
Designers Attic	M & M Nautical Imports	Sadek	

Phone orders accepted:	**Yes**
Discount:	**30%-40% off mfrs. suggested retail**
Payment methods:	**Personal checks. No credit cards.**
In-house financing available:	**No**
Deposits required:	**30% deposit when order is placed, balance due when furniture is ready to be shipped**
Catalog available:	**No**
Clearance center:	**Yes**
Delivery:	**Full service in-home delivery and set-up. Customer pays freight company directly for shipping costs.**

Directions: From I-40, take exit #123 and drive north on Hwy. 321 to Hudson, NC. Franklin Furniture is on the right side of the road.

French Heritage Factory Store

The Atrium
430 S. Main St.
High Point, NC 27260

Phone:	**(336) 884-0022**	**Hours:**	**M-F 9:00-6:00, Sat 9:00-5:00**
Toll Free:	**None**	**E-mail:**	**french@theatrium.com**
Fax:	**(336) 837-0020**	**Web site:**	**www.theatrium.com**

This is the only factory outlet for French Heritage, which specializes in French reproduction furniture. The outlet also carries a line of English country reproductions. The quality is quite good.

The prices here range from 50%-75% off, and most of the furniture is in new first-quality condition. If you're looking for quality French or English reproduction furniture, this is definitely an outlet you should visit.

Lines carried:

Country Club
Crosswinds Corner
De Bournais
French Heritage
Richelieu

Phone orders accepted:	**No**
Discount:	**50%-75% off mfrs. suggested retail**
Payment methods:	**VISA, MC, personal checks**
In-house financing available:	**No**
Deposits required:	**Not applicable**
Catalog available:	**Not applicable**
Clearance center:	**Not applicable**
Delivery:	**Full service in-home delivery and set-up. Customer pays freight company directly for shipping costs.**

Directions: French Heritage is located inside the Atrium complex in downtown High Point. Please see *The Atrium* for complete directions.

Furniture Clearance Center - Hickory

66 Hwy. 321 NW
Hickory, NC 28601

Phone:	(828) 323-1558	**Hours:**	M-F 9:00-6:00, Sat 9:00-5:00
Toll Free:	None	**E-mail:**	None
Fax:	(828) 326-9846	**Web site:**	None

The Furniture Clearance Center in Hickory, NC, is a combined factory-owned factory outlet for Drexel-Heritage, La Barge, Maitland-Smith, Sedgewick Rattan, Carrington Court, and Craftique. It occupies a huge warehouse building.

The stock consists of floor samples, customer returns, photography samples, and discontinued styles. Virtually all of the furniture here is in new first-quality condition. The discounts run from 50%-70% off retail, with most pieces around 60% off. They usually have a big sale every January and May when they mark most pieces an extra 10%-20% off.

If you travel to Hickory to shop for high-end traditional furniture, this outlet is a "must visit"!

Phone orders accepted:	No
Discount:	50%-70% off mfrs. suggested retail
Payment methods:	VISA, MC, personal checks
In-house financing available:	No
Deposits required:	Not applicable
Catalog available:	Not applicable
Clearance center:	Not applicable
Delivery:	Full service in-home delivery and set-up. Customer pays freight company directly for shipping costs.

Directions: From I-40, take exit #123 and drive north on Hwy. 321 into Hickory. Furniture Clearance Center is about two miles down on the right.

Furniture Clearance Center - High Point

1107 Tate St.
High Point, NC 27260

Phone:	(336) 882-1688	**Hours:**	M-Sat 9:00-5:00
Toll Free:	None	**E-mail:**	None
Fax:	(336) 882-8423	**Web site:**	None

The Furniture Clearance Center in High Point, NC, serves as the clearance center for Utility Craft and Wood-Armfield, two major High Point furniture discounters. The stock here consists of floor samples, photography samples, discontinued styles, and customer returns. The discounts run about 50%-75% off retail, with most pieces marked at about 60% off. Virtually all of the furniture here is in first-quality condition.

This place is a gold mine for high end furniture. Most of the furniture is from very high-end lines, such as Hickory White, Century, Maitland-Smith, Baker, etc.

On my most recent visit here, I found a terrific deal on a Century dining room table (pictured on the following page). The retail on this piece is normally $6,860.00, but the clearance center had this one for only $2,625.00. It was in perfect condition.

From the outside, this place doesn't look like much. I'm sure most people (except the interior designers who are always here) drive right on past it. In reality, though, this is one of the very best sources in High Point for furniture that you can take home the same day. If you plan to visit High Point to buy high-end traditional furniture, this should be your first stop.

Phone orders accepted:	No
Discount:	50%-75% off mfrs. suggested retail
Payment methods:	Personal checks. No credit cards.
In-house financing available:	No
Deposits required:	Not applicable
Catalog available:	Not applicable
Clearance center:	Not applicable
Delivery:	Customers must make own arrangements to take furniture home.

Directions: From I-85, take exit #111 (Hwy. 311), and head northwest into High Point. After several miles, when you reach downtown High Point, Hwy. 311 will become S. Main St. Shortly after you pass Business 85, turn right on Wheeler St. One block down, turn right again on Tate St. Furniture Clearance Center will be on your left.

Furniture Clearance Center - High Point (cont.)

Furniture Clearance Center

Dining room table from Century Furniture

Retail: $6,860.00   Discounted price: $2,625.00
Savings at Furniture Clearance Center: $4,235.00 = 62% off retail

Furniture Collections Of Carolina

3197 NC Hwy. 127 S.
Hickory, NC 28602

Phone:	(828) 294-3593	**Hours:**	M-F 9:00-5:30, Sat 9:00-4:00
Toll Free:	(800) 968-9079	**E-mail:**	None
Fax:	(828) 294-4276	**Web site:**	www.users.twave.net/fcc/

Furniture Collections Of Carolina is a small but well-furnished store on the edge of Hickory, NC. Their discounts run about 40%-50% off retail. In addition to adult furniture lines, this source also has a nice selection of baby and juvenile furniture from Simmons, Childcraft, Bassett, Lexington, Welch, and others.

There aren't any discontinued items or floor samples available, and they have no clearance center. For this reason, if you plan to travel directly to the Hickory area to shop for furniture, you would be better off to stick with the many other discounters and factory outlets in the area that do have deeper discounts for customers who shop in person.

However, if you plan to order furniture over the phone, do give these people a call. They have some of the most pleasant and helpful salespeople I've come across, and their prices are quite good.

Lines carried:

ABCO	Childcraft	Highland House	Morgan Stewart
American Drew	Chromecraft	Hon	Null
American Of Martinsville	Clayton Marcus	Hooker	Pulaski
Action By Lane	Cochrane	Johnston Casuals	Riverside Desk
Bassett	Dar/Ran	Kincaid	Serta
Bassett Baby/Juvenile	Design Horizon	Lane	Simmons
Bean Station	Dresher	La-Z-Boy	Stanley
Berkshire	Elan Beds	Lea	Stoneville
Bob Timberlake	Flexsteel	Lexington	Universal
Brooks Glider Rockers	Hammary	Link Taylor	Welch
Broyhill	Henry Link	Lynn Hollyn	
Cal Style	Hickory Hill	Miller Desks	
Cambridge Chair	Hickory Tavern	Mobel	

Phone orders accepted:	Yes
Discount:	40%-50% off mfrs. suggested retail
Payment methods:	VISA, MC, personal checks
In-house financing available:	No
Deposits required:	50% deposit when order is placed, balance due when furniture is delivered.
Catalog available:	No
Clearance center:	No
Delivery:	Full service in-home delivery and set-up. Customer pays freight company directly for shipping costs.

Directions: From I-40, take exit #123 and drive south on Hwy. 127. Furniture Collections Of Carolina is several miles down on the right.

Furniture Collections Of Carolina (cont.)

Furniture Collections Of Carolina

Furniture Factory Outlet Shoppes
930 Hwy. 70 SW
Hickory, NC 28602

The Furniture Factory Outlet Shoppes is a small strip-mall type complex in Hickory with four furniture factory outlets and discounters. There is no main office as there is for the Hickory Furniture Mart nearby.

Some of the showrooms here have good deals; some don't. Please check the individual listings for details on discounts, stock, payment, shipping, lines carried, etc:

Mitchell Gold Factory Outlet	(828) 261-0051
Repetes	(828) 328-9440
Seconds & Samples	(828) 261-2108
Vanguard Showroom	(828) 261-0051

Directions: **From I-40, take exit #123 (Hwy. 321), and go north toward Hickory. After a few miles, take the Hwy. 70 exit, and go east. The Furniture Factory Outlet Shoppes is immediately on your left as you exit onto Hwy. 70.**

Furniture Gallery (formerly Furniture Direct)

1280 S. Powerline Rd., Suite 189
Pompano Beach, FL 33069

Phone:	**None**	**Hours:**	**M-F 9:00-5:00**
Toll Free:	**(800) 444-4154**	**E-mail:**	**sales@furnituredir.com**
Fax:	**(954) 958-9996**	**Web site:**	**www.furnituredir.com**

Furniture Gallery, formerly knows as Furniture Direct, sells furniture directly to the public through phone sales only. They have excellent prices due to their low overhead, and they will allow you to pay for your entire order with a major credit card, which greatly reduces any chance of problems with your order.

This is a great source. Anyone who is planning to order furniture by phone should compare prices here.

Phone orders accepted:	**Yes**
Discount:	**35%-65% off mfrs. suggested retail**
Payment methods:	**VISA, MC, Discover, AMEX, personal checks**
In-house financing available:	**No**
Deposits required:	**50% deposit when order is placed, balance due when furniture is ready to be shipped**
Catalog available:	**No**
Clearance center:	**No**
Delivery:	**Full service in-home delivery and set-up. Customer pays freight company directly for shipping costs.**

Directions: Furniture Direct has no showroom open to the public.

Furniture Gallery (cont.)

Lines carried:

Action By Lane
Alexvale
American Drew
American Of Martinsville
Anna French
Arnold Palmer
Artifacts
Artistica Metal
Aston Garrett
B. Berger
Bamboo Odyssey
Barcalounger
Beachley
Bed Design/Lazar
           Industries
Bob Timberlake
Bonart Lamps
Carsons
Casa Bique
Casual Of California
Cebu Imports
Chair Design/Lazar
           Industries
Charleston Forge
Cochrane
Design Master
Distinction Leather
Duralee
Elements By Grapevine
Elite Leather
Emerson et Cie
Fashion Bed Group
Fine Art Lamps
Flat Rock
Flexsteel
Fremarc
Garcia Imports
Global Furniture
Gordon International
Greysen
Habersham Plantation
Hammary
Hart Associates
Hekman
Henry Link
Hickory Chair
Hickory White
Hooker
HTB Lane

Jasper Cabinet
Jordi Mere
Johnston Casuals
JSF Industries
Kasmir
Keller
Kessler
K. I.
Kiani
Kincaid
King Hickory
Kravet
Kusch
L & B Industries
Lane
Lane/Venture
Lazar Industries
Lea
Leathercraft
Lexington
Lorts
Lowenstein
Marge Carson
Michael Thomas
Miles Talbot
Modern Classics
Natural Light
Nichols & Stone
OFS
Oriental Lacquer
Originals 22
Pacific Coast
Paoli
Park Place
Pearson
Pulaski
Richardson Bros.
Robert Allen
Romweber
Ron Fisher
Sam Moore
San Miguel
Sarreid
Schnadig International
Seabrook
Sherrill
Sligh
Stanley
Stone Collection

Stone International
Sumter Cabinet
Taylor King
Tellus
Troy Westridge
Universal
Virco
Weiman
Wellington Hall
Wesley Allen
Winston

The Furniture Shoppe

3351 Hickory Blvd.
Hudson, NC 28638

Phone:	(828) 396-1942	**Hours:**	M-Sat 9:00-5:00
Toll Free:	None	**E-mail:**	furnitureshoppe@abts.net
Fax:	(828) 396-2376	**Web site:**	www.furnitureshoppe.com

The Furniture Shoppe in Hudson, NC, just north of Hickory, has a very good selection of case goods, along with some upholstery and juvenile furniture.

Their discounts on new furniture range from 45%-55% off retail, whether you shop in person or order by phone. They also have a 3,000 square foot clearance center in the back where they sell off floor samples, discontinued items, and customer returns. Discounts there range from 65%-75% off retail.

This source has been in business for over twenty years, and they do a huge volume of phone sales. Their prices on many lines are quite good. If you plan to order furniture by phone, definitely call this source and give them a chance to bid on your business.

If you plan to be in the Hickory, NC, area to shop for furniture, their clearance center is worth a look.

Lines carried:

Action By Lane	Clayton Marcus	Kincaid	Sealy
American Drew	Cochrane	King Koil	Serta
American Of Martinsville	Craftique	Lane	Skillcraft
Bassett	Decorative Crafts	Lane/Venture	Spring Air
Bassett Mirror	Dinaire	Lexington	Stanley
Best Chair	Fairfield	Lloyd/Flanders	Swann Brass
Bob Timberlake	Flexsteel	Lyon Shaw	Telescope
Brady	Hammary	Mobel	Thayer Coggin
Broyhill	Henry Link	Mohawk	Universal
Cambridge	Hooker	Phillip Reinisch	Wesley Allen
Canal Dover	Jasper Cabinet	Pulaski	Winston
Carolina Mirror	Johnston Casuals	Ridgeway Clocks	
Chatham County	Keller	Riverside	
Chromecraft	Kimball	Sam Moore	

Phone orders accepted:	Yes
Discount:	**45%-55% off mfrs. suggested retail**
Payment methods:	**VISA, MC, AMEX, Discover, personal checks**
In-house financing available:	Yes
Deposits required:	**50% deposit when order is placed, balance due when furniture is ready to be shipped**
Catalog available:	No
Clearance center:	Yes
Delivery:	**Full service in-home delivery and set-up. Customer pays freight company directly for shipping costs.**

Directions: From I-40, take exit #123 and drive north on Hwy. 321 to Hudson. The Furniture Shoppe is 12 miles from I-40 on the left side of the highway.

The Furniture Shoppe (cont.)

The Furniture Shoppe

Furnitureland South

5635 Riverdale Dr.
Jamestown, NC 27282

Phone:	(336) 841-4328	**Hours:**	M-W & Sat 8:30-5:30, Th-F 8:30-8:30
Toll Free:	None	**E-mail:**	Dick_Cottam@furniturelandsouth.com
Fax:	(336) 841-7026	**Web site:**	www.furniturelandsouth.com

Furnitureland South is an enormous complex in Jamestown, NC, right on the outskirts of High Point. Just to give you an idea of how big the main building (pictured on the following page is), look at the top of the ball and claw foot on the faux highboy that decorates the front of the building. When I stand next to it, the top of the claw comes up to my waist.

Furnitureland South is by far one of the biggest and best-established telephone discounters of furniture in North Carolina, rivaled only by Boyles and Rose Furniture. They are very reputable, and they carry <u>everything</u>.

The first three floors of the new building are devoted to galleries of new furniture discounted at about 40% off, which is also the standard discount they offer on most lines sold by phone.

The fourth floor is occupied by a factory-owned Drexel-Heritage factory outlet. It's huge, and it has an enormous selection of overstocks, floor samples, discontinued styles, etc., at 60%-70% off retail. Virtually all of the furniture here is in new first-quality condition. There's an even mix of upholstery and case goods.

The fifth floor houses Furnitureland South's clearance center, called "Rooms Now". It sells floor samples, customer returns, discontinued styles, and photography samples from all the lines sold by Furnitureland South. They have a very wide selection of case goods and upholstery at about 60%-70% off retail. Furnitureland South has just closed their old "Odds & Ends" store in Asheboro and moved its stock into "Rooms Now".

This is a terrific source to visit if you plan to be in High Point personally to shop for furniture. The fourth and fifth floor clearance centers have some amazing deals. However, the new furniture on sale on the first three floors and over the phone isn't discounted as much as it is from other sources that sell by phone. So, if you plan to buy your furniture over the phone, check prices here, but check prices elsewhere, too.

Lines carried:	Please see pages 138-140
Phone orders accepted:	Yes
Discount:	40%-70% off mfrs. suggested retail
Payment methods:	Personal checks. No credit cards.
In-house financing available:	No
Deposits required:	1/3 deposit when order is placed, balance due when furniture is ready to be shipped
Catalog available:	No
Clearance center:	Yes- See *Rooms Now*
Delivery:	Full service in-home delivery and set-up. Customer pays freight company directly for shipping costs.

Directions: From I-85, take exit #118, and turn west on Business 85. Furnitureland South will be about one mile down on your right at the Riverdale Rd. exit.

Furnitureland South (cont.)

Furnitureland South

Furnitureland South (cont.)

Lines carried:

A. A. Lane
Action by Lane
A La Carte
Alexander Julian
Allusions
Ambiance Imports
Ambiance Lighting
American Drew
American Impressions
Ancor Concepts
Andrew Pearson
Aquarius Mirrorworks
Archiped Classics
Ardley Hall
Art & Commerce
Artagraph
Arteriors Imports
Artisan House
Artistica Metal Designs
As You Like It
Ashley Manor
Athol Table
Atlanta Glasscrafters
Austin Sculpture
Azzolin Bros. Importers
Balangier
Baldwin
Barcalounger
Bard International
Barn Door Furniture
Bassett Mirror
Basta Sole by Tropitone
Bean Station
Benchcraft
Benchcraft Rattan
Benicia
Bernhardt
Berkline
Bestar
Betty Ginsberg
Bevan Funnell
Bibi
Blacksmith Shop
Bob Timberlake
Boling
Bomar
Bradington Young
Brasscrafters
Braxton Culler

Brett Austin
Brown Jordan
Broyhill
Butler Specialty
Cal-Bear
Cambridge Lamps
Cape Craftsmen
Capel Rugs
Carole Fabrics
Carolina Mirror
Carsons
Carter Upholstery
Carvers Guild
Casa Bique
Casa Stradivari
Casey Collection
Castilian Imports
Casual Lamps
Cebu Imports
Centurion Leather
Century
Chapala Imports
Chapman
Charles Alan
Charles Sadek
Chatham County
Chelsea House
Child Craft
China Trader
Chromecraft
CIC Bed Linens
Clark Casual
Classic Art
Classic Gallery
Classic Leather
Classic Rattan
Clay, Metal, & Stone
Clayton Marcus
Cochrane
Coja Leather
Collections 85
Collezione Europa
Colonial Furniture
Comfort Designs
Conant Ball
Conover Chair
Copper Canyon
Cooper Connection
Correia

Corsican
Country Originals Inc.
Cox Manufacturing
Craft-Tex
Craftique
Craftwork Guild
Crawford
Creations at Dallas
Creative Decor
Creative Fine Arts
Creative Ideas
Cresswell Lighting
Crishawn
Crystal Clear
Currey & Co.
D & F Wicker & Rattan
Dale Tiffany
Dar-Ran
David Landis
Decorative Arts
Decorative Crafts
Design Guild
Design South Furniture
Designer's Attic
Dessau Brass
Deszign Inc.
Dietz
Dillon
Dimplex
Dinaire
Directional
Distinction Leather
Distinctive Designs
Dr. Livingstone
Dream Weavers
Drexel-Heritage
Duralee Fabrics
Dutalier
Edward Art
Ekornes
Elements by Grapevine
Elliott's Designs
Ello
Entree
Eric Morgan
Evans Designs
Excelsior
Excursions by Venture
Expressive Designs Rugs

Fabric To Frame
Fairfield Chair
Fashion Bed Group
Ficks Reed
Fine Arts Ltd.
Fire Farm
Flair Design
Flair Upholstery by
        Bernhardt
Flexsteel
Floria Nova
Forma Design
Foundry
Framed Picture Ent.
Frames and Arts Inc.
Franklin Pictures
Frederick Cooper
French Heritage
        Reproductions
Friedman Brothers
Ganz
Garden Wrenn
George Kovacs
Georgian Furnishings
Gianni
Glober
Glass Arts
Gloster
Goodwin Weavers
Grace Manufacturing
Great City Traders
Guardsman
Guildmaster
Gunlocke
H. Studios
Hamilton Collections
Hammary
Harley Furniture
Harris Lamps
Harris Strong
Harrison Imports
Hartford Prospect
Heirloom
Hekman
Hen Feathers
Henry Link Wicker
Hickory Hill
Hickory House
Hickory White

Furnitureland South (cont.)

Lines carried (cont.):

High Point Furniture
Highland House
Hilda Flack Accessories
Historic Golf Prints
Holly Woods
House Parts
Howard Miller Clocks
Hubbardton Forge
Humane Trophies
Hyundai Furniture
Idea Industries
Ideal Originals
Inmon Enterprises
Interlude
International China Co.
Italia
Jackson of Danville
James R. Cooper
Jamestown Manor
Jasper Cabinet
Jay Willfred
JDI Group Cal-Style
Jean Wilkes
J. J. Hyde
Johnston Benchworks
Johnston Casuals
Jon Elliott Upholstery
JSF Industries
Kaiser/Kuhn Lighting
Kalanik
Karges
Kathryn Clarke Limited
Keller
Kennebunk Weavers
Kessler
Key City
Kimball Reproductions
Kinder Harris
King Hickory
Knobler
Koch & Lowy
Koch Originals
Kravet Fabrics
La Barge
Labs Inc.
Ladybug
Ladyslipper
Lambs & Ivy
Lane

Lane Action
Lankol Inc.
Latin Accents
Lea
Leathercraft
Leathertrend
Leeazanne
Legacy
Lenox Lighting
Lexington
Light & Sight
Lillian August
Link Works
Little Souls
Lloyd/Flanders
Lodi Down & Feather
Lorraine Headboards
Lotus Arts
Lucia Designs
Luna Bella Lamps
Lux Art Silks
Lyon Shaw
M & M Nautical
   Imports
MAC Sculpture
Madison Square
Magnussen Presidential
Maitland-Smith
Marbro
Markel
Marlow
Marvel
Maryland Classics
Masland Carpets
Masterlooms Rugs
Masterpiece Accessories
Maxton
Meadowcraft
Melinda Trent
Merida Meridian
Metropolitan Galleries
McKay Table Pads
Mikhail Darafeev
Millender
Miller Desk
Minoff Lamps
Mirror Craft
Mission Trade
Mohawk

Montaage
Monticello Studio
MTS
Multiplex
Murobello
Murray Feiss
Mystic Valley Traders
Natural Light
Natuzzi
New Century Pictures
Nichols & Stone
Norman Perry
Normans Of Salisbury
North Bay Collections
Null
OFS
Oklahoma Casting
Oklahoma Importing
Old Hickory Tannery
OLF Lamps Inc.
Orbit
P & P Chair Co.
Pacific Coast Lighting
Palecek
Paragon Pictures
Park Avenue Lamps
Parker Southern
Payne Street Imports
Pearson
Pennsylvania Classics
Pennsylvania House
Peoplelounger
Peters Revington
Peter Vitalie
Phillips Collection
Piage & Pietan Art Stone
Picture Source
Plant Plant
Pompeii
Powell
Preview
Privilege House
Pulaski
Quiedan
Quintessa
Regency House
Rainbow Graphics
Reliance Lamp Co.
Rembrandt Lamps

Remi
Remington Lamp
Reprocrafters
Rex Furniture
Richardson Brothers
Ridgeway Clocks
Ridgewood
Riverside
Robert Abbey Lamps
Robert Allen Fabrics
Roma
Royal Designs Inc.
Royal Patina
Rug Barn
Rug Market
Sadek Imports
San Diego Designs II
Sagefield Leather
Salem Square
Saloom
Sam Moore
Samsonite
Sanctuary Fine Linens
Sandicast
Sarreid
Savoir Faire
Schnadig
Schumacher Fabrics
Schweiger Industries
Sealy
Second Avenue
Second Impressions
Sedgefield Lamps
Serta
Shadow Catchers
Shae Designs
Sheffield & Galloway
Shuford
Sidney Arthur
Signature Designer
   Rugs
Signature Lighting
Silver
Simmons
Sirmos
Skanse
Sligh
Sligh Clocks

Furnitureland South (cont.)

Lines carried (cont.):

Southern Craftsman Guild
Southern Furniture
      Reproductions
Spiral Collection
Spring Air
St. Timothy
Stakmore
Stanley Furniture
Statesville Chair
Statton
Stiffel Lamp
Stone International
Stoneleigh
Stoneville
Straits
Stratford/Stratolounger
Strong
Stylecraft Lamps
Sumter Cabinet
Superior Furniture
Swaim Classics
Swaim Designs
Swan Brass Beds
Table Designs
Telescope
Temple Upholstery
Tempo
Thayer Coggin
Thief River Linens
Timmerman
Toyo
Tradition House
Traditions by Kimball
Tree Factory
Triad Butcher Block Inc.
Triune
Tropitone
Trowbridge Gallery
Tubb Woodcrafters
Tyndale
Ultegra
Union City Mirrors &
      Tables
Unique Originals
United Design
Universal
Urban Woods
Uttermost
Uwharrie Chair

Van Teal
Vanguard
Vanguard Studios
Vaughan
Vaughan Bassett
Velcro
Veneman
Venture By Lane
Versteel
Victorian Classics
Vietri
Virginia House
Virginia Metalcrafters
Vogel Peterson
Wal-Kitecture
Wara Tapestries
Waverly Fabrics
Weiman
Wellington Hall
Wesley Allen
Westwood Lamps
Whitecraft
Wildwood Lamps
Willow Lamps
Windsor Art
Winners Only
Winston Outdoor
Woodard
Woodlands
Woodmark
Ziro Clocks

Gordon's Furniture Store

214 N. Center St.
Statesville, NC 28687

Phone:	**(704) 873-4329**	**Hours:**	**M-F 9:00-6:00, Sat 9:00-5:00**
Toll Free:	**None**	**E-mail:**	**lgordon@i-america.net**
Fax:	**(704) 873-4397**	**Web site:**	**www.ncnet.com/ncnw/gordons.html**

Gordon's Furniture Store has occupied most of one city block in downtown Statesville, NC, since 1917. Their showroom is huge, and their discounts are quite good. On several lines, including Pennsylvania House, Gordon's has the best order-by-phone discounts I've found.

On my most recent trip here, I found a great deal on a queen-size solid cherry rice bed from Pennsylvania House (pictured at right). The retail on this bed is normally $2,267.00, but Gordon's will special-order it or sell you this one off the floor for only $1,133.50, exactly 50% off. This piece, like all of the other furniture on display, was new and in first-quality condition.

If you live within a sixty mile radius of Statesville (an area which includes Charlotte, Greensboro, and Winston-Salem), Gordon's will deliver your furniture free in their own trucks. As in any other case where free delivery is offered, you may be able to negotiate an extra discount if you wish to pick up your furniture in your own truck. Ask.

If you're ordering furniture by phone, you should definitely call Gordon's for a price comparison.

Lines carried:	**Please see page 143**
Phone orders accepted:	**Yes**
Discount:	**50%-55% off mfrs. suggested retail**
Payment methods:	**VISA, MC, personal checks**
In-house financing available:	**No**
Deposits required:	**30% deposit when order is placed, balance due when furniture is ready to be shipped.**
Catalog available:	**No**
Clearance center:	**No**
Delivery:	**Full service in-home delivery and set-up. Customer pays freight company directly for shipping costs. Customers within 60 miles of Statesville, NC can have their furniture delivered free in Gordon's own trucks.**

Directions: From I-40, take exit #150 (Hwy. 115) and head south. Hwy. 115 will become Center St. as you enter Statesville. Gordon's is downtown on the left.

Gordon's Furniture Store (cont.)

Gordon's Furniture Store

Solid cherry rice bed from Pennsylvania House

Retail: $2,267.00   Discounted price: $1,133.00
Savings at Gordon's Furniture Store: $1,134.00 = 50% off retail

Gordon's Furniture Stores

Lines carried:

Acacia
Alexander Julian
American Of Martinsville
American Drew
Arnold Palmer Collection
Bassett
Best Chairs
Blacksmith Shop
Bob Timberlake
Broyhill
Builtright Chair
Cabin Craft Carpet
Carolina Mirror
Chair Co.
Charleston Forge
Chatham County
China Traders Lamps
Chromecraft
Clayton-Marcus
Councill Craftsmen
Custom Rugs
Denny Lamp
Distinction Leather
Ducks Unlimited
Fairfield Chair
Fashion Beds
Grace Iron Beds
Hammary
Hekman
Henry Link
Hooker
J-Royale
Kincaid
La-Z-Boy
Lane
Lea
Lexington
Ligo
Lloyd/Flanders
Lyon Shaw
Masland Carpet
Minoff Lamps
Nora Fenton
Ohio Table Pad
Pennsylvania House
Philadelphia Carpet
Pulaski
Riverside
SK Products

Sarreid
Sedgefield Lamp
Shaw Carpets
Simmons Bedding
Stanley
Stoneville
Stratolounger
Telescope
Universal
Vanguard Studios
Velco
Virginia House
Winston
WundaWeve

Green Front Furniture

316 N. Main St.
Farmville, VA 23901

Phone:	(804) 392-5943	**Hours:**	M-F 9:00-5:00, Sat 9:00-5:30
Toll Free:	None	**E-mail:**	sales@greenfront.com
Fax:	None	**Web site:**	www.greenfront.com

Green Front Furniture's main store and telephone sales operation is located in Farmville, VA, just west of Richmond. The store complex is huge, covering 4 city blocks. There are large galleries for Henredon, Sherrill, Henkel Harris, Statton, and Thomasville. They also carry many other medium to high-end lines of furniture and accessories.

The discounts on brand new first-quality furniture, whether bought in person or over the phone, run from 40%-50% off retail. There is also a clearance center on site which has even better deals.

If you're in the Richmond or Washington, DC, areas, it's worth a side trip to check out Green Front's Clearance Center. Otherwise, it's best to compare their prices over the phone. They do have very good deals on many lines, and they have a reputation for reliable service. Anyone planning to order furniture by phone should check them out.

Phone orders accepted:	Yes
Discount:	40%-50% off mfrs. suggested retail
Payment methods:	VISA, MC, Discover, personal checks
In-house financing available:	Yes
Deposits required:	50% deposit when order is placed, balance due when furniture is ready to be shipped
Catalog available:	No
Clearance center:	Yes -- See *Green Front Furniture Clearance Ctr.*
Delivery:	Full service in-home delivery and set-up. Customer pays freight company directly for shipping costs.

Directions: From I-95, on the south side of Richmond, VA, take exit #62 and go west on Hwy. 288. Then, take Hwy. 360 west to Hwy. 307, and go west. Then, take Hwy. 307 to Hwy. 460, and continue west into downtown Farmville, VA. The three main Green Front buildings surround the intersection of Main St. and 2nd St. in downtown Farmville.

Green Front Furniture

Lines carried:

Aubusson
Baldwin
Barcalounger
Basta Sole
Best Chair
Big Fish
Boling
Bradington Young
Brown Street
Bucks County
Capel Rugs
Cassady
Cibola
Colonial
Colonial Mills
Connoisseur
Craftwork Guild
CTH Occasional
Durham
Eastern Accents
E. J. Victor
Eldred Wheeler
Feizy Imports
Ficks Reed
Fine Art Import
Friedman Brothers
Giemme
Hancock Moore
Hen Feathers
Henkel Harris
Henkel Moore
Henredon
Henry Link
High Point Furniture
Hooker
Jasper Cabinet
Jessica Michaels
John Richard Lamps
John Richards
Keller
King Hickory
Kingsley Bate
La Barge
Lane
Lane-Venture
Leathercraft
Leisters
Lexington
Lloyd/Flanders

Lyon Shaw
Madison Square
Maitland Smith
Malden
Meadowcraft
Michael Thomas
Miles Talbott
Mobel
Motioncraft
Mystic Valley Traders
Nichols & Stone
Old Hickory Tannery
Palecek Baskets
Pawley's Island
Peacock Alley
Pimpernel
Pinehurst
Precedent
Pulaski
Quoizel
Renaissance Art
Sadek
Saloom
Shadow Catchers
Sherrill
Sleep Works
Sligh
Southern Furniture
        Reproductions
Southern Of Conover
Southwood Reproductions
Speer
Stanford
Stanley
Statton
Taylor-King
Thomasville
Tomlin
Tropitone
Waterford
Wellington Hall
Wesley Allen
Whittemore-Sherrill
Wildwood
Winston
Woodard
Wright Table Co.

Green Front Furniture

1304-A Severn Way
Sterling, VA 20166

Phone:	**(703) 406-0761**	**Hours:**	**M-Sat 10:00-6:00,**
Toll Free:	**None**		**Sun 12:00-5:00**
Fax:	**(703) 406-0763**	**E-mail:**	**sales@greenfront.com**
		Web site:	**www.greenfront.com**

Green Front Furniture's Northern Virginia location is located in Sterling, VA, just a few miles west of Washington, DC. They have a very nice selection of medium to high-end lines, including Lexington, Hooker, Sherrill, and Maitland-Smith.

All of Green Front's floor samples and discontinued styles from their two stores and their phone sales service are all sent to their clearance center at their other location in Farmville, VA. For this reason, there is no monetary advantage to shopping at this location in person. All the furniture here is new, and you get the same price whether you buy in person or over the phone.

If you are near Farmville, VA, it's worth making a stop at their clearance center. Otherwise, most people would be better off saving the drive and just ordering from this source over the phone. They do have very good prices, and anyone planning to order furniture by phone should definitely call this source to compare their discounts.

Lines carried:

Bradington Young	Keller	Miles Talbott	Stanford
Brown Street	King Hickory	Mobel	Statton
Cibola	Lane	Nichols & Stone	Taylor-King
Colonial	Leathercraft	Precedent	Wellington Hall
CTH Occasional	Lexington	Pulaski	Wesley Allen
Durham	Madison Square	Sherrill	Whittemore-Sherrill
Hancock Moore	Maitland Smith	Sligh	
Hooker	Michael Thomas	Southwood Reproductions	

Phone orders accepted:	**Yes**
Discount:	**40%-50% off mfrs. suggested retail**
Payment methods:	**VISA, MC, Discover, personal checks**
In-house financing available:	**Yes**
Deposits required:	**50% deposit when order is placed, balance due when furniture is ready to be shipped**
Catalog available:	**No**
Clearance center:	**Yes -- See *Green Front Furniture Clearance Ctr.***
Delivery:	**Full service in-home delivery and set-up. Customer pays freight company directly for shipping costs.**

Directions: From the I-495 perimeter around Washington, DC, take exit #12 and go west on the Dulles Toll Rd. Take exit #9B, and go left on 28N Sally Rd. After 4 miles, turn left on Severn Way. Green Front's is one block down on the right.

Green Front Furniture Clearance Center

316 N. Main St.
Farmville, VA 23901

Phone:	(804) 392-5943	**Hours:**	M-F 9:00-5:00, Sat 9:00-5:30
Toll Free:	None	**E-mail:**	sales@greenfront.com
Fax:	None	**Web site:**	www.greenfront.com

Green Front Furniture's clearance center liquidates floor samples, discontinued styles, and returns from Green Front's two main locations in Farmville and Sterling, VA, as well as their huge phone sales operation.

They have great deals. The discounts run from 50%-75% off. Virtually all of the furniture here is in new first-quality condition. They have a nice selection of medium to high-end brands.

If you're in the Richmond or Washington, DC, areas, it's worth a side trip to check out Green Front's Clearance Center.

Phone orders accepted:	No
Discount:	50%-70% off mfrs. suggested retail
Payment methods:	VISA, MC, Discover, personal checks
In-house financing available:	Yes
Deposits required:	Not applicable
Catalog available:	Not applicable
Clearance center:	Not applicable
Delivery:	Full service in-home delivery and set-up. Customer pays freight company directly for shipping costs.

Directions: From I-95, on the south side of Richmond, VA, take exit #62 and go west on Hwy. 288. Then, take Hwy. 360 west to Hwy. 307, and go west. Then, take Hwy. 307 to Hwy. 460, and continue west into downtown Farmville, VA. The clearance center is on Main St. on the first floor of Green Front's Building #8.

Greenhill Furniture Co.

1308 Hwy. 70 SW
Hickory, NC 28602

Phone:	(704) 327-2024	**Hours:**	M-F 9:00-5:00, Sat 9:00-3:00
Toll Free:	None	**E-mail:**	None
Fax:	None	**Web site:**	None

Greenhill Furniture Co. is located on the west side of Hickory, NC. They have a good selection of medium to high-end lines, including Lexington, Hekman, Hooker, and Universal.

They don't have a clearance center or any floor samples or discontinued pieces on display. For this reason, there is no monetary advantage to visiting in person. They do have great deals on many lines sold over the phone, though. So, if you're planning to order your furniture by phone, definitely give this source a call to compare their prices.

Lines carried:

Action By Lane	Cochrane	Howard Miller Clocks	Rex Furniture
American Drew	C. R. Laine	J/B Ross	Riverside
American Of Martinsville	Dinaire	Jasper Cabinet	Skillcraft
Artistry Design	Dresher	Keller	Stanley
Bassett	Emerson Leather	Kingsdown Bedding	Sterling Taylor
Bassett Mirror	Fairfield	Lane	Tropitone
Benchcraft	Glass Fashions	Lea	Universal
Berkshire	Greene Brothers	Lexington	Venture
Blacksmith Shop	Hekman	Link Taylor	Virginia House
BMC	Henry Link	Moosehead	Young-Hinkle
Broyhill	Highland House	Nathan Hale	Winners Only
Carolina Mirror	Home Lamp Co.	Ohio Table Pad Co.	
Chatham County	Hooker	Pulaski	

Phone orders accepted:	Yes
Discount:	40%-50% off mfrs. suggested retail
Payment methods:	VISA, MC, personal checks
In-house financing available:	No
Deposits required:	50% deposit when order is placed, balance due when furniture is ready to be shipped
Catalog available:	No
Clearance center:	No
Delivery:	Full service in-home delivery and set-up. Customer pays freight company directly for shipping costs.

Directions: From I-40, take exit #123 and drive north on Hwy. 321 into Hickory, NC. Turn left on Hwy. 70. Greenhill Furniture will be 1 mile on the right.

Grindstaff's Interiors

1007 W. Main St.
Forest City, NC 28043

Phone:	(828) 245-4263	**Hours:**	M-Sat 9:00-6:00
Toll Free:	None	**E-mail:**	None
Fax:	(828) 245-7758	**Web site:**	None

Grindstaff's Interiors is located in Forest City, NC, about an hour southwest of Hickory, NC. They have a very nice 80,000 square foot store with a good selection of high-end lines, including Bernhardt, Hekman, La Barge, Baker, Century, and Maitland-Smith.

They don't have a clearance center or any floor samples or discontinued pieces on display. For this reason, there is no monetary advantage to visiting in person. They do have great deals on many lines sold over the phone, though. So, if you're planning to order your furniture by phone, definitely give this source a call to compare their prices.

Lines carried:

Baker	Frederick Cooper Lamps	Karges	Pennsylvania House
Baldwin	Friedman Brothers	Kincaid	Philadelphia
Bernhardt	Hancock Moore	La Barge	Sarreid
Bevan Funnell	Hekman	Lane	Serta
Bradington Young	Henkel Harris	Lexington	Southwood
Brown Jordan	Hickory Chair	Lloyd/Flanders	Reproductions
Casa Stradivari	Hitchcock Chair	Madison Square	Stanley
Century	Hon	Maitland Smith	Statton
Chapman	Hooker	Meadow Craft	Stiffel Lamps
Classic Leather	Jasper Cabinet	Miller	Waterford
Councill Craftsmen	Jeffco	National Mt. Airy	Wildwood
DMI	John Widdicomb	Pande Cameron	Woodard
Ekornes	Karastan	Pennsylvania Classics	Woodmark Originals

Phone orders accepted:	**Yes**
Discount:	**35%-50% off mfrs. suggested retail**
Payment methods:	**VISA, MC, Discover, personal checks**
In-house financing available:	**No**
Deposits required:	**50% deposit when order is placed, balance due when furniture is ready to be shipped**
Catalog available:	**No**
Clearance center:	**No**
Delivery:	**Full service in-home delivery and set-up. Customer pays freight company directly for shipping costs.**

Directions: **From I-40, take the Hwy. 221 exit south (the exit is about one hour west of Hickory, NC). In downtown Forest City, turn left on Hwy. 74. Grindstaff's Interiors is one and a half blocks down on the right.**

Hamilton's

506 Live Oak St.
Beaufort, NC 28516

Phone:	**(919) 728-4720**	**Hours:**	**M-Sat 9:00-5:30**
Toll Free:	**(800) 488-4720**	**E-mail:**	**None**
Fax:	**None**	**Web site:**	**None**

Hamilton's is located in Beaufort, NC, on the Atlantic Coast. They have a very nice selection of medium to high-end lines, including Jasper Cabinet, Classic Leather, Lane, and Kincaid.

They don't have a clearance center or any floor samples or discontinued pieces on display. For this reason, there is no monetary advantage to visiting in person. Also, this store is about five hours drive from the main furniture discounting centers of Hickory and High Point, NC.

They do have great deals on many lines sold over the phone, though. So, if you're planning to order your furniture by phone, definitely give this source a call to compare their prices.

Lines carried:

Action By Lane	D & F Wicker	Lane	Telescope Furniture
American Of Martinsville	Distinction Leather	Lea	Temple
Barcalounger	Dixie	Leister	Tinsley Clark
Barn Door	Ducks Unlimited	Lexington	Troutman Chair
Bassett	Fairfield Chair	Lineal	Universal
Beechbrook	Fortress	Murphy Furniture	Vaughan
Bemco	Fortune Rattan	Null Industries	Vaughan Bassett
Braxton Culler	H & H Furniture	Ohio Table Pad Co.	Victorian Classic
Brookwood	Hickory Hill	P & P Chair	Virginia House
Broyhill	Hooker	Pennsylvania Classics	Webb Furniture
Butler Specialty Co.	Hyundai Furniture	Pulaski	Winston
Cambridge Chair	Jasper Cabinet	Ridgewood	Young America
Carlton McClendon	Keller	Samsonite	by Stanley
Casual Crates	Key City	Serta	Young Hinkle
Classic Leather	Kincaid	Stanley	
Cochrane	Klaussner	Statesville Chair	

Phone orders accepted:	**Yes**
Discount:	**40%-50% off mfrs. suggested retail**
Payment methods:	**VISA, MC, Discover, personal checks**
In-house financing available:	**No**
Deposits required:	**50% deposit when order is placed, balance due when furniture is ready to be shipped**
Catalog available:	**No**
Clearance center:	**No**
Delivery:	**Full service in-home delivery and set-up. Customer pays freight company directly for shipping costs.**

Directions: From I-95, take Hwy. 70 all the way east to Beaufort, NC. You'll see signs for the store as you enter downtown.

Hammary Furniture Factory Outlet

2464 Norwood St. SW
Lenoir, NC 28645-0760

Phone:	**(828) 726-3333**	**Hours:**	**M-F 9:00-5:00**
Toll Free:	**None**	**E-mail:**	**None**
Fax:	**None**	**Web site:**	**None**

This is Hammary Furniture's only factory-owned factory outlet, adjacent to their main factory in Lenoir, NC. Most of the stock here is wrought iron and case goods, primarily armoires and occasional tables. There are a few sofas and occasional chairs.

The furniture here is very nice quality and priced well. The discounts here are 20% off the usual wholesale price, which normally translates to 60%-70% off of retail.

On my most recent visit here, I found a good deal on an end table (pictured on the following page). It normally retails for $300.00, but this one was only $145.00.

If you're in the Lenoir/Hickory, NC, area looking for wrought iron tables, occasional tables, or armoires, this is a great place to check out.

Phone orders accepted:	**No**
Discount:	**60%-70% off mfrs. suggested retail**
Payment methods:	**Personal checks. No credit cards.**
In-house financing available:	**No**
Deposits required:	**Not applicable**
Catalog available:	**Not applicable**
Clearance center:	**Not applicable**
Delivery:	**Customer must make own arrangements to take furniture home.**

Directions: **From I-40, take exit #123, and drive north on Hwy. 321 to Lenoir, NC. Turn left on Hwy. 321-A South. Then, turn left on Norwood St. The Hammary outlet will be on the right.**

Hammary Furniture Factory Outlet (cont.)

Hammary Furniture Factory Outlet

End table from Hammary Furniture

Retail: $300.00   Discounted price: $145.00
Savings at the Hammary Furniture Factory Outlet: $155.00 = 52% off retail

Harden Factory Outlet

Mill Pond Way
McConnellsville, NY 13401

Phone:	**(315) 245-1000**	**Hours:**	**M-Sat 10:00-5:00, Sun 1:00-5:00**
Toll Free:	**None**		**Closed first two weeks of July**
Fax:	**(315) 245-2884**	**E-mail:**	**None**
		Web site:	**None**

This is Harden Furniture's only factory outlet, located in the Harden factory itself in McConnellsville, NY, near Oneida Lake just east of Syracuse, NY. Actually, the outlet is what they call an "overpile" room, where they store photography samples, seconds, floor samples, discontinued styles, and overruns.

Most of the stock here is solid cherry case goods. This is a very high-quality traditional furniture line. The discounts here run from 50%-75% off retail.

Harden conducts business a bit differently from most outlets. If you come by to look through their overpile room, and you find something you like, they won't allow you to buy it on the spot. They tag it and ship it free of charge to the Harden dealer nearest you on the next Harden truck delivering furniture to that particular store. This can take up to a month. Then, when it arrives at your local Harden dealer, you'll be notified to come pick it up and pay the dealer for it directly. You do still pay the outlet price however.

If you plan to stop by this outlet, you may wish to plan your visit on a Wednesday morning. The Harden factory gives one-hour factory tours every Wednesday at 10:00. It's quite interesting, and it's free.

This is a good source. Harden has very high-quality gorgeous furniture, and the prices are quite good.

Phone orders accepted:	**No**
Discount:	**50%-75% off mfrs. suggested retail**
Payment methods:	**Personal checks. No credit cards.**
In-house financing available:	**No**
Deposits required:	**Not applicable**
Catalog available:	**Not applicable**
Clearance center:	**Not applicable**
Delivery:	**Furniture will be tagged and delivered free of charge via a Harden truck to the Harden dealer nearest the customer. The customer then picks up the furniture and pays for it at the local Harden dealer.**

Directions: **From I-90, take exit #34, and go north on Hwy. 13. The Harden factory and outlet are just off Hwy. 13 in downtown McConnellsville.**

Hendricks Furniture Galleries

I-40, Exit #174
182 Farmington Rd.
Mocksville, NC 27028

Phone:	**(336) 998-7712**	**Hours:**	**M-Sat 9:00-6:00**	
Toll Free:	**(888) 316-3351**	**E-mail:**	**None**	
Fax:	**(336) 998-9598**	**Web site:**	**www.boyles.com**	

Hendricks Furniture Galleries is part of the Boyles conglomerate. Boyles also has 11 more locations, and they've become one of the biggest furniture discounters in North Carolina.

Like the other Boyles locations, this store has an extensive high-end gallery. All of the furniture in stock is new first-quality. The discounts range from 30%-50% off retail. All of Hendricks' floor samples and discontinued items are sent to Boyles' clearance center in Hickory, NC, located right behind Boyles' Country Shop.

On my most recent visit, I found a great deal on a Bernhardt "Embassy Row" bedroom set (pictured on the following page). This set (bed, dresser, bachelor's chest, and master chest) normally retails for $16,020.00, but it was marked down to $7,059.00, 56% off. The extra discount was due to their annual January "winter sale", when most items are marked 55%-60% off retail.

One significant advantage to buying from Hendricks/Boyles is that, unlike most discounters, they will allow you to make your final payment for your furniture on delivery instead of requiring that you pay the rest of your bill before the furniture is shipped to your home.

If you're buying furniture by phone, you should compare prices with this source. If you're traveling to the Hickory, NC, area in person to shop, you should definitely check out Boyles' clearance center.

Lines carried:	**Please see page 156**
Phone orders accepted:	**Yes**
Discount:	**30%-50% off mfrs. suggested retail**
Payment methods:	**VISA, MC, personal checks**
In-house financing available:	**No**
Deposits required:	**1/3 deposit when order is placed, balance due when furniture is delivered to your home**
Catalog available:	**No**
Clearance center:	**Yes -- See *Boyles Clearance Center***
Delivery:	**Full service in-home delivery and set-up. Customer pays freight company directly for shipping costs.**

Directions: From I-40, take exit #174 (Farmington Rd.). You'll see Hendricks right next to the expressway exit.

Hendricks Furniture Galleries (cont.)

Hendricks Furniture Galleries

Embassy Row bedroom set from Bernhardt Furniture

Retail: $16,020.00   Discounted price: $7,059.00
Savings at Hendricks Furniture Galleries: $8,961.00 = 56% off retail

Hendricks Furniture Galleries (cont.)

Lines carried:

American Drew
Baker
Bernhardt
Bevan Funnell
Bob Timberlake
Bradington Young
Broyhill
Cape Craftsmen
Casa Bique
Century
Charleston Forge
Councill Craftsmen
Hancock & Moore
Harden
Hekman
Henkel-Harris
Henkel-Moore
Henredon
Hickory Chair
Hickory White
Hooker
Jasper Cabinet
Jeffco
J. Royale
Karges
Kincaid
Kingsdown
La Barge
Lane
Leathercraft
Lexington
Madison Square
Maitland Smith
Marge Carson
Motioncraft
National Mt. Airy
Nichols & Stone
Pennsylvania House
Precedent
Rex
Riverside
Sam Moore
Sealy
Sherrill
Shuford
Sligh
Southwood Reproductions
Stanley
Thomasville

Tradition House
Universal
Weiman
Wellington Hall
Wesley Allen
Whittemore-Sherrrill

Henredon Factory Clearance Center

Rte 3, Box 379
Henredon Rd.
Spruce Pine, NC 28777

Phone:	**(828) 765-1320**	**Hours:**	**M-Sat 9:00-4:30**
Toll Free:	**None**	**E-mail:**	**None**
Fax:	**None**	**Web site:**	**None**

The Henredon Factory Clearance Center in Spruce Pine is a huge warehouse with a nice selection of case goods. There are very few upholstered pieces in stock here, though. For Henredon upholstery, it's better to visit their other outlets at the Hickory Furniture Mart in Hickory, NC, and in Raleigh, NC.

This outlet does have a great selection of case goods. There's one large room with dozens of occasional tables, another with beds and chests, and a third one with nothing but armoires. Don't forget to check the front loading dock for more beds. There's also a semi-hidden back room with more armoires.

On my most recent visit here, I found a great deal on a solid ash burl veneer entertainment center (pictured on the following page). This piece normally retails for $9,500.00, but the outlet had this one for only $2,300.00. It was a photography sample with no damage.

The vast majority of the furniture at this outlet are discontinued styles, photography samples, floor samples, and a few seconds. The discounts range from 75% to 80% off retail. Nearly all of the pieces are in first quality condition.

Important note: The roads up to this outlet go essentially straight up a mountain. It takes nearly one hour of very challenging driving through the edge of the Smoky Mountains to reach this outlet from I-40. This is not a place you want to visit in bad weather or after dark. Also, this is not a good place for anyone to rent a truck or trailer and drive it up to the outlet to pick up their own furniture. Unless you are very experienced driving large vehicles on very bad roads, please let the outlet ship your furniture to you.

This outlet is wonderful, but very difficult to get to. Most people will be better off to visit the Henredon outlet in Hickory, NC, which also has a terrific selection and great bargains. However, if you're in the Asheville area or on a vacation to the Smoky Mountains, and you feel up to the drive, by all means check out this outlet. It is definitely worth a visit.

Phone orders accepted:	**No**
Discount:	**75%-80% off mfrs. suggested retail**
Payment methods:	**VISA, MC, personal checks**
In-house financing available:	**No**
Deposits required:	**Not applicable**
Catalog available:	**Not applicable**
Clearance center:	**Not applicable**
Delivery:	**Full service in-home delivery and set-up. Customer pays freight company directly for shipping costs.**

Directions: From I-40, take exit #86 (the Marion exit), and take Hwy. 221/226 north to Spruce Pine. There are many signs all along the way to Spruce Pine. Near the top of the mountain, you will cometo a Shell station. Turn right at the station onto Hall Town Rd. Go 3-4 miles until you reach a dead end and turn right. Follow the Henredon signs to the outlet.

Henredon Factory Clearance Center (cont.)

Henredon Factory Clearance Center

Solid ash burl veneer entertainment center from Henredon

Retail: $9,500.00   Discounted price: $2,300.00
Savings at the Henredon Factory Clearance Center: $7,200.00 = 76% off retail

Henredon Factory Outlet

3004-A Parquet Dr.
Dalton, GA 30720

I'm sorry to have to report that this terrific outlet closed on February 1, 1999. I was told that the outlet was closed at the request of certain furniture retailers in the Atlanta area who objected to having this outlet located 75 miles away from their stores.

It is an unfortunate fact of life in the home furnishings industry that manufacturers who sell directly to the public are often subjected to extreme pressure from the retailers whose profit margins shrink as a result. Every time this kind of bullying from retailers results in the closure of another factory outlet or deep discounter, you and I all pay higher prices for furniture as a result.

The best way to combat this problem is for all consumers to pressure manufacturers to keep selling through factory outlets and deep discounters. Vote with your checkbook. Pressure manufacturers to sell in a way that is in YOUR best interests, rather than in the middlemen's best interests.

Fortunately, there are still three terrific Henredon factory outlets in North Carolina, and this line is sold over the phone by a number of deep discounters.

Henredon Factory Outlet

Level 2
Hickory Furniture Mart
U. S. Hwy. 70 SE
Hickory, NC 28602

Phone:	**(828) 322-7111**	**Hours:**	**M-Sat 9:00-6:00**
Toll Free:	**None**	**E-mail:**	**info@hickoryfurniture.com**
Fax:	**None**	**Web site:**	**www.hickoryfurniture.com**

The Henredon Factory Outlet at the Hickory Furniture Mart has a huge selection of Henredon case goods and upholstery. This is one of only three Henredon factory outlets, and it's probably the best one consumers to visit in person.

Most of the pieces here are floor samples and discontinued items, although there are some seconds. Even the seconds have extremely small flaws, however. The discounts are very good: 65%-70% off retail.

On my most recent visit, I found a wonderful deal on a solid mahogany bed (pictured on the following page). This queen mahogany bed normally retails for $7,485.00, but the outlet had this one for only $2,745.00, a discount of almost 65% off retail. This particular bed was a floor sample in first-quality condition.

This outlet normally has sales in January and May when all items are marked down an extra 10%-20%, so you may wish to consider this in making your travel plans to North Carolina. Many other outlets and showrooms have special sales in January and May, as well.

The outlet will not special order new Henredon furniture, but if you see a Henredon piece you like at a local furniture store, you can call the outlet to see if they might have a floor sample or a similar discontinued style. The outlet will take these types of orders by phone and have your furniture shipped to you.

Anyone considering purchasing Henredon furniture should definitely check this outlet out before they buy, preferably in person. This outlet is a "must-visit".

Phone orders accepted:	Yes
Discount:	**65%-70% off mfrs. suggested retail**
Payment methods:	**VISA, MC, personal checks**
In-house financing available:	**No**
Deposits required:	**Not applicable**
Catalog available:	**Not applicable**
Clearance center:	**Not applicable**
Delivery:	**Full service in-home delivery and set-up. Customer pays freight company directly for shipping costs.**

Directions: Please see *Hickory Furniture Mart* for complete directions.

Henredon Factory Outlet (cont.)

Carved solid mahogany bed from Henredon

Retail: $7,485.00   Discounted price: $2,745.00
Savings at the Henredon Factory Outlet: $4,740.00 = 63% off retail

Henredon Factory Outlet

3943 New Bern Ave.
Raleigh, NC 27610

Phone:	**(919) 212-8250**	**Hours:**	**M-Sat 9:00-6:00**
Toll Free:	**None**	**E-mail:**	**None**
Fax:	**None**	**Web site:**	**None**

The Henredon Factory Outlet in Raleigh has a huge selection of Henredon case goods and upholstery. This is one of only three Henredon factory outlets nationwide.

Most of the pieces here are floor samples and discontinued items, although there are some seconds. Even the seconds have extremely small flaws, however. The discounts are very good: 60%-70% off retail.

On my most recent visit, I found a great deal on a solid mahogany armoire that had been returned by a customer because the wrong item had been ordered by the interior designer. It normally retails for $7,485.00, but this one at the outlet was only $2,745.00. It was brand-new and in perfect condition.

The outlet will not special order new Henredon furniture, but if you see a Henredon piece you like at a local furniture store, you can call the outlet to see if they might have a floor sample or a similar discontinued style. The outlet will take these types of orders by phone and have your furniture shipped to you.

Anyone traveling in or near the Raleigh area really should check out this outlet. However, if you're planning a general shopping trip to North Carolina, you would probably be better off to shop at the other Henredon Factory Outlet in Hickory, NC. Unlike this outlet, the one in Hickory is surrounded by outlets from many other manufacturers. This outlet is terrific, but it's several hours away from the main furniture discounting centers of Hickory and High Point.

Phone orders accepted:	**Yes**
Discount:	**60%-70% off mfrs. suggested retail**
Payment methods:	**VISA, MC, personal checks**
In-house financing available:	**No**
Deposits required:	**Not applicable**
Catalog available:	**Not applicable**
Clearance center:	**Not applicable**
Delivery:	**Full service in-home delivery and set-up. Customer pays freight company directly for shipping costs.**

Directions: From I-40, take the Wade Ave. exit. There is only one direction to go when you exit on Wade Ave. Go about one and a half miles until you see a sign for 440-N ("Wake Forest/Rocky Mount/Inner Beltloop"). Take that exit, and get on the inner beltloop. Take exit #13-B (Rocky Mount). Go to the third traffic light, and take a left. The Henredon Factory Outlet is in the shopping center immediately on your left after you turn.

Henredon Factory Outlet (cont.)

Solid mahogany armoire from Henredon

Retail: $7,485.00   Discounted price: $2,745.00
Savings at the Henredon Factory Outlet: $4,740.00 = 63% off retail

kory Chair Factory Outlet

1120 Hwy. 16 N.
Conover, NC 28613

Phone:	**(828) 464-9940**		**Hours:**	**M-Sat 9:00-6:00**
Toll Free:	**None**		**E-mail:**	**None**
Fax:	**(828) 464-9964**		**Web site:**	**None**

The Hickory Chair Factory Outlet is a part of Factory Direct Furniture in Conover, NC. This showroom also serves as the factory outlet for Century and Councill-Craftsmen. This location and their other showroom in the Hickory Furniture Mart, operated by the same company, are the only two factory-owned factory outlets for these three brands.

The discounts on the outlet furniture generally runs a straight 60% off across the board. Virtually all of the furniture here is in new first-quality condition.

At both locations, the sales staff immediately volunteers to customers that they can come down even further from the price marked, so be sure to haggle. Factory Direct Furniture also runs periodic sales, usually giving another 10%-20% off the marked discount. These sales normally run in January, March, May, and September.

Both locations have an excellent selection. Most of the pieces are traditional, but there are usually a few contemporary styles.

If you're traveling to the Hickory area, this outlet is a "must-visit". If you don't find what you're looking for here, be sure to check their other location about ten minutes away at the Hickory Furniture Mart.

Phone orders accepted:	**No**
Discount:	**60% off mfrs. suggested retail**
Payment methods:	**VISA, MC, personal checks**
In-house financing available:	**No**
Deposits required:	**Not applicable**
Catalog available:	**Not applicable**
Clearance center:	**Not applicable**
Delivery:	**Full service in-home delivery and set-up. Customer pays freight company directly for shipping costs.**

Directions: From I-40, take exit #131, and go one-quarter mile north on Hwy. 16 North. Factory Direct Furniture will be on the right side of the highway.

Hickory Chair Factory Outlet

Level 4
Hickory Furniture Mart
U. S. Hwy. 70 SE
Hickory, NC 28602

Phone:	(828) 324-9400	**Hours:**	M-Sat 9:00-6:00
Toll Free:	None	**E-mail:**	info@hickoryfurniture.com
Fax:	(828) 464-9964	**Web site:**	www.hickoryfurniture.com

The Hickory Chair Factory Outlet is a part of the National Furniture Outlets space at the Hickory Furniture Mart. This showroom also serves as the factory outlet for Councill-Craftsmen and Hickory Chair. This location and one more warehouse in nearby Conover, NC, operated by the same company are the only two factory-owned factory outlets for these three brands.

This location is about half-stocked with antiques and accessories, with the other half of the showroom devoted to discontinued styles and floor samples from the above-mentioned three brands. The discounts on the outlet furniture generally runs a straight 60% off across the board. Virtually all of the furniture here is in new first-quality condition.

At both locations, the sales staff immediately volunteers to customers that they can come down even further from the price marked, so be sure to haggle. National Furniture Outlets also runs periodic sales, usually giving another 10%-20% off the marked discount. These sales normally run in January, March, May, and September.

Both locations have an excellent selection. Most of the pieces are traditional, but there are usually a few contemporary styles.

If you're traveling to Hickory, this outlet is a "must-visit". If you don't find what you're looking for here, be sure to check their other location about ten minutes away in Conover, NC.

Phone orders accepted:	No
Discount:	60% off mfrs. suggested retail
Payment methods:	VISA, MC, personal checks
In-house financing available:	No
Deposits required:	Not applicable
Catalog available:	Not applicable
Clearance center:	Not applicable
Delivery:	Full service in-home delivery and set-up. Customer pays freight company directly for shipping costs.

Directions: Please see *Hickory Furniture Mart* for complete directions.

Hickory Furniture Mart

U. S. Hwy. 70 SE
Hickory, NC 28602

Phone:	**(828) 322-3510**	**Hours:**	**M-Sat 9:00-6:00**
Toll Free:	**(800) 462-MART**	**E-mail:**	**info@hickoryfurniture.com**
Fax:	**(828) 322-1132**	**Web site:**	**www.hickoryfurniture.com**

The Hickory Furniture Mart is big. How big is it? Well, they have pagers available for loan at all the information counters in case you get separated from your friends and family. That's big.

The Mart does have some excellent deals from legitimate discounters and true factory outlets. Be aware though, that not every store in the Mart sells at bargain prices. Some Mart stores were omitted from this book because they are just regular retailers.

Please see the individual listings in this book for each gallery or outlet for details on payment, shipping, lines carried, etc:

Beacon Hill Clearance Center	(828) 324-2220
Boyles Galleries	(828) 326-1740
Boyles Showcase Gallery	(828) 326-1735
Bradington Young Gallery	(828) 328-5257
Broyhill Showcase Gallery	(828) 324-9467
Century Factory Outlet	(828) 324-2442
Councill-Craftsmen Outlet	(828) 324-2442
Don Lamor	(828) 324-1776
Drexel-Heritage Outlet	(828) 324-2220
Henredon Factory Outlet	(828) 322-7111
Hickory Chair Factory Outlet	(828) 324-2442
Home Focus	(828) 324-7742
Ironstone Galleries	(828) 304-1094
La Barge Factory Outlet	(828) 324-2220
Maitland-Smith Outlet	(828) 324-2220
Rhoney Furniture House	(828) 328-8688
Robert Bergelin Company	(828) 345-1500
Wildermere	(828) 322-6602

The Mart has some good bargains on airfares and trip packages to the Hickory area, so definitely call their main office above when making your travel plans. There is a Holiday Inn Express connected to the Mart building that has some very good trip packages. Please call the Mart's main office above for details.

Many discounters and outlets have special sales in May and November, right after the bi-annual High Point International Home Furnishings Market, as well as in January when business is traditionally slow. Many other factory outlets and showrooms in the High Point area have special sales during these months, too, so you may wish to plan any trips to High Point to take advantage of these extra discounts.

If you're looking for furniture, you can't afford not to come here. If you had to choose one shopping destination in the entire state of North Carolina, this would be the one.

Directions: **From I-40, take exit #125 and turn right. Head south on Hwy. L-R. After about a mile, turn left onto Hwy. 70. You'll see the outlet a couple of miles down on the right.**

Hickory Furniture Mart (cont.)

Hickory Furniture Mart

Hickory Park Furniture Galleries

Level 3
Hickory Furniture Mart
U. S. Hwy. 70 SE
Hickory, NC 28602

Phone:	**(828) 322-4440**	**Hours:**	**M-Sat 9:00-6:00**
Toll Free:	**None**	**E-mail:**	**hparksales@hickorypark.com**
Fax:	**(828) 322-1454**	**Web site:**	**www.hickorypark.com**

Although Hickory Park Furniture carries furniture for any room in the home, their specialty is upholstery. Their Hickory Furniture Mart showroom has a special section called "The Comfort Zone" which stocks leather, upholstery, sectionals, and recliners. They also have a fairly good selection of children's furniture from Child Craft, ID Kids, Little Miss Liberty, and others.

Do check Hickory Park's contract carefully if you should decide to order from them. I've seen contracts from other discounters that were far more favorable to the consumer.

One provision that Hickory Park insists on that particularly concerns me is their $7.50 per day storage fee for furniture that isn't picked up or shipped to the customer within 7 days of its arrival at Hickory Park. This is not a standard contract clause for a discounter, and it can result in significant additional storage and/or freight costs to the consumer. This clause alone may be enough reason for you to shop elsewhere.

Lines carried:

Action By Lane	Dinaire	Lane	Sidney Arthur
Alexvale	Dutailier	Lea	Simmons
Barcalounger	GMS Imports	Little Bridge Lane	Spring Air
Barn Door	Hammary	Little Miss Liberty	Style Upholstery
Benchcraft	Hekman	McKay Table Pads	Timmerman
Berkline	Hickory-Fry	McKinley Leather	Vermont Precision
Bermex	ID Kids	Parker Southern	Wambold
C. R. Laine	JSF Industries	Reflections	Whitecraft
Cebu	Jensen Jarrah	Regency House	Winners Only
Charleston Forge	Kincaid	Riverside	Woodard
Child Craft	Kingsdown	Ron Fisher	
Creative Ideas	KNF Designs	Rowe	

Phone orders accepted:	**Yes**
Discount:	**40%-50% off mfrs. suggested retail**
Payment methods:	**VISA, MC, personal checks**
In-house financing available:	**No**
Deposits required:	**25% deposit when order is placed, balance due when furniture is ready to be shipped**
Catalog available:	**No**
Clearance center:	**No**
Delivery:	**Full service in-home delivery and set-up. Customer pays freight company directly for shipping costs.**

Directions: Please see *Hickory Furniture Mart* for complete directions.

Hickory Park Furniture Galleries

The Atrium
430 S. Main St.
High Point, NC 27260

Phone:	**(336) 883-3800**	**Hours:**	**M-F 9:00-6:00, Sat 9:00-5:00**
Toll Free:	**None**	**E-mail:**	**hparksales@hickorypark.com**
Fax:	**(336) 883-9047**	**Web site:**	**www.hickorypark.com**

Hickory Park's gallery at The Atrium Furniture Mall has a nice selection of upholstery, leather, sectionals, and recliners. They have a particularly good Action By Lane gallery at this location. They also have a good selection of entertainment centers, desks, and other office furniture here.

Do check Hickory Park's contract carefully if you should decide to order from them. I've seen contracts from other discounters that were far more favorable to the consumer.

One provision that Hickory Park insists on that particularly concerns me is their $7.50 per day storage fee for furniture that isn't picked up or shipped to the customer within 7 days of its arrival at Hickory Park. This is not a standard contract clause for a discounter, and it can result in significant additional storage and/or freight costs to the consumer. This clause alone may be enough reason for you to shop elsewhere.

Lines carried:

Action By Lane	Dinaire	Lane	Sidney Arthur
Alexvale	Dutailier	Lea	Simmons
Barcalounger	GMS Imports	Little Bridge Lane	Spring Air
Barn Door	Hammary	Little Miss Liberty	Style Upholstery
Benchcraft	Hekman	McKay Table Pads	Timmerman
Berkline	Hickory-Fry	McKinley Leather	Vermont Precision
Bermex	ID Kids	Parker Southern	Wambold
C. R. Laine	JSF Industries	Reflections	Whitecraft
Cebu	Jensen Jarrah	Regency House	Winners Only
Charleston Forge	Kincaid	Riverside	Woodard
Child Craft	Kingsdown	Ron Fisher	
Creative Ideas	KNF Designs	Rowe	

Phone orders accepted:	**Yes**
Discount:	**40%-50% off mfrs. suggested retail**
Payment methods:	**VISA, MC, personal checks**
In-house financing available:	**No**
Deposits required:	**25% deposit when order is placed, balance due when furniture is ready to be shipped**
Catalog available:	**No**
Clearance center:	**No**
Delivery:	**Full service in-home delivery and set-up. Customer pays freight company directly for shipping costs.**

Directions: Hickory Park is located inside the Atrium complex in downtown High Point. Please see *The Atrium* for complete directions.

Hickory White Factory Outlet

2679 Ramada Rd.
Burlington, NC 2715

Phone:	**(336) 229-0831**	**Hours:**	**M-F 9:00-5:00**
Toll Free:	**None**	**E-mail:**	**None**
Fax:	**None**	**Web site:**	**None**

This is one of only two Hickory White factory-owned factory outlets. The first floor has an extensive selection of case goods and upholstery. The smaller second floor has a nice selection of occasional chairs, ottomans, and odd sets of dining room chairs.

The stock here consists of floor samples, discontinued styles, overruns, customer returns, photography samples, and a few seconds. Virtually all of the furniture here is new and in first-quality condition. The discounts range from 60%-75% off retail, with most items marked about 65% off. Most of the furniture here is traditional, but there are a few contemporary pieces.

On my most recent visit here, I found a great deal on a white silk ottoman (pictured on the following page). This ottoman normally retails for $1,450.00, but this one was on sale for only $545.00. It was a floor sample in new first-quality condition.

This outlet is situated almost next door to factory outlets for Pennsylvania House and Classic Leather, which makes it a good side trip for anyone who travels to High Point, NC, to shop. Burlington is less than an hour's drive east of High Point, and these three outlets have some really terrific deals.

Phone orders accepted:	**No**
Discount:	**60%-75% off mfrs. suggested retail**
Payment methods:	**Personal checks. No credit cards.**
In-house financing available:	**No**
Deposits required:	**Not applicable**
Catalog available:	**Not applicable**
Clearance center:	**Not applicable**
Delivery:	**Full service in-home delivery and set-up. Customer pays freight company directly for shipping costs.**

Directions: From I-85, take exit #143, and go north on Hwy. 62. The Hickory White outlet is just off the interstate on the frontage road.

Hickory White Factory Outlet (cont.)

Hickory White Factory Outlet in Burlington, NC

Silk ottoman from Hickory White

Retail: $1,450.00   Discounted price: $545.00
Savings at the Hickory White Factory Outlet: $905.00 = 62% off retail

Hickory White Factory Outlet

1537 E. Broad St.
Statesville, NC 28625

Phone:	**(704) 838-0855**	**Hours:**	**M-F 9:00-5:00**
Toll Free:	**None**	**E-mail:**	**None**
Fax:	**None**	**Web site:**	**None**

This is one of only two Hickory White factory-owned factory outlets. This one is a bit bigger than the one in Burlington, and it has a quite a bit more furniture in stock. About two-thirds of the furniture here is upholstery, but there is still a nice selection of case goods, too.

The stock here consists of floor samples, discontinued styles, overruns, customer returns, photography samples, and a few seconds. Virtually all of the furniture here is new and in first-quality condition. The discounts range from 60%-75% off retail, with most items marked about 65% off. Most of the furniture here is traditional, but there are a few contemporary pieces.

On my most recent visit here, I found a terrific deal on a solid maple buffet (pictured on the following page). It normally retails for $5,099.00, but this one was on sale for $999.00, over 80% off retail. This piece was a floor sample with very minor use. It had two tiny half-moon shaped dings about one centimeter across and a superficial scratch about an inch long.

I got an estimate from a local refinisher to invisibly repair the damage. I was told that it would cost no more than $200.00. That $200.00 repair charge is a fine trade-off for a $4,100.00 savings off of retail. This is the kind of "fixer-upper" that can be a terrific bargain. This piece was the exception, though. The vast majority of the furniture here had no damage of any kind.

Statesville is right in-between Hickory and High Point, about an hour's drive from either. Anyone traveling to either city might want to consider taking an extra day to go to Statesville. This outlet has some marvelous deals, and there are several other sources nearby that are well worth a visit.

Phone orders accepted:	**No**
Discount:	**60%-75% off mfrs. suggested retail**
Payment methods:	**Personal checks. No credit cards.**
In-house financing available:	**No**
Deposits required:	**Not applicable**
Catalog available:	**Not applicable**
Clearance center:	**Not applicable**
Delivery:	**Full service in-home delivery and set-up. Customer pays freight company directly for shipping costs.**

Directions: From I-77, take exit #50, and go east on Broad St. The Hickory White Outlet is just off the interstate.

Hickory White Factory Outlet (cont.)

Hickory White Factory Outlet in Statesville, NC

Solid maple buffet from Hickory White

Retail: $5,099.00   Discounted price: $999.00
Savings at the Hickory White Factory Outlet: $4,100.00 = 80% off retail

High Point Furniture Sales

2000 Baker Rd.
High Point, NC 27260

Phone:	**(336) 841-5664**	**Hours:**	**M-F 9:00-5:00**
Toll Free:	**(800) 334-1875**	**E-mail:**	**None**
Fax:	**(336) 885-7034**	**Web site:**	**None**

High Point Furniture Sales has a very nice store on the east side of High Point with large galleries for Thomasville and Lexington. They have very good prices, 48% off retail on most of the brands they carry.

They have no discontinued styles or floor samples on display, but they will give you an extra 5% off on any new furniture purchased off the sales floor if you ask. Of course, this is only helpful if you are a North Carolina resident. Residents of other states won't benefit from the extra discount because shopping in person rather than over the phone would obligate you to pay North Carolina sales tax.

This source has made special arrangements to carry Wexford Furniture. Wexford Furniture manufactures all of the furniture for Crate & Barrel. Now, any furniture from Crate & Barrel can be ordered here at about half price.

Don't let the plain exterior fool you. This is a terrific source. Unless you're a North Carolina resident, there isn't any monetary advantage to shopping in person, but anyone considering buying furniture over the phone should definitely compare prices here. The staff is extremely helpful, and the discounts are very impressive on many lines.

Phone orders accepted:	Yes
Discount:	40%-50% off mfrs. suggested retail
Payment methods:	Personal checks. No credit cards.
In-house financing available:	No
Deposits required:	25% deposit when order is placed, balance due when furniture is ready to be shipped
Catalog available:	No
Clearance center:	No
Delivery:	Full service in-home delivery and set-up. Customer pays freight company directly for shipping costs.

Directions: From Business I-85, take the Baker Rd. exit, on the east side of High Point, NC. Go north on Baker Rd. High Point Furniture Sales is just off the interstate on the right side of the road.

High Point Furniture Sales (cont.)

Lines carried:

Ace Crystal
Action By Lane
Alexander Julian
American Drew
American Mirror
American Of Martinsville
Andrew Pearson
Arnold Palmer Collection
Artistic Impressions
Austin Art
Balangier
Baldwin Brass
Baldwin Clocks
Barcalounger
Barn Door
Bauer Lamps
Benicia Beds
Berkline
Berkshire
Blacksmith Shop
Bob Timberlake
Bradington Young
Brass Craft Inc.
Braxton Culler
Brown Jordan
Broyhill
Cal-Style
Cambridge Lamps
Cape Craftsman
Carlton McLendon
Carolina Mirror
Carsons
Carter Furniture
Casa Bique
Castilian Imports
Casual Lamps
Cebu
Charisma Chairs
Chatham County
Charter Table Co.
Chromcraft
Clark Casual
Classic Rattan
Clayton Marcus
Cochrane Furniture
Conover Chair
Cox Mfg.
Crate & Barrel (Wexford)
Crawford Mfg.

Creations At Dallas
Crystal Clear Ind.
Dar Ran
Darafeau
Daystrom
Decorative Crafts
Design Masters
Design Trees
Design Trends
            by Cochrane
Dillon
Dinaire
Distinctive Designs
Dresher
Dutailier
Ello
Excelsior
Fabricoate
Fairfield Chair
Fashion Bed Group
Ficks Reed
Fine Arts Lamps
Flexsteel
Floral Arts
Frederick Cooper Lamps
Friedman Brothers
Friendship Upholstery
Fitz & Floyd
Glass Arts
Grace
Great American
            Trading Co.
Great City Traders
Greene Brothers
Guildmaster
Halcyon
Hollywoods
Hubbardton Forge
Hammary
Hekman
Henry Link
Hickory Hill
High Point Furniture
Hitchcock Chair
Hood Furniture
Hooker
Howard Miller Clocks
Huntington House
Hyundai Furniture

International Furniture
Jasper Cabinet
Jeffco
Johnston Casuals
Keller
Key City
Kimball
Kincaid
Kinder Harris
Kingsdown
Lane
Lane-Venture
Laurier
Lea
Leisters
Lexington
Link Taylor
Lloyd/Flanders
Lyon Shaw
Marlow
Mary Dale Lamp
Master Design
Miller Desk
Mirror Craft
Mobel
Murray Feiss
Natural Light
Null Industries
Oriental Lacquer
Ohio Table Pad Co.
Palecek
Paragon
Park Place
Patrician
Peoplelounger
Peter Revington
Phillips Furniture
Pieri
Pinnacle
Plant Plant
Preview
Pulaski
Regency House
Remington Lamps
Rex Furniture
Richardson Brothers
Ridgeway
Riverside
Rowe Furniture

Rug Barn
Sam Moore
Samsonite
San Diego Design
Santee
Schnadig
Schweiger
Sealy Mattress
Sedgefield Lamps
Serta Mattress
Skillcraft
Shafer Seating
Sherrill
Signature Rugs
Stanley
Stiffel Lamps
Stratalounger
Stratford
Swaim Originals
Taylorsville
            Upholstery
Telescope
Thayer Coggin
Thomasville
Timeless Bedding
Toyo
Tropitone
Universal
U. S. Furniture
Uttermost Mirrors
Uwharrie Chair
Van Patten
Van Teal
Vanguard
Vaughan
Vaughan Bassett
Victorian Classics
Weiman
Wesley Allen
Wexford
Winston
Woodard
Woodmark

Highland House Factory Outlet

Manufacturer-Owned Factory Outlets (Lenoir Mall)
1031 Morganton Blvd.
Lenoir, NC 28645

Phone:	**(828) 758-8899**	**Hours:**	**M-Sat 10:00-7:00, Sun 1:00-5:00**
Toll Free:	**None**	**E-mail:**	**None**
Fax:	**(828) 754-5038**	**Web site:**	**None**

This is Highland House's only factory outlet, near their factory in Hickory, NC. The outlet is actually located inside the Broyhill Factory Outlet in Lenoir Mall. Unfortunately, the outlet had less than a dozen pieces on display from Highland House.

The Manufacturer-Owned Factory Outlets in Lenoir Mall are definitely worth a visit, primarily because of the Thomasville and Bernhardt outlets here, but I wouldn't make a special trip just to visit the Highland House outlet. It's simply too small and too poorly stocked.

Phone orders accepted:	**No**
Discount:	**65%-75% off mfrs. suggested retail**
Payment methods:	**VISA, MC, personal checks.**
In-house financing available:	**No**
Deposits required:	**Not applicable**
Catalog available:	**Not applicable**
Clearance center:	**Not applicable**
Delivery:	**Full service in-home delivery and set-up. Customer pays freight company directly for shipping costs.**

Directions:	**From I-40, take exit #123 (Hwy. 321) and head north through Hickory toward Lenoir. Turn left on Hwy. 64, then turn left again on the Hwy. 18S Bypass. The outlet is on the left inside Lenoir Mall.**

Hitchcock Chair Factory Outlet

Route 20
Riverton, CT 06065

Phone:	**(860) 379-4826**	**Hours:**	**M-F 10:00-5:00, Sat 10:00-6:00,**
Toll Free:	**None**		**Sun 12:00-5:00**
Fax:	**(860) 379-4185**	**E-mail:**	**None**
		Web site:	**None**

The Hitchcock Chair Factory Outlet is located in the original house and factory owned by the company's original founder, Lambert Hitchcock. Aside from being very quaint and located in a gorgeous area of Connecticut, this outlet also has some terrific bargains.

The discounts here run from 40%-60% off retail. New furniture runs around 40% off, and discontinued styles and floor samples run from 50%-60% off. The outlet has a nice selection of case goods that covers just about every style Hitchcock Chair makes.

The outlet will allow you to order any new styles from the Hitchcock Chair line at about 40% off retail. They take orders over the phone, and they have a very nice full-color catalog.

On my most recent visit here, I found a great deal on a solid cherry entertainment center (pictured on the following page). All three pieces together normally retail for $4,947.00, but this set was available at the outlet for only $2,997.00. This was a brand-new first-quality entertainment center directly from the factory. It could have been ordered by phone at the same price, 40% off retail.

This is a great outlet. It is a bit of a drive to get to, but it's in such a pretty area of the country. If you are ever in Northwest Connecticut, you really should consider visiting this outlet.

Phone orders accepted:	**Yes**
Discount:	**40%-60% off mfrs. suggested retail**
Payment methods:	**VISA, MC, AMEX, personal checks.**
In-house financing available:	**No**
Deposits required:	**Not applicable**
Catalog available:	**Yes**
Clearance center:	**Not applicable**
Delivery:	**Full service in-home delivery and set-up. Customer pays freight company directly for shipping costs.**

Directions: **From I-84, take exit #52, and go northwest on Hwy. 44. After about an hour, you'll run into Hwy. 8. Take Hwy. 8 north for a few miles, then turn east on Route 20 into downtown Riverton, CT. The Hitchcock Chair Factory Outlet is on Route 20 in the center of town.**

Hitchcock Chair Factory Outlet (cont.)

Hitchcock Chair Factory Outlet

Solid cherry entertainment center from Hitchcock Chair

Retail: $4,947.00   Discounted price: $2,997.00
Savings at the Hitchcock Chair Factory Outlet: $1,950.00 = 40% off retail

Holton Furniture

805 Randolph St.
Thomasville, NC 27361

Phone:	**(336) 472-0400**	**Hours:**	**M-F 9:00-5:30, Sat 9:00-5:00**
Toll Free:	**None**	**E-mail:**	**holtonfurn@aol.com**
Fax:	**(336) 472-0415**	**Web site:**	**www.holtonfurniture.com**

Holton Furniture in Thomasville has a very upscale store with a large Thomasville gallery. They also carry many other high-end lines such as Hooker, Thayer Coggin, Flexsteel, Pennsylvania House, and Hickory Chair. Their discounts aren't quite as good as others in the High Point area, only 30% to 50% off retail. Due to manufacturer restrictions, Thomasville carries a lesser discount.

If you're traveling to the High Point/Thomasville area, you would be much better off to visit Holton's huge clearance warehouse a few miles away. The prices there are much better.

Lines carried:	**Please see page 180**
Phone orders accepted:	**Yes**
Discount:	**30%-50% off mfrs. suggested retail**
Payment methods:	**VISA, MC, personal checks**
In-house financing available:	**Yes**
Deposits required:	**35% deposit when order is placed, balance due when furniture is ready to be shipped**
Catalog available:	**No**
Clearance center:	**Yes - See *Holton Furniture Clearance Center***
Delivery:	**Full service in-home delivery and set-up. Customer pays freight company directly for shipping costs.**

Directions: From I-85, take exit #103, and head one mile north on Hwy. 109, which will become Randolph St. Holton Furniture is about one mile from the interstate on the right side of the road.

Holton Furniture (cont.)

Lines carried:

Action By Lane
American Drew
Arnold Palmer Collection
As You Like It Lamps
Athol Tables
Barcalounger
Bassett
Bassett Mirror
Bassett Table
Bassett Upholstery
Benchcraft
Benecia Beds
Berkline
Berkshire
Bevan Funnell
Blacksmith Shop
Bob Timberlake
Bradington Young
Broyhill
Builtright
Butler
Cambridge Lamps
Carolina Mirror
Carolina Tables
Casa Bique
Casual Lamps
Chatham County
Classic Leather
Classic Rattan
Classic Traditions
Cochrane
Cox
Crawford
Craftique
D & F Wicker
Denny Lamps
Ducks Unlimited
Executive Leather
Fairfield Chair
Fashion Bed Group
Ficks Reed
Flexsteel
Frederick Cooper
Froelich Companies
Georgian Furnishings
Hammary
Henry Link Wicker
Hickory Chair
Hooker

Hoyle Lamps
Jasper Cabinet
Karges
Kingsdown Mattress
Kingsley Bate
L & S Imports
La Barge
Lane
Lane/Venture
Lea
Leisters
Lexington
Lloyd/Flanders
Lyon Shaw
Meadowcraft
Miller Desk
Mobel
Motion Craft
Nichols and Stone
North Hickory
Null Industries
Ohio Table Pad
P & P Chair
Palmer Home Collection
Pennsylvania House
Peopleloungers
Peters Revington
Pulaski
Rex
Riverside
S K Furniture
Sam Moore
Sealy Upholstery
Serta Mattress
Sherrill Occasional
Skillcraft
Stiffel Lamps
Taylorsville Upholstery
Telescope
Thayer Coggin
The Chair Co.
Thomasville
Tropitone
Universal
Vaughan
Vaughan Bassett
Virginia House
Weiman
Wellington Hall

Wesley Allen
Wildwood Lamps
Wildwood Tables
Winston
Woodard
Woodmark Originals
Yorkshire Leather
Younger Furniture

Holton Furniture Clearance Center

409 Julian Ave.
Thomasville, NC 27361

Phone:	(336) 475-1427	**Hours:**	M-Thurs 9:00-3:00, Fri 9:30-1:00
Toll Free:	None	**E-mail:**	holtonfurn@aol.com
Fax:	None	**Web site:**	www.holtonfurniture.com

Holton Furniture's Clearance Center in Thomasville is huge. It consists of two large adjoined warehouses crammed with floor samples, discontinued styles, and customer returns from their main showroom and order-by-phone service in downtown Thomasville.

Discounts here range from about 50% to 75% off retail. Most of the furniture here is in first-quality condition and from very high-end lines such as Hooker, Pennsylvania House, and Hickory Chair.

If you plan to be in the Thomasville area, this clearance center is definitely worth a visit.

Phone orders accepted:	No
Discount:	50%-75% off mfrs. suggested retail
Payment methods:	VISA, MC, personal checks
In-house financing available:	No
Deposits required:	Not applicable
Catalog available:	Not applicable
Clearance center:	Not applicable
Delivery:	Full service in-home delivery and set-up. Customer pays freight company directly for shipping costs.

Directions: From I-85, take exit #103, and head one mile north on Hwy. 109, which will become Randolph St. Holton Furniture's main store is about one mile from the interstate on the right side of the road. Right next to the main store is a side street called Royal Oaks. Follow Royal Oaks about a block until it dead ends into Julian Ave., and turn left. The Holton Furniture Clearance Center is a large warehouse on right side of the road at the first stop light.

Holton Furniture Clearance Center (cont.)

Lines carried:

Action By Lane
American Drew
Arnold Palmer Collection
As You Like It Lamps
Athol Tables
Barcalounger
Bassett
Bassett Mirror
Bassett Table
Bassett Upholstery
Benchcraft
Benecia Beds
Berkline
Berkshire
Bevan Funnell
Blacksmith Shop
Bob Timberlake
Bradington Young
Broyhill
Builtright
Butler
Cambridge Lamps
Carolina Mirror
Carolina Tables
Casa Bique
Casual Lamps
Chatham County
Classic Leather
Classic Rattan
Classic Traditions
Cochrane
Cox
Crawford
Craftique
D & F Wicker
Denny Lamps
Ducks Unlimited
Executive Leather
Fairfield Chair
Fashion Bed Group
Ficks Reed
Flexsteel
Frederick Cooper
Froelich Companies
Georgian Furnishings
Hammary
Henry Link Wicker
Hickory Chair
Hooker

Hoyle Lamps
Jasper Cabinet
Karges
Kingsdown Mattress
Kingsley Bate
L & S Imports
La Barge
Lane
Lane/Venture
Lea
Leisters
Lexington
Lloyd/Flanders
Lyon Shaw
Meadowcraft
Miller Desk
Mobel
Motion Craft
Nichols and Stone
North Hickory
Null Industries
Ohio Table Pad
P & P Chair
Palmer Home Collection
Pennsylvania House
Peopleloungers
Peters Revington
Pulaski
Rex
Riverside
S K Furniture
Sam Moore
Sealy Upholstery
Serta Mattress
Sherrill Occasional
Skillcraft
Stiffel Lamps
Taylorsville Upholstery
Telescope
Thayer Coggin
The Chair Co.
Thomasville
Tropitone
Universal
Vaughan
Vaughan Bassett
Virginia House
Weiman
Wellington Hall

Wesley Allen
Wildwood Lamps
Wildwood Tables
Winston
Woodard
Woodmark Originals
Yorkshire Leather
Younger Furniture

Home Focus

Level 1
Hickory Furniture Mart
U. S. Hwy. 70 SE
Hickory, NC 28602

Phone:	**(828) 324-7742**	**Hours:**	**M-Sat 9:00-6:00**
Toll Free:	**None**	**E-mail:**	**homefocus@newwave.net**
Fax:	**(828) 327-3825**	**Web site:**	**www.homefocusfurniture.com**

Home Focus at the Hickory Furniture Mart is owned by Palliser Furniture, a maker of leather upholstery, wall units, bedroom furniture, and juvenile furniture. There is a large Palliser gallery here, along with galleries for Kimball, Canadel, and J. Royale.

Unfortunately, Home Focus is not a discounter or factory outlet. Despite being located among so many true discounters and outlets at the Hickory Furniture Mart, Home Focus' prices aren't much better than those you'll find at your local retailer.

Occasionally, Home Focus does have clearance sales at their main warehouse in Troutman, NC (about 30 miles from Hickory), but even these rare sales don't approach the everyday bargains at the true discounters and factory outlets in Hickory.

If you're interested in going to a Home Focus warehouse sale, they occur on weekends 3-4 times a year. Please call the showroom above for the dates of the next sale. However, there's really no need to drive all the way to Troutman when there are so many good bargains right in Hickory every day.

Lines carried:	**Please see page 184**
Phone orders accepted:	**Yes**
Discount:	**This source prices at or near full retail**
Payment methods:	**VISA, MC, Discover, personal checks**
In-house financing available:	**Yes**
Deposits required:	**50% deposit when order is placed, balance due when furniture is ready to be shipped**
Catalog available:	**No**
Clearance center:	**No**
Delivery:	**Full service in-home delivery and set-up. Customer pays freight company directly for shipping costs.**

Directions: Please see *Hickory Furniture Mart* for complete directions.

Home Focus (cont.)

Lines carried:

101 Country Workshop
Accents Etc.
Accessories
Alan White Company
All Continental Inc.
Anthony's Art Design Ltd.
Ant Gifts
Antigua
Art & Frame Direct
Art and Frame Source
Artisan House
Artistry Design, Inc.
Artmaster
Artmaster Studios
Art Under Glass
Aspen Bay Company
Bard International
Baroque Designs, Inc.
Beach Manufacturing
Big Fish Inc.
Bonavita
Boyd Furniture Co. Inc.
Brasscrafters
Carolina Brass
Cal-Bear
Cape Craftsman
Cargo
Carole Dalton
Carole Fabrics
Caspari
Castillian Imports
Catna
Cleveland Chair Co.
Chic Table Pad Co.
Cisco Bros. Corp.
Classic Georgian Fur Inc.
Classic Picture Co.
Clay, Metal, and Stone
Cleveland Chair Co.
Creative Lifestyles
Cogan Books
Collections '85 Inc.
Container Marketing Inc.
Consolidated Glass
          & Mirror
Cooper Classics
Corinthian Rugs
Country Originals Inc.
Cozy Country Works

Creative Art Flowers Inc.
Creative Images
Cristalery
Craft-Tex/Ladyrug
Culprit Ltd.
D & W Silks
Decorative Crafts Inc.
Dewoolfson Down
Distinctive Designs
Douglas Furniture
Earth Elements
Eden LLC
Empire Art Products
Fancy Frames
Floral Art
Florita Nova
Focal Point
F. O. Moire & Co. Inc.
Forjo Designs
Franklin Picture
Genesis
Goldhill Enterprises
Grace Manufacturing Co.
Greenleaf
Guardsman Leather Protect
Harris Lamps
Harris Marcus Furniture
Head Over Heels
High Point Furniture Ind.
Inantino
Inmon Enterprises
International Craftsmen
Jaru
Jay Willipred
My Dog Spot
New Feathers Corp.
O. L. F. Lam Lee Group
Pacer
Pacific Coast Lighting
Pacific Rim
Pacific Sun Casual Furniture
Paddywax
Panasonic
Paragon Picture Gallery
Peacock Alley
Peopleloungers
Petite Amie
Phoenix Galleries
Poundex

Powell
Palliser
Rainbow Graphics
Raj
Royce Casey
Randy Ouzts/Garden Sense
Renoir
Riverwalk Furniture
San Miguel Arts & Crafts
Sarreid
Somerset Studios Inc.
Spiral Collection
Stainsafe
Stoneville
Straits Furniture Co.
Studio International
Stylecraft
Taylorsville Upholstering
Tracey's Originals
Tree Masters Inc.
Trunks By Barbara
Two's Company
Turkart
Ultimate Manufacturing
Uni
United Design
Vanguard
Vietri
Wal-Kitecture
Wayborn Furniture & Accessories
Whitaker Furniture Co.
Wood Craft Co.
Wurlitzer Juke Boxes
Zocalo Imports

Home Focus

The Atrium
430 S. Main St.
High Point, NC 27260

Phone:	**(336) 882-7031**	**Hours:**	**M-F 9:00-6:00, Sat 9:00-5:00**
Toll Free:	**None**	**E-mail:**	**homefocus@newwave.net**
Fax:	**(336) 886-7607**	**Web site:**	**www.homefocusfurniture.com**

Home Focus at the Atrium Furniture Mall is owned by Palliser Furniture, a maker of leather upholstery, wall units, bedroom furniture, and juvenile furniture.

Unfortunately, Home Focus is not a discounter or factory outlet. Despite being located among so many true discounters and outlets in the High Point area, Home Focus' prices aren't much better than those you'll find at your local retailer.

Occasionally, Home Focus does have clearance sales at their main warehouse in Troutman, NC (about one hour's drive west of High Point), but even these rare sales don't approach the everyday bargains at the true discounters and factory outlets in High Point.

If you're interested in going to a Home Focus warehouse sale, they occur on weekends 3-4 times a year. Please call the showroom above for the dates of the next sale. However, there's really no need to drive all the way to Troutman when there are so many good bargains right in High Point every day.

Lines carried:	**Please see page 186**
Phone orders accepted:	**Yes**
Discount:	**This source prices at or near full retail**
Payment methods:	**VISA, MC, Discover, personal checks**
In-house financing available:	**Yes**
Deposits required:	**50% deposit when order is placed, balance due when furniture is ready to be shipped**
Catalog available:	**No**
Clearance center:	**No**
Delivery:	**Full service in-home delivery and set-up. Customer pays freight company directly for shipping costs.**

Directions: **Home Focus is located inside the Atrium complex in downtown High Point. Please see *The Atrium* for complete directions.**

Home Focus (cont.)

Lines carried:

101 Country Workshop
Accents Etc.
Accessories
Alan White Company
All Continental Inc.
Anthony's Art Design Ltd.
Ant Gifts
Antigua
Art & Frame Direct
Art and Frame Source
Artisan House
Artistry Design, Inc.
Artmaster
Artmaster Studios
Art Under Glass
Aspen Bay Company
Bard International
Baroque Designs, Inc.
Beach Manufacturing
Big Fish Inc.
Bonavita
Boyd Furniture Co. Inc.
Brasscrafters
Carolina Brass
Cal-Bear
Cape Craftsman
Cargo
Carole Dalton
Carole Fabrics
Caspari
Castillian Imports
Catna
Cleveland Chair Co.
Chic Table Pad Co.
Cisco Bros. Corp.
Classic Georgian Fur Inc.
Classic Picture Co.
Clay, Metal, and Stone
Cleveland Chair Co.
Creative Lifestyles
Cogan Books
Collections '85 Inc.
Container Marketing Inc.
Consolidated Glass
        & Mirror
Cooper Classics
Corinthian Rugs
Country Originals Inc.
Cozy Country Works

Creative Art Flowers Inc.
Creative Images
Cristalery
Craft-Tex/Ladyrug
Culprit Ltd.
D & W Silks
Decorative Crafts Inc.
Dewoolfson Down
Distinctive Designs
Douglas Furniture
Earth Elements
Eden LLC
Empire Art Products
Fancy Frames
Floral Art
Florita Nova
Focal Point
F. O. Moire & Co. Inc.
Forjo Designs
Franklin Picture
Genesis
Goldhill Enterprises
Grace Manufacturing Co.
Greenleaf
Guardsman Leather Protect
Harris Lamps
Harris Marcus Furniture
Head Over Heels
High Point Furniture Ind.
Inantino
Inmon Enterprises
International Craftsmen
Jaru
Jay Willipred
My Dog Spot
New Feathers Corp.
O. L. F. Lam Lee Group
Pacer
Pacific Coast Lighting
Pacific Rim
Pacific Sun Casual Furniture
Paddywax
Panasonic
Paragon Picture Gallery
Peacock Alley
Peopleloungers
Petite Amie
Phoenix Galleries
Poundex

Powell
Palliser
Rainbow Graphics
Raj
Royce Casey
Randy Ouzts/Garden Sense
Renoir
Riverwalk Furniture
San Miguel Arts & Crafts
Sarreid
Somerset Studios Inc.
Spiral Collection
Stainsafe
Stoneville
Straits Furniture Co.
Studio International
Stylecraft
Taylorsville Upholstering
Tracey's Originals
Tree Masters Inc.
Trunks By Barbara
Two's Company
Turkart
Ultimate Manufacturing
Uni
United Design
Vanguard
Vietri
Wal-Kitecture
Wayborn Furniture &
Accessories
Whitaker Furniture Co.
Wood Craft Co.
Wurlitzer Juke Boxes
Zocalo Imports

Homeway Furniture

121 W. Lebanon St.
Mount Airy, NC 27030

Phone:	**(336) 786-6151**	**Hours:**	**M-F 9:00-5:30, Sat 9:00-5:00**
Toll Free:	**(800) 334-9094**	**E-mail:**	**homeway@advi.net**
Fax:	**(336) 786-1822**	**Web site:**	**www.homewayfurniture.com**

Homeway Furniture is located in Mt. Airy, NC, about an hour's drive north of High Point, NC. They have a very nice selection of high end lines, including Lexington, Councill Craftsmen, Hooker, and Hickory Chair.

They don't have a clearance center or any floor samples or discontinued pieces on display. For this reason, there is no monetary advantage to visiting in person. They do have great deals on many lines sold over the phone, though. So, if you're planning to order your furniture by phone, definitely give this source a call to compare their prices.

Lines carried:	**Please see pages 188-189**
Phone orders accepted:	**Yes**
Discount:	**40%-50% off mfrs. suggested retail**
Payment methods:	**Personal checks. No credit cards.**
In-house financing available:	**No**
Deposits required:	**50% deposit when order is placed, balance due when furniture is ready to be shipped**
Catalog available:	**No**
Clearance center:	**No**
Delivery:	**Full service in-home delivery and set-up. Customer pays freight company directly for shipping costs.**

Directions: From I-77, take exit #100, and go east on Hwy. 89. Go to the sixth stoplight, and turn left on Business 52. Go to the third stoplight, and turn left. Homeway Furniture will be on the left side of the road.

Homeway Furniture (cont.)

Lines carried:

A. A. Laun
Acacia
Action By Lane
Alexvale
American Chair & Table
American Drew
American Mirror
American Of High Point
Andrew-Pearson
A. P. Industries
Arbek
Arnold Palmer Collection
As You Like It
Athens Furniture
Athol Table
Baldwin Brass
Barcalounger
Barn Door
Bassett Furniture
Bassett Motion
Bean Station
Beechbrook
Benchcraft
Benicia Beds
Bentwood
Berkline
Best Chair
Bevan Funnell
Blacksmith Shop
Bob Timberlake
Boyd
Brady
Braxton Culler
Brown Jordan
Broyhill
Brunschwig & Fils
Butler Specialty
Canal Dover
Canadel
Capel Rugs
Carolina Comfort
Carolina Mirror
Carson's
Carter
Casa Bique
Casa Rustica
Castilian Imports
Catalina
Catnapper

Chapman Mfg.
Charleston Forge
Chatham County
Chatham Novelties
Chromcraft
Clark Casual
Classic Gallery
Classic Leather
Classic Rattan
Clayton Marcus
Cochrane
Colonial
Conover Chair
Councill Craftsmen
County Seat
Cox
Craftique
Craftmaster
Crawford
Crescent
Crystal Clear
D & F Wicker and Rattan
D. Scan
Darafeev
Daystrom
Decorative Crafts
Denny Lamp
Design Connection
Design Master
Dillon
Dinaire
Distinction Leather
Dutailier
Eagle Craft
Ekornes
Elliott's Designs
Ello
Emerald Craft
Emerson Leather
Executive Leather
Fairfield Chair
Fairmont Designs
Fashion Bed Group
Fashion Bedding
Ficks-Reed
Flexsteel
Frederick Cooper
Fremarc
Friendship Upholstery

Froelich
Gardner Mirror
Gentry Upholstery
Georgian Furnishings
Glenncraft
Greene Brothers
Greystone Victorian
Habersham Plantation
Halcyon
Hammary
Harris Marcus
Hekman
Hickory Chair
Hickory Hill
Hickory International
Hickory Mark
High Point Furniture
Highland House
Hippopotamus
Hitchcock Chair
Hooker
Howard Miller Clocks
Huntington House
Hyundai Furniture
International Furniture
J. Royale
J. S. F. Oriental
James David JDI
Jasper Cabinet
Jetton Furniture
Johnston Benchworks
Johnston Casuals
Johnston Tombigbee
Jon Elliott
Kaiser Kuhn Lighting
Keller
Kettler
Kessler
Key City
Kimball Reproductions
Kincaid
King Hickory
Kingcraft
Kingsdown
Kingsley Upholstery
Klaussner
Koch Originals
Kravet Fabrics
La Barge

Lane
Lane/Venture
Largo
Lea
Leather Mart
Leather Trends
Leisters
Lexington
Lloyd/Flanders
Lyon Shaw
Madison Square
Maitland Smith
Marlow
Master Design
Masterfield
Meadow Craft
Michael Howard
Miller Desk
Mobel
Mohawk Furniture
Morgan Stewart Uph.
Murphy
Murray Iron Works
Nichols & Stone
Null Industries
Oakwood Interiors
Ohio Table Pad
Old Hickory Tannery
Oriental Accent
Overnight Sleepers
Palliser
Palmer Home Coll.
Paragon Pictures
Parker Southern
Paul Robert
Pearson
Pennsylvania Classics
Pennsylvania House
Peoplelounger
Peters Revington
Philip Reinisch
Pinnacle
Powell
Preview
Pulaski
Regency House
Reliance Lamp
Rembrandt Lamp
Remington Lamp

Homeway Furniture (cont.)

Lines carried (cont.):

Restonic Carolinas
Rex Furniture
Richardson Brothers
Ridgewood
Riverside
Robert Allen
Robinson
Ross Accessories
Royal Patina
Saloom
Sam Moore
Samsonite
Sarreid
Schnadig
Schumacher
Schweiger
Sealy Upholstery
Sealy Mattress
Sedgefield
Serta Mattress
Shenandoah
Sherrill Occasional
Skillcraft
South Sea Rattan
Spring Air
St. Timothy
Statesville Chair
Statton
Stein World
Stewart
Stiffel Lamps
Stoneville
Stratford
Stratolounger
Stroupe Mirror
Style Upholstery
Stylecraft Lamps
Superior
Swaim
Taylorsville Upholstery
Temple
Temple Stuart
Thayer Coggin
Three Coins
Tom Seeley
Towne Square
Tropitone
Tyndale
U. S. Furniture

Union City Chair Co.
Universal
Uwharrie Chair
Vargas
Vaughan
Vaughan Bassett
Venture By Lane
Victorian Classics
Walker Marlen
Waverly Fabrics
Webb
Weiman
Wellington Hall
Wesley Allen
Wesley Hall Upholstery
Westwood
Whitaker
Wildwood Lamps
Winners Only
Winston
Woodard Classics
Woodmark Originals

House Dressing

3608 W. Wendover Ave.
Greensboro, NC 27407

Phone:	**(336) 294-3900**	**Hours:**	**M-Thurs 8:30-5:30**
Toll Free:	**(800) 322-5850**		**Fri 8:30-5:00, Sat 10:00-2:00**
Fax:	**(336) 294-0004**	**E-mail:**	**None**
		Web site:	**None**

House Dressing is a great source for ordering furniture over the phone. They are very well established and reputable, and they carry a wide range of brands.

Their store in Greensboro, NC, has a good selection of medium to high-end furniture. The standard discount on new furniture, whether purchased in person or over the phone, is 40%-50% off retail.

They have a small clearance area in the back with floor samples and discontinued styles, but the discounts are only 50%-60%, and the selection is very limited. There really isn't much reason to travel here in person.

If you plan to order furniture by phone, however, you really should compare House Dressing's prices.

Phone orders accepted:	**Yes**
Discount:	**40%-50% off mfrs. suggested retail**
Payment methods:	**VISA, MC, personal checks**
In-house financing available:	**No**
Deposits required:	**50% deposit when order is placed, balance due when furniture is ready to be shipped**
Catalog available:	**No**
Clearance center:	**Yes**
Delivery:	**Full service in-home delivery and set-up. Customer pays freight company directly for shipping costs.**

Directions: **From I-40, take exit #215, and go northeast into Greensboro on Wendover Ave. House Dressing is about two miles down on the left.**

House Dressing (cont.)

House Dressing

Lines carried:

Action By Lane
Alexander Julian
Alexvale
American Drew
American Mirror
Andre Originals
Andrew Pearson
Arbek
Arlington House
Artisan House
Artistica Metal
Ashley
Ashley Manor
As You Like It
Athol
Baker
Barcalounger
Bassett
Bassett Mirror
Bauer Lighting
Beachly Upholstery
Bean Station
Benchcraft Rattan
Benecia Brass Beds
Berkline
Bernhardt
Beth Weisman

Bevan Funnell
Blacksmith Shop
Bob Timberlake
Bradington Young
Brasscrafters
Braxton Culler
Brown Jordan
Brown Street
Broyhill
Butler Specialty
C. R. Laine
Cal-Style
Cambridge Lamps
Canadel
Carlton McLendon
Carolina Mirror
Carson's Contemporary
Carter
Casa Rustica
Casa Bique
Casual Crates
Cellini
Chapel Hill
Charleston Forge
Chatham County
Chromcraft
Clark Casual

Classic Gallery
Clayton Marcus
Cochrane
Comfort Designs
Contemporary Furniture
        Design
Cox
Craftique
Crawford
Crystal Clear
Darafeev
Decorative Arts
Decorative Crafts
Design South
Dillon
Dinaire
Directional
Distinction Leather
D-Scan
Ducks Unlimited
Dutailier
Eaglecraft
Ecco
Ekornes
Elliott's Designs Inc.
Ello Contemporary
Emerson Leather

Excelsior
Fairfield Chair
Fashion Bed Group
Fine Art
Flexsteel
Frederick Cooper
Friedman Brothers
Garcia
George Kovacs
Georgian Furnishings
Glass Arts
Godwin Weavers
Great City Traders
Halcyon
Hammary
Hekman
Henry Link
Hickory Chair
Hickory Fry
Hickory Hill
Highland House
Hood
Hooker
Howard Miller Clocks
Hyundai Furniture
International Furniture
J. Berdou

House Dressing (cont.)

Lines carried (cont.):

J. Strasborg
JRW Contemporary
Jack Houseman
        Chandeliers
Jasper Cabinet
John Boos
John Widdicomb
Johnston Benchworks
Johnston Casuals
Kaiser Kuhn Lamps
Keller
Kessler
Key City
Kimball
Kincaid
King Hickory
Kingsley
Klaussner
Koch Originals
La Barge
Lane
Lane Action Recliners
Lane A La Carte
Lane Upholstery
Lane/Venture
Laurier
Lea
Leather Trend
Leazanne
Lexington
Link Taylor
Lloyd Flanders
Lowenstein
Lyon Shaw
Madison
Madison Square
Mario Lamps
Maryland Classics
Master Design
McEnroe
McKay Table Pad
McKinley Leather
Meadowcraft
Michael Thomas
Mikhail Darafeev
Millennium
Montaage
Morganton Chair
Murray Feiss

Najarian
Nathan Hale
National Mt. Airy
Natural Light
Natuzzi
Null Industries
Ohio Table Pad
Old Hickory Tannery
Olympia Lighting
Oriental Lacquer
Pacific Rattan
Paoli
Pennsylvania Classics
Pennsylvania House
Peters Revington
Phillip Reinisch
Plant Plant
Powell
Preview
Pulaski
Reliance Lamps
Remington Lamps
Rex
Richardson Brothers
Ridgeway Clocks
Riverside
Robert Allen Fabrics
Rowe
Royal Patina
S. K. Products
Salem Square
Saloom
Sam Moore
Samsonite
Sarreid
Schnadig
Schumacher
Schweiger
Sealy
Sedgefield Lamps
Serta Mattress
Shenandoah Leather
Spring Air
Stakmore
Stanley
Statesville Chair
Stiffel Lamps
Stoneleigh
Stratolounger

Stratford
Stout Chair
Straits
Stylecraft
Summer Classics
Superior
Swaim Originals
Swan Brass Beds
Thayer Coggin
Thousand Islands
Timmerman Iron
Tradition-France
Tropitone
Tubb
Universal
Van Teal
Vargas
Vaughan
Vaughan Bassett
Veneman
Venture By Lane
Vietri
Virginia House
Virginia Metalcrafters
Walburg
Wambold
Waverly
Weiman
Wellesley Guild
Wesley Allen
Whitaker
Whitecraft
Wildwood Lamp
Winston

Hudson Discount Furniture

940 Highland Ave. NE
Hickory, NC 28601

Phone:	(828) 322-4996	**Hours:**	M-Sat 8:30-5:00
	(828) 322-5717	**E-mail:**	jehfurn@twave.net
Toll Free:	None	**Web site:**	www.hudsonfurniture.com
Fax:	(828) 322-6953		

Hudson Discount Furniture has been discounting furniture for over 75 years. They have an excellent reputation and very good prices. Their store in Hickory has very few floor samples and discontinued styles, which makes it less efficient to visit in person. However, any customer who plans to order their furniture over the phone would do well to call this source and compare their prices.

Lines carried:

Action By Lane	Craftique	Lexington	Stearns & Foster
American Drew	Ducks Unlimited	Link Taylor	Stiffel Lamp
American Of Martinsville	Emerson Leather	Null Industries	Sumter Cabinet
Athol Table	Fashion Bed Group	Ohio Table Pad Co.	Superior
Barn Door	Hekman	Palmer Home Collection	Temple
Bassett	Henry Link	Parker Southern	Timmerman
Berkline	Highland House	Parliament	Universal
Blacksmith Shop	Hooker	Peters Revington	U. S. Furniture
Bob Timberlake	Hyundai Furniture	Pulaski	Uwharrie Chair
Broyhill	Jasper Cabinet	Regency House	Vaughan
Builtrite Chair Co.	J. Royale	Ridgeway Clocks	Vaughan Bassett
Cambridge Chair	Keller	Riverside	Victorian Classics
Carlton McLendon	Kincaid	Sealy Bedding	Wellington Hall
Carolina Mirror	Lane	Seay	Wesley Allen
Cochrane	Lane/Venture	Simmons Bedding	
Cox	Lea	Stanley	

Phone orders accepted:	Yes
Discount:	40%-50% off mfrs. suggested retail
Payment methods:	VISA, MC, personal checks
In-house financing available:	No
Deposits required:	25% deposit when order is placed, balance due when furniture is ready to be shipped
Catalog available:	No
Clearance center:	No
Delivery:	Full service in-home delivery and set-up. Customer pays freight company directly for shipping costs.

Directions: From I-40, take exit #125 and drive north on Lenoir-Rhyne Rd. to Hickory. The road will bear right and change name to Highland Ave. Hudson Furniture is a few miles down on the right side of the road.

Interior Furnishings

P. O. Box 1644
Hickory, NC 28603

Phone:	**(704) 328-5683**	**Hours:**	**M-F 9:00-5:00, Sat 9:00-3:00**
Toll Free:	**None**	**E-mail:**	**None**
Fax:	**None**	**Web site:**	**None**

Interior Furnishings is located in Hickory, NC. They have no showroom open to the public, but they do a booming phone order business. They have a very nice selection of medium to high-end lines, including Lexington, Broyhill, Stanley, and Hooker.

They don't have a clearance center or any floor samples or discontinued pieces on display. For this reason, there is no monetary advantage to visiting in person. They do have great deals on many lines sold over the phone, though. So, if you're planning to order your furniture by phone, definitely give this source a call to compare their prices.

Lines carried:

Action By Lane	Cochrane	Howard Miller Clocks	Ohio Table Pad Co.
American Drew	Craftique	J/B Ross	Peters Revington
American Of Martinsville	Davis Chair	Jasper Cabinet	Pulaski
Artistry Design	Dinaire	Keller	Park Place
Barcalounger	Dixie	Kincaid	Riverside
Bassett	Dresher	Kingsdown Bedding	Skillcraft
Bassett Mirror	Emerson Leather	L & S Imports	Stanley
Benchcraft	Fairfield Chair	La Barge Mirrors	Serta Bedding
Berkshire	Glass Fashions	Lane	Tell City
Blacksmith Shop	Greene Brothers	Lane/Venture	Tropitone
BMC	Hekman	Lea	Universal
Broyhill	Henry Link	Lexington	Vaughan
C. R. Laine	Hickory Hill	Link Taylor	Virginia House
Carolina Mirror	Highland House	Mersman	Young Hinkle
Charleston Forge	Home Lamp Co.	Moosehead	
Chatham County	Hooker	Nathan Hale	

Phone orders accepted:	**Yes**
Discount:	**40%-50% off mfrs. suggested retail**
Payment methods:	**Personal checks. No credit cards.**
In-house financing available:	**No**
Deposits required:	**30% deposit when order is placed, balance due when furniture is ready to be shipped**
Catalog available:	**No**
Clearance center:	**No**
Delivery:	**Full service in-home delivery and set-up. Customer pays freight company directly for shipping costs.**

Directions: Interior Furnishings has no showroom open to the public.

Ironstone Galleries Factory Outlet

Level 4
Hickory Furniture Mart
U. S. Hwy. 70 SE
Hickory, NC 28602

Phone:	(828) 304-1094	**Hours:**	M-Sat 9:00-6:00
Toll Free:	None	**E-mail:**	info@hickoryfurniture.com
Fax:	(828) 304-1095	**Web site:**	www.hickoryfurniture.com

This is the only factory outlet for Ironstone Galleries, a manufacturer of stone, metal, and glass furniture. They have very nice quality and a unique contemporary look. They don't have a catalog, but the staff at the outlet will mail you copies of product sheets if you have a basic idea what you're looking for.

They will special order new furniture from their own line, as well as from Michael Thomas Upholstery. The normal discount on new special-order furniture is about 40% off retail. There are also some floor samples and discontinued styles in stock from both lines priced at about 50% off retail.

For example, on my most recent visit here, I found a very nice leather-topped table with 4 chairs (pictured on the following page) that normally retails for $4,956.00 on sale for $2,691.00. I was able to further haggle the saleswoman down to $2,500.00 even on this set, a discount of just over 50% off retail.

If you're in the Hickory area and you're looking for contemporary furniture, this is a source you should check out. Their quality is excellent, and their prices are quite good for what you get.

Lines carried:

Ironstone Galleries
Michael Thomas Upholstery

Phone orders accepted:	Yes
Discount:	40%-50% off mfrs. suggested retail
Payment methods:	VISA, MC, personal checks
In-house financing available:	No
Deposits required:	50% deposit when order is placed, balance due when furniture is ready to be shipped
Catalog available:	Not applicable
Clearance center:	Not applicable
Delivery:	Full service in-home delivery and set-up. Customer pays freight company directly for shipping costs.

Directions: Please see *Hickory Furniture Mart* for complete directions.

Ironstone Galleries Factory Outlet (cont.)

Leather-topped table and chairs from Ironstone Galleries

Retail: $4,956.00   Discounted price: $2,500.00
Savings at the Ironstone Galleries Factory Outlet: $2,456.00 = 50% off retail

Jones Brothers Furniture

1324 N. Bright Leaf Blvd.
Smithfield, NC 27577

Phone:	(919) 934-4162	**Hours:**	Mon & Fri 9:00-9:00
Toll Free:	None		Tues, Wed, Thurs, Sat 9:00-5:30
Fax:	(919) 989-7500	**E-mail:**	None
		Web site:	None

Jones Brothers Furniture is located in Smithfield, NC, just west of Raleigh, NC. They have a good selection of medium to high-end lines, including Lexington, Wellington Hall, Hekman, and Hooker.

They don't have a clearance center or any floor samples or discontinued pieces on display. For this reason, there is no monetary advantage to visiting in person. They do have great deals on many lines sold over the phone, though. So, if you're planning to order your furniture by phone, definitely give this source a call to compare their prices.

Lines carried:

Action By Lane	Craftique	La Barge	Stanley
American Drew	Disque	Lane	Stiffel Lamps
American Of Martinsville	Dixie	Lane/Venture	Sumter Cabinet
Athol	Fairfield Chair	Lexington	Taylor King
Bevan Funnell	Frederick Cooper Lamps	Link Taylor	Thomasville
Blacksmith Shop	Hammary	Madison Square	Tradition House
Bob Timberlake	Hancock & Moore	Maitland Smith	Universal
Bradington Young	Hekman	Michael Thomas	Venture By Lane
Broyhill	Henkel-Harris	Miles Talbot	Waterford
C. R. Laine	Henkel-Moore	Nathan Hale	Wellington Hall
Casa Bique	Henry Link	Pearson	Wildwood Lamps
Charleston Forge	Hickory Chair	Pulaski	Woodmark
Classic Rattan	Hooker	Rex	Young-Hinkle
Cochrane	Jasper Cabinet	Riverside	
Colonial	John Richard	Sealy	
Cox	Kimball	Sligh	

Phone orders accepted:	Yes
Discount:	35%-50% off mfrs. suggested retail
Payment methods:	Personal checks. No credit cards.
In-house financing available:	No
Deposits required:	25% deposit when order is placed, balance due when furniture is ready to be shipped
Catalog available:	No
Clearance center:	No
Delivery:	Full service in-home delivery and set-up. Customer pays freight company directly for shipping costs.

Directions: From I-95, take exit #97, and go west on Hwy. 70. Turn left on Hwy. 301. Jones Brothers is one-half mile down on the left side of the road.

Kagan's American Drew

The Atrium
430 S. Main St.
High Point, NC 27260

Phone:	**(336) 885-8568**	**Hours:**	**M-F 9:00-6:00, Sat 9:00-5:00**
Toll Free:	**None**	**E-mail:**	**kagan@northstate.net**
Fax:	**(336) 889-9316**	**Web site:**	**www.theatrium.com**

Kagan's American Drew gallery at the Atrium Furniture Mall in High Point has a beautiful showroom, but the prices here aren't as impressive as the prices at other area discounters. The discounts here only range from 30%-50% off retail. Also, Kagan's does not accept phone orders, customers must order in person.

All of the furniture here is new and first-quality. Kagan's has a clearance center on the south side of High Point where they liquidate their floor samples and discontinued styles.

If you're planning a trip to High Point to shop in person, your time would be far better spent shopping at the many true factory outlets in the area.

Lines carried:

American Drew	Flexsteel	Millennium	Universal
Clayton Marcus	Hooker	Pulaski	Weiman
Excelsior	Leda	Rowe	

Phone orders accepted:	**No**
Discount:	**30%-50% off mfrs. suggested retail**
Payment methods:	**Personal checks. No credit cards.**
In-house financing available:	**No**
Deposits required:	**50% deposit when order is placed, balance due when furniture is ready to be shipped**
Catalog available:	**No**
Clearance center:	**Yes - See *Kagan's Clearance Center***
Delivery:	**Full service in-home delivery and set-up. Customer pays freight company directly for shipping costs.**

Directions: Kagan's American Drew is located inside the Atrium complex in downtown High Point. Please see *The Atrium* for complete directions.

Kagan's Clearance Center

1628 S. Main St.
High Point, NC 27261

Phone:	**(336) 889-89210**	**Hours:**	**M-Sat 9:00-6:00**
Toll Free:	**None**	**E-mail:**	**kagan@northstate.net**
Fax:	**None**	**Web site:**	**www.theatrium.com**

Kagan's Clearance Center on the south side is just not very impressive, unfortunately. They do have a large selection of furniture, but most of it is medium quality, not the high end lines listed on the sign out front.

Also, the discounts aren't very good. On my most recent visit, I saw quite a few floor samples, discontinued items, and even damaged pieces priced at only 30%-40% off retail. Anyone can get better discounts than that on brand-new first quality furniture at dozens of other discounters and factory outlets all over the High Point area.

If you're traveling to High Point to shop, you would be better off to visit the many true factory outlets in the area.

Lines carried:

Alexander Julian	Clayton Marcus	JD Originals	Rex
American Impressions	Creative Furniture	Kingsley	Rowe/Capitol Leather
American Of Martinsville	Chateau D'Ax	Leda	Rowe Gold
Aquarius Mirror Works	Carson's	Limelight	San Diego Designs
Artmax	Excelsior Designs	McKay Custom Pads	Sealy Upholstery
Ashley	Flexsteel	Millennium	Simmons Bedding
Athens	Glober	Modern Classics	Straits
Atlanta Glass Crafters	Grace Manufacturing	Muniz	Swaim
Austin Sculpture	Hooker	Najarian	Temple
Barclay	H. Studios By Shlomi	Ohio Table Pads	Universal
Bassett	Hyundai	Pulaski Pool Tables	Vaughan Bassett
Bassett Mirror	Howard Miller	RCA Home Theater/	Villageois
Cherry Grove	Interline Italia	Proscan	Wambold
Chromcraft	Johnston Casuals	Reuben's	

Phone orders accepted:	**No**
Discount:	**30%-50% off mfrs. suggested retail**
Payment methods:	**Personal checks. No credit cards.**
In-house financing available:	**No**
Deposits required:	**Not applicable**
Catalog available:	**Not applicable**
Clearance center:	**Not applicable**
Delivery:	**Full service in-home delivery and set-up. Customer pays freight company directly for shipping costs.**

Directions: From I-85, take exit #111 (Hwy. 311), and head northwest into High Point. After several miles, when you reach downtown High Point, Hwy. 311 will become S. Main St. Kagan's is on the left side of Main St.

Kagan's Gallery

The Atrium
430 S. Main St.
High Point, NC 27260

Phone:	**(336) 885-1333/885-8300**	**Hours:**	**M-F 9:00-6:00, Sat 9:00-5:00**
Toll Free:	**None**	**E-mail:**	**kagan@northstate.net**
Fax:	**(336) 889-9316**	**Web site:**	**www.theatrium.com**

Kagan's Gallery at the Atrium Furniture Mall in High Point has a beautiful showroom, but the prices here aren't as impressive as the prices at other area discounters. The discounts here only range from 30%-50% off retail. Also, Kagan's does not accept phone orders, customers must order in person.

All of the furniture here is new and first-quality. Kagan's has a clearance center on the south side of High Point where they liquidate their floor samples and discontinued styles.

If you're planning a trip to High Point to shop in person, your time would be far better spent shopping at the many true factory outlets in the area.

Lines carried:

Alexander Julian	Clayton Marcus	JD Originals	Rex
American Impressions	Creative Furniture	Kingsley	Rowe/Capitol Leather
American Of Martinsville	Chateau D'Ax	Leda	Rowe Gold
Aquarius Mirror Works	Carson's	Limelight	San Diego Designs
Artmax	Excelsior Designs	McKay Custom Pads	Sealy Upholstery
Ashley	Flexsteel	Millennium	Simmons Bedding
Athens	Glober	Modern Classics	Straits
Atlanta Glass Crafters	Grace Manufacturing	Muniz	Swaim
Austin Sculpture	Hooker	Najarian	Temple
Barclay	H. Studios By Shlomi	Ohio Table Pads	Universal
Bassett	Hyundai	Pulaski Pool Tables	Vaughan Bassett
Bassett Mirror	Howard Miller	RCA Home Theater/	Villageois
Cherry Grove	Interline Italia	Proscan	Wambold
Chromcraft	Johnston Casuals	Reuben's	

Phone orders accepted:	**No**
Discount:	**30%-50% off mfrs. suggested retail**
Payment methods:	**Personal checks. No credit cards.**
In-house financing available:	**No**
Deposits required:	**50% deposit when order is placed, balance due when furniture is ready to be shipped**
Catalog available:	**No**
Clearance center:	**Yes - See *Kagan's Clearance Center***
Delivery:	**Full service in-home delivery and set-up. Customer pays freight company directly for shipping costs.**

Directions: Kagan's Gallery is located inside the Atrium complex in downtown High Point. Please see *The Atrium* for complete directions.

Kincaid Factory Outlet

Manufacturer-Owned Factory Outlets (Lenoir Mall)
1031 Morganton Blvd.
Lenoir, NC 28645

Phone:	**(828) 754-2126**	**Hours:**	**M-Sat 10:00-7:00, Sun 1:00-5:00**
Toll Free:	**None**	**E-mail:**	**None**
Fax:	**(828) 754-8052**	**Web site:**	**None**

This is Kincaid's only true factory outlet. It's a medium-size outlet occupying two spaces in the Manufacturer-Owned Factory Outlets at Lenoir Mall, just north of Hickory, NC.

This outlet also serves as a factory outlet for La-Z-Boy, which owns Kincaid Furniture, so there is a small area with La-Z-Boy and Kincaid recliners. There is also a nice selection of Kincaid case goods: china cabinets, beds, chests, sideboards, etc.

There are virtually no seconds here. Most of the recliners are floor samples from the bi-annual wholesale furniture markets in High Point. Most of the case goods are samples and discontinued styles.

On my most recent visit here, I found a great deal on a cherry china cabinet from Kincaid (pictured on the following page). This piece normally retails for $3,068.00, but the outlet had this overstock piece for only $1,250.00. There were no flaws of any kind.

If you're in the Lenoir area, and you're looking for medium-quality furniture, you may wish to visit this outlet.

Phone orders accepted:	**No**
Discount:	**50%-75% off mfrs. suggested retail**
Payment methods:	**VISA, MC, personal checks**
In-house financing available:	**No**
Deposits required:	**Not applicable**
Catalog available:	**Not applicable**
Clearance center:	**Not applicable**
Delivery:	**Full service in-home delivery and set-up. Customer pays freight company directly for shipping costs.**

Directions:	**From I-40, take exit #123 (Hwy. 321) and head north through Hickory toward Lenoir. Turn left on Hwy. 64, then turn left again on the Hwy. 18S Bypass. The outlet is on the left inside Lenoir Mall.**

Kincaid Factory Outlet (cont.)

Kincaid Factory Outlet at the Manufacturer Owned Furniture Outlets in Lenoir, NC

Solid cherry china cabinet from Kincaid

Retail: $3,068.00   Discounted price: $1,250.00
Savings at the Kincaid Factory Outlet: $1,818.00 = 59% off retail

Kincaid Galleries

The Atrium
430 S. Main St.
High Point, NC 27260

Phone:	(336) 883-1818	**Hours:**	M-F 9:00-6:00, Sat 9:00-5:00
Toll Free:	(800) 527-2570	**E-mail:**	kincaidg@netmcr.com
Fax:	(336) 883-1850	**Web site:**	www.kincaidgalleries.com

Kincaid Galleries is a retail store, not a factory outlet. The prices here are a bit better than your local retailer, but they aren't comparable to the prices at discounters who carry the same brands.

If you're looking for the best deals on Kincaid, try the true factory-owned Kincaid factory outlet in Lenoir, NC.

Lines carried:

Ducks Unlimited	Lane	Morganton Chair	Woodmark Leather
Fashion Bed Group	Legacy Leather	Serta	
Kincaid	Lloyd/Flanders	Temple	

Phone orders accepted:	Yes
Discount:	At or near full retail
Payment methods:	VISA, MC, Discover, personal checks
In-house financing available:	No
Deposits required:	1/3 deposit when order is placed, balance due when furniture is delivered to your home
Catalog available:	Yes
Clearance center:	No
Delivery:	Full service in-home delivery and set-up. Customer pays freight company directly for shipping costs.

Directions: Kincaid Galleries is located inside the Atrium complex in downtown High Point. Please see *The Atrium* for complete directions.

Klaussner Furniture Factory Outlet

214 Hwy. 49 South
Asheboro, NC 27203

Phone:	**(336) 629-1985**	**Hours:**	**M-F 9:00-5:00**
Toll Free:	**None**	**E-mail:**	**None**
Fax:	**(336) 626-0905**	**Web site:**	**None**

Klaussner Furniture manufactures the Sealy Upholstery line. This is their only factory outlet. The stock here is primarily floor samples, overruns, returns, and discontinued styles. There is no specific discount structure. Everything is just tagged with one flat price.

Unfortunately, you aren't likely to get the most for your money here. The prices aren't very good, and the quality is only low to medium. There are so many places in the nearby High Point area that have much better quality upholstery for little or no more money.

Phone orders accepted:	**No**
Discount:	**Varies**
Payment methods:	**Personal checks. No credit cards.**
In-house financing available:	**No**
Deposits required:	**Not applicable**
Catalog available:	**Not applicable**
Clearance center:	**Not applicable**
Delivery:	**Customer must make own arrangements to take furniture home.**

Directions: From I-85, take exit #122, and go south for about half an hour on Hwy. 220. Take the Hwy. 49 exit. The Klaussner outlet is right off Hwy. 220.

Knight Galleries Inc.

835 Creekway Dr. NW
Lenoir, NC 28645

Phone:	**(828) 758-8422**	**Hours:**	**M-F 9:00-5:00**
Toll Free:	**(800) 334-4721**	**E-mail:**	**None**
Fax:	**(828) 754-1592**	**Web site:**	**None**

    Knight Galleries is located in Lenoir, just a few miles north of Hickory, NC. They have a fairly small store with a few pieces of furniture from Lexington and Stanley. Most of their business is done by phone.

    They don't have a clearance center or any floor samples or discontinued pieces on display. For this reason, there is no monetary advantage to visiting in person. They do have good deals on many lines sold over the phone, though. So, if you're planning to order your furniture by phone, definitely give this source a call to compare their prices.

Lines carried:

Action By Lane	Dixie	Lea	Serta Mattress
American Drew	Fairfield Chair	Lexington	Southern Reproductions
American Of Martinsville	Flexsteel	Link Taylor	Stanley
Barcalounger	Hammary	Lyon Shaw	Stanton Cooper
Bassett	Hekman	Mobel	Stratford
Blacksmith Shop	Henry Link	Nathan Hale	Stratolounger
Broyhill	Hickory Tavern	National Mt. Airy	Swan Brass Beds
C & M Furniture	Hickory White	Nichols & Stone	Tell City Chair
C. R. Laine	Highland House	Null Industries	Temple
Clark Casual	Hooker	Ohio Table Pad Co.	Universal
Clayton Marcus	Jasper Cabinet	Pearson	Venture By Lane
Cochrane	Keller	Peoplelounger	Virginia House
Corsican Beds	King Hickory	Pulaski	Young Hinkle
Craftique	Lane	Richardson Brothers	
Crawford	Lane/Venture	Riverside	

Phone orders accepted:	**Yes**
Discount:	**40%-50% off mfrs. suggested retail**
Payment methods:	**VISA, MC, personal checks**
In-house financing available:	**No**
Deposits required:	**1/3 deposit when order is placed, balance due when furniture is ready to be shipped**
Catalog available:	**No**
Clearance center:	**No**
Delivery:	**Full service in-home delivery and set-up. Customer pays freight company directly for shipping costs.**

Directions: **From I-40, take exit #123 and drive north on Hwy. 321 to Lenoir. Turn left on 321A South, and go 1 mile to the first traffic light. Then, turn right on Creekway Dr. Knight Galleries is immediately on the right.**

La Barge Factory Outlet

Inside the Henredon/Drexel Heritage Factory Outlet
3004-A Parquet Dr.
Dalton, GA 30720

I'm sorry to have to report that this terrific outlet closed on February 1, 1999. I was told that the outlet was closed at the request of certain furniture retailers in the Atlanta area who objected to having this outlet located 75 miles away from their stores.

It is an unfortunate fact of life in the home furnishings industry that manufacturers who sell directly to the public are often subjected to extreme pressure from the retailers whose profit margins shrink as a result. Every time this kind of bullying from retailers results in the closure of another factory outlet or deep discounter, you and I all pay higher prices for furniture as a result.

The best way to combat this problem is for all consumers to pressure manufacturers to keep selling through factory outlets and deep discounters. Vote with your checkbook. Pressure manufacturers to sell in a way that is in YOUR best interests, rather than in the middlemen's best interests.

Fortunately, there are still two terrific La Barge factory outlets in Hickory, NC, and this line is sold over the phone by a number of deep discounters. There are also some La Barge clearance pieces available at the Maitland-Smith Factory Outlet in High Point, NC.

La Barge Factory Outlet

Level 1 & 2
Hickory Furniture Mart
U. S. Hwy. 70 SE
Hickory, NC 28602

Phone:	**(828) 324-2220**	**Hours:**	**M-Sat 9:00-6:00**
Toll Free:	**None**	**E-mail:**	**info@hickoryfurniture.com**
Fax:	**(828) 323-8445**	**Web site:**	**www.hickoryfurniture.com**

The Drexel-Heritage/La Barge Factory Outlet at the Hickory Furniture Mart is huge, covering over one-eighth of the entire square footage of the Mart between its two levels. This outlet also serves as a factory-owned factory outlet for Drexel-Heritage, Beacon Hill, Baldwin Brass, and Maitland Smith.

Most of the stock here is in new first-quality condition: floor samples, customer returns, discontinued items, and stock overruns. There is a fairly even mix of case goods and upholstery.

Their normal discount runs between 50% to 80%. In January, the outlet runs a month long sale with even bigger discounts. During the sale, all items are 75% to 80% off retail. The outlet also runs shorter sales in May and September with the same discounts.

The outlet will not take phone orders for new furniture from La Barge's current lines, but if you know exactly which item you want, they will see if they have that particular style in stock at the outlet and allow you to order it by phone. They do accept credit cards for payment, and they will arrange shipping.
They do require you to pay in full for the item when your order is placed, but they also ship almost immediately.

This outlet, along with the Hickory Furniture Mart in general, is a "must-visit" on any trip to Hickory, NC. If you don't find exactly what you want at this outlet, Drexel Heritage/La Barge does have another outlet nearby in Hickory that is also very impressive.

Please also see the listings under Hickory Furniture Mart for more information on travel bargains to the Mart and ways of saving money on shipping.

Phone orders accepted:	**Yes**
Discount:	**50%-80% off mfrs. suggested retail**
Payment methods:	**VISA, MC, AMEX, personal checks**
In-house financing available:	**No**
Deposits required:	**Full payment due with order**
Catalog available:	**No**
Clearance center:	**Not applicable**
Delivery:	**Full service in-home delivery and set-up. Customer pays freight company directly for shipping costs.**

Directions: Please see *Hickory Furniture Mart* for complete directions.

La Barge Factory Outlet

Furniture Clearance Center
66 Hwy. 321 NW
Hickory, NC 28601

Phone:	**(828) 323-1558**	**Hours:**	**M-F 9:00-6:00, Sat 9:00-5:00**
Toll Free:	**None**	**E-mail:**	**None**
Fax:	**(828) 326-9846**	**Web site:**	**None**

The Furniture Clearance Center in Hickory, NC, is a combined factory-owned factory outlet for Drexel-Heritage, La Barge, Maitland-Smith, Sedgewick Rattan, Carrington Court, and Craftique. It occupies a huge warehouse building.

The stock consists of floor samples, customer returns, photography samples, and discontinued styles. Virtually all of the furniture here is in new first-quality condition. The discounts run from 50%-70% off retail, with most pieces around 60% off.   They usually have a big sale every January and May when they mark most pieces an extra 10%-20% off.

If you travel to Hickory to shop for high-end traditional furniture, this outlet is a "must visit"!

Phone orders accepted:	**No**
Discount:	**50%-70% off mfrs. suggested retail**
Payment methods:	**VISA, MC, personal checks**
In-house financing available:	**No**
Deposits required:	**Not applicable**
Catalog available:	**Not applicable**
Clearance center:	**Not applicable**
Delivery:	**Full service in-home delivery and set-up.**
	Customer pays freight company directly for shipping costs.

Directions: From I-40, take exit #123 and drive north on Hwy. 321 into Hickory. Furniture Clearance Center is about two miles down on the right.

Lake Hickory Furniture

4360 Hickory Blvd.
Granite Falls, NC 28630

Phone:	**(828) 396-2194**	**Hours:**	**M-Sat 9:00-5:00**
Toll Free:	**None**	**E-mail:**	**None**
Fax:	**(828) 396-1226**	**Web site:**	**None**

Lake Hickory Furniture is located just a few miles north of Hickory, NC. They have a good selection of medium to high-end lines, including Lexington, Lane, Universal, and Stanley.

They don't have a clearance center, and they have very few floor samples or discontinued pieces on display. There really isn't much reason to go by this store in person. They do have good deals on many lines sold over the phone, though. So, if you're planning to order your furniture by phone, give this source a call to compare their prices.

Lines carried:

American Drew	Crawford	Lexington	Southern Reproductions
American Of Martinsville	Distinction Leather	Marlow	Stanley
Benicia Brass Beds	Habersham Plantation	Mobel	Superior
Bob Timberlake	Hammary	Null Industries	Tell City Chair
Bork Holder	Hitchcock Chair	Old Salem	Timeless Bedding
Brady Furniture	Hooker	Peters Revington	Two Day Designs
Brown Street	Huntington House	Phillips Leather	Universal
Cambridge Glider Rockers	Jasper Cabinet	Pulaski	Virginia House
Chatham County	Johnston Casuals	Richardson Brothers	Wisconsin Furniture
Conover Chair	Key City	Simply Southern	
County Seat	Lane	Sleepworks	

Phone orders accepted:	**Yes**
Discount:	**35%-50% off mfrs. suggested retail**
Payment methods:	**VISA, MC, personal checks**
In-house financing available:	**No**
Deposits required:	**50% deposit when order is placed, balance due when furniture is ready to be shipped**
Catalog available:	**No**
Clearance center:	**No**
Delivery:	**Full service in-home delivery and set-up. Customer pays freight company directly for shipping costs.**

Directions: From I-40, take exit #123 and drive north on Hwy. 321 to Granite Falls. Lake Hickory Furniture is on the right side of the road.

La-Z-Boy Factory Outlet

Manufacturer-Owned Factory Outlets (Lenoir Mall)
1031 Morganton Blvd.
Lenoir, NC 28645

Phone:	**(828) 754-2126**	**Hours:**	**M-Sat 10:00-7:00, Sun 1:00-5:00**
Toll Free:	**None**	**E-mail:**	**None**
Fax:	**(828) 754-8052**	**Web site:**	**None**

This is La-Z-boy's only true factory outlet. Unfortunately, it's only a small corner of the Kincaid Factory Outlet at the Manufacturer-Owned Factory Outlets in Lenoir Mall, just north of Hickory, NC.

There just isn't much of a selection at this outlet. On my most recent visit, they had only about 30 recliners on display. Most of these were discontinued styles and floor samples from the bi-annual wholesale furniture markets in High Point. The selection does improve a bit in May and November, right after the High Point markets end.

The selection here just doesn't justify a special trip. If you're in the Lenoir area anyway, and you're looking for a recliner, by all means stop by. Others will be better off to order their La-Z-Boy recliners over the phone from Thomas Home Furnishings or Gordon's Furniture Stores.

Phone orders accepted:	**No**
Discount:	**50%-75% off mfrs. suggested retail**
Payment methods:	**VISA, MC, personal checks**
In-house financing available:	**No**
Deposits required:	**Not applicable**
Catalog available:	**Not applicable**
Clearance center:	**Not applicable**
Delivery:	**Full service in-home delivery and set-up. Customer pays freight company directly for shipping costs.**

Directions:	**From I-40, take exit #123 (Hwy. 321) and head north through Hickory toward Lenoir. Turn left on Hwy. 64, then turn left again on the Hwy. 18S Bypass. The outlet is on the left inside Lenoir Mall.**

Lindy's Furniture Co.

Hwy. 70
Connelly Springs, NC 28612

Phone:	**(828) 879-4530**	**Hours:**	**Mon, Tues, Thurs, & Fri 8:30-5:00**
Toll Free:	**None**		**Sat 8:30-3:00**
Fax:	**(828) 327-6088**	**E-mail:**	**purg@twave.net**
		Web site:	**www.lindysfurniture.com**

Lindy's Furniture Co. takes Southern style <u>very</u> seriously. The store, perched high on a hill in the tiny town of Connelly Springs, looks a lot like "Tara" from *Gone With the Wind*. Thankfully, this makes it very easy to spot going down the road.

The store is huge. In addition to the four-story main building, there are 6 interconnected warehouses behind it filled with wall-to-wall furniture. The staff estimates that it takes one and a half hours to tour the entire facility straight through.

Virtually all of the furniture in-stock is new first-quality. There are a very few discontinued styles and samples scattered around marked at about 65% to 75% off retail, but these are few and far between.

It's much better to order by phone from this source. They have a very unusual policy for North Carolina discounters. They actually charge a "restocking" fee if you buy furniture off the floor to cover the difficulty of bringing a replacement into the building. This is the only discounter I have ever heard of that sells at a cheaper price over the phone than they do if you shop in person.

They carry hundreds of lines, far more than their published list on the following page. They also promise to meet or beat any competitor's written price quote, so hold them to it!

Anyone who is planning to order furniture by phone should check prices with this source. As interesting as the store is, however, it really isn't worth visiting in person. You pay more to shop in person, not less, and the store is located some distance from the main cluster of outlets and discounters in nearby Hickory, NC.

Lines carried:	**Please see page 212**
Phone orders accepted:	**Yes**
Discount:	**40%-60% off mfrs. suggested retail**
Payment methods:	**Personal checks. No credit cards.**
In-house financing available:	**No**
Deposits required:	**25% deposit when order is placed. The balance can be paid either before shipment or COD.**
Catalog available:	**No**
Clearance center:	**No**
Delivery:	**Full service in-home delivery and set-up. Customer pays freight company directly for shipping costs.**

Directions: From I-40, take exit #113, and go south on Connelly Springs Rd. At the first stop sign, turn left. Go about 3 miles until you reach Hwy. 70. Turn right on Hwy. 70. Lindy's is about one mile down on the right side of the road. It's the large building at the top of the hill that looks like "Tara" from *Gone With the Wind*.

Lindy's Furniture Co. (cont.)

Lindy's Furniture Co.

Lines carried:

American Drew
American Of Martinsville
Arnold Palmer Collection
Athens
Barclay
Bassett
Berkline
Berkshire
Best Chair
Blacksmith Shop
Bob Timberlake
Broyhill
Capital Leather
Catnapper
Chatham County
Chromecraft
Clayton Marcus
Cochrane
Craftique
Douglas Dinettes
Dresher
Ducks Unlimited
England Corsair
Fairfield

Fashion Bed
Flexsteel
Florida Furniture
Hammary
Hekman
Henry Link
Hickory Hill
Hood
Hooker
Howard Miller Clocks
J/B Ross
Keller
Kincaid
Kingsdown Bedding
Kroehler
Lane
La-Z-Boy
Lea
Lexington
Ligo
Millennium
Morgan Stewart
National Mt. Airy
Ohio Table Pad

Palmer Home Collection
Pulaski
Richardson Bros.
Ridgewood
Riverside
Rock City
Rowe
Stanley
Stoneville
Universal
U. S. Furniture
Vaughan
Vaughan-Bassett
Victorian Classics
Winners Only

L. J. Best Furniture Distributors

12-16 W. Main
Thomasville, NC 27360

Phone:	**(919) 475-9101**	**Hours:**	**M-F 9:00-5:00, Sat 9:00-Noon**
Toll Free:	**(800) 334-8000**	**E-mail:**	**None**
Fax:	**None**	**Web site:**	**None**

L. J. Best Furniture Distributors is located in downtown Thomasville, NC, just south of High Point. They have a very nice selection of high end lines, including Lexington, Hickory White, and Classic Leather.

They don't have a clearance center or any floor samples or discontinued pieces on display. For this reason, there is no monetary advantage to visiting in person. They do have great deals on many lines sold over the phone, though. So, if you're planning to order your furniture by phone, definitely give this source a call to compare their prices.

Lines carried:

A. A. Laun	Binnie's	Casual Lamps	Clayton Marcus
A. L. Shaver	Blacksmith Shop	Carson's Of High Point	Clover Lamp
Acco	Boatable Furniture	Carter	Clyde Pearson
Ainsley Inc.	Bradington Young	Carver's Guild	Cochrane
Airguide Weather Inst.	Brass Originals	Casa Bique	Coja Leather
American Drew	Brasscrafters	Castilian Imports	Comfort Designs
American Of High Point	Broyhill	Chaircraft	Conover Chair
American Of Martinsville	C. M. Furniture	Charisma Chairs	Conant Ball
Art Flo	C. R. Laine	Chatham County	Councill Craftsmen
Ayers Chairmakers	Cachet Upholstery	Childcraft	Cox
Bali Blinds	Cal-Style	Chelsea House	Crestline
Barcalounger	Capel Rugs	Chromcraft	Crystal Clear
Baroody-Spence	Carlton McLendon	Clark Casual	D & F Wicker
Bassett	Carolina Mirror	Classic Gallery	Dansen Contemporary
Benchcraft	Carolina Seating	Classic Leather	Dapha
Bevan Funnell	Carolina Tables	Classic Rattan	Dar-Ran

Phone orders accepted:	**Yes**
Discount:	**35%-50% off mfrs. suggested retail**
Payment methods:	**VISA, MC, personal checks**
In-house financing available:	**No**
Deposits required:	**50% deposit when order is placed, balance due when furniture is ready to be shipped**
Catalog available:	**No**
Clearance center:	**No**
Delivery:	**Full service in-home delivery and set-up. Customer pays freight company directly for shipping costs.**

Directions: From I-85, take exit #103, and go north on Randolph St. After a few miles, turn right on Main St. L. J. Best Furniture is on the left.

L. J. Best Furniture Distributors (cont.)

Lines carried:

David Thomas Lamps
Daystrom
Decorative Crafts
Dillon
Directional
Dixie
Dresher
Ecco
Ello
Emerson Leather
Erwin Lambeth
Excelsior
Fairfield Chair
Fine Arts Lamps
Finkel
Fitz & Floyd
Flexsteel
Frederick Cooper Lamps
Garcia Imports
Georgian Reproductions
Georgian Lighting
Gerald Stein Brass Beds
Glass Arts Of California
HTB Contemporary
Halcyon
Hammary
Hart Country Shop
Hekman
Henry Link
Hickory Fry
Hickory Hill
Hickory Tavern
Hickory White
Highland House
High Point Desk
High Point Woodworking
Hitchcock Chair
Homecrest
Hood
Hooker
Howard Miller Clocks
Hyundai Furniture
International Furniture
J. B. Ross
Jasper Cabinet
Jeffco
Johnson Casuals
Joanna Blinds
Karedsen

Karges
Karpen
Keller
Key City
Kincaid
Kirsch Blinds
La Barge
Lane
Lane/Venture
Lea
Leathermen's Guild
Leonard Silver
Lewittes
Lexington
Link Taylor
Lucite & Lacquer
Lyon Shaw
Madison Square
Mark Thomas Lamps
Martinsville Novelty
Masland Carpets
Mersman Tables
Motion Only
Murray Feiss
Nathan Hale
National Mt. Airy
Nichols & Stone
Norman Perry Lamps
Normans Of Salisbury
Null Industries
O'Asian
Ohio Table Pads
Old Country
        Reproductions
Old Hickory Tannery
P & P Chair Co.
Paoli
Paul Hansen Lamps
Peopleloungers
Pennsburg
Pennsylvania Classics
Peters Revington
Plant Plant
Plymouth Harlee
Pouliot
Pulaski
Reliance Lamp
Reprodux
Richardson Brothers

Ridgeway Clocks
Riverside
Sam Moore
Sarreid
Schweiger
Sealy Bedding
Sedgefield
Selig
Serta Bedding
Seth Thomas Clocks
Sherrill
Singer
Sligh
Smith Wood Products
Solid Brass USA
Somma Waterbeds
Speer Lamps
Sprague Carlton
Stanley
Stanton Cooper
Stiffel Lamps
Stratford
Stratolounger
Sunset Lamps
Swaim Originals
Swan Brass Beds
Taylor Woodcraft
Telescope
Tell City Chair
Temple Stuart
Thayer Coggin
Through the
        Barn Door
Trim Trac
Tropitone
TRS Upholstery
Tyndale Lamp
Typhoon
Umbrella Factory
Union National
Upper Deck Brass
U. S. Furniture
Vanguard
Velda Leather
Venture By Lane
Virginia House
Virginia Metalcrafters
Webb
Weiman

Wesley Allen
Westwood
White Furniture
Widdicomb
Wildwood Lamps
Wildwood Tables
Winston Furniture
Woodfield, Ltd.
Woodlee
Woodmark
Young Hinkle

Loftin Black Furniture Co.

111 Sedgehill Dr.
Thomasville, NC 27360

Phone:	**(336) 472-6117**	**Hours:**	**M-F 8:30-5:30, Sat 8:30-4:30**
Toll Free:	**(800) 745-3876**	**E-mail:**	**None**
Fax:	**(336) 472-2052**	**Web site:**	**www.ncnet.com/ncnw/tho-loft.html**

Loftin-Black Furniture Co. has a good selection of medium to high-end lines: Hooker, Lexington, Universal, Stanley, etc. Their discounts run about 35%-50% off retail on new first-quality furniture.

They have very few discontinued pieces and floor samples available, and these are only discounted about 30%, which is far less than the discounts offered on comparable furniture by other discounters and factory outlets.

Loftin-Black does have an excellent reputation for customer service. They've been in business for over 50 years, and they're very reliable. If you're planning to order furniture over the phone, you should definitely compare their prices. However, if you're planning to visit the High Point/Thomasville area in person to shop, there are many other discounters and factory outlets in the area that have much better bargains.

Lines carried:	**Please see page 216**
Phone orders accepted:	**Yes**
Discount:	**35%-50% off mfrs. suggested retail**
Payment methods:	**VISA, MC, Discover, personal checks**
In-house financing available:	**No**
Deposits required:	**50% deposit when order is placed, balance due when furniture is ready to be shipped**
Catalog available:	**No**
Clearance center:	**No**
Delivery:	**Full service in-home delivery and set-up. Customer pays freight company directly for shipping costs.**

Directions: From I-85, take exit #103 (Hwy. 109). Turn left on Sedgehill Dr. You'll see a Shoney's on the corner. Loftin-Black is right behind Shoney's.

Loftin Black Furniture Co. (cont.)

Lines carried:

A. A. Laun
Accentrics
Action By Lane
Alexvale
Alexander Julian
Alva
American Drew
American Of High Point
American Of Martinsville
Baldwin Brass
Barcalounger
Barn Door
Bassett
Bassett Mirror
Beechley Upholstery
Benchcraft
Best Chairs
Blacksmith Shop
Bob Timberlake
Bradington Young
Braxton Culler
Brown Street
Broyhill
Butler Specialty
C. R. Laine
Cal-Style
Cape Craftsmen
Carolina Mirror
Carson's
Carter
Casa Bique
Century
Charleston Forge
Chatham County
Chromcraft
Classic Gallery
Classic Leather
Classic Rattan
Clayton Marcus
Cochrane
Colonial
Comfort Designs
Conover Chair
Continental Accents
Corsican Beds
Councill Craftsmen
Cox
Craftique
Crawford

Crystal Clear Lamps
Daystrom
Dillon
Dinaire
Directional
Distinction Leather
Dutailier Gliders
Eaglecraft Desks
Edward Art
Elliott Designs
Emerson Leather
Emissary
Excelsior
Executive Leather
Fairfield Chair
Fancher
Fashion Bed Group
Feathermade Mattress
Ficks Reed
Fine Art Lamps
Flexsteel
Floral Art
Franklin Chair
Frederick Cooper Lamps
Frederick Edward
Froelich
Futuristic Recliners
Georgian Reproductions
Glass Arts
Goodwin Weavers
Hale Of Vermont
Hammary
Hekman
Henry Link
Hickory Hill
Hickory Mark
Hickory Tavern
Highland House
Hitchcock Chair
Hood
Hooker
Howard Miller Clocks
HTB Upholstery
Hyundai Furniture
International Glass Corp.
Jasper Cabinet
Jetton Upholstery
Johnston Casuals
KNF Designs

Keller
Kimball
Kincaid
King Hickory
Kingsdown
Knob Creek
La Barge
Lane
Lane/Venture
Lea
Leisters
Lexington
Lillian August
Link Taylor
Lloyd/Flanders
Lyon Shaw
Madison Square
Mark Thomas Lamps
Marlowe
Maryland Classics
McKinley Leather
Millender
Millennium
Moosehead
Najarian
Nathan Hale
National Mt. Airy
Nichols & Stone
North Hickory
Null Industries
O'Asian
Ohio Table Pad Co.
Palecek
Pearson Upholstery
Pennsylvania Classics
Peoplelounger
Peters Revington
Precedent
Pulaski
Rex
Richardson Brothers
Ridgeway Clocks
Ridgewood
Riverside
Rochelle
Rock City
Rowe
S. K. Products
Saloom

Sam Moore
Samsonite
Sarreid
Schumacher Fabrics
Schweiger
Sealy Mattress
Sealy of Maryland
Sedgefield Lamps
Selig Upholstery
Serta Mattress
Skillcraft
Sligh
Southampton
Southwood
        Reproductions
Stanley
Stanton Cooper
Statesville Chair
Straits
Stratford
Stratolounger
Stiffel Lamps
Superior Furniture
Swaim Designs
Swan Brass Beds
Taylor Woodcraft
Thayer Coggin
Through the Barn Door
Universal
Uwharrie Chair
Venture By Lane
Victorian Classics
Virginia House
Virginia Metalcrafters
Weiman
Wesley Allen
Westwood Lamps
Wildwood Lamps
Winston Outdoor
Woodard
Woodmark
Yorkshire Leather

The Lounge Shop

2222 E. Patterson St.
Greensboro, NC 27410

Phone:	(828) 726-3333	**Hours:**	M-F 9:30-8:00, Sat 9:30-6:00
Toll Free:	None		Sun 1:00-6:00
Fax:	None	**E-mail:**	None
		Web site:	None

   The Lounge Shop doesn't publish a list of the lines they can special order, but they have access to about 250 brands, including most popular medium to high-end lines. The discounts on phone orders or in person sales run about 60%-75% off retail. They have particularly good deals on Lexington.

   This is a very impressive store. On my most recent visit here, I found a great deal on a Henry Link wicker set (pictured on the following page). Normally, the sofa, chair, and two end tables retail for $3,928.00, but The Lounge Shop had this set in stock for $1,848.00, including the cushions.

   There's no real monetary advantage to going in person because they will match their store prices on orders placed by phone. However, anyone ordering furniture by phone should definitely compare prices here. I was very impressed with the staff at this store, as well as the service and the discounts.

Phone orders accepted:	Yes
Discount:	**60%-75% off mfrs. suggested retail**
Payment methods:	**Personal checks. No credit cards.**
In-house financing available:	No
Deposits required:	**50% deposit when order is placed, balance due when furniture is ready to be shipped**
Catalog available:	No
Clearance center:	No
Delivery:	**Full service in-home delivery and set-up. Customer pays freight company directly for shipping costs.**

Directions: **From I-85, take the Holden Rd. exit and head north into Greensboro. Then, after a few miles, turn right on Patterson St. The Lounge Shop is a few miles down on the left.**

The Lounge Shop (cont.)

The Lounge Shop

Wicker living room set from Henry Link

Retail: $3,928.00   Discounted price: $1,848.00
Savings at The Lounge Shop: $2,080.00 = 53% off retail

Mackie Furniture Co.

13 N. Main St.
Granite Falls, NC 28630

Phone:	(828) 396-3313	**Hours:**	M-F 9:00-5:00
Toll Free:	None	**E-mail:**	None
Fax:	(828) 396-3314	**Web site:**	None

Mackie Furniture Co. is a very quaint small-town furniture store in tiny Granite Falls, NC. It's been in business since 1917. The store isn't very big, but they do have some nice pieces in stock from medium to high-end lines such as Lexington, Lane, Stanley, and Hooker.

They don't have a clearance center or any floor samples or discontinued pieces on display. For this reason, there is no monetary advantage to visiting in person. They do have good deals on many lines sold over the phone, though. So, if you're planning to order your furniture by phone, give this source a call to compare their prices.

Lines carried:

Action By Lane	Chatham County	Keller	Morgan Stewart
American Drew	Clayton Marcus	Kincaid	Pulaski
Ashley Furniture	Cochrane	Kingsdown Mattress	Riverside
Bassett	Ducks Unlimited	Lane	Sarreid
Betsy Cameron	Fairfield Chair	Lea	Telescope
Blacksmith Shop	Fashion Bed Group	Lexington	Thera-A-Pedic Mattress
Bob Timberlake	Hammary	Link Taylor	Timmerman
Bradington Young	Henry Link	Lloyd/Flanders	Universal
Broyhill	Hooker	McKay Table Pads	U. S. Furniture
Carolina Mirror	Jasper Cabinet	Morganton Chair	Vaughan

Phone orders accepted:	Yes
Discount:	35%-50% off mfrs. suggested retail
Payment methods:	VISA, MC, personal checks
In-house financing available:	No
Deposits required:	50% deposit when order is placed, balance due when furniture is ready to be shipped
Catalog available:	No
Clearance center:	No
Delivery:	Full service in-home delivery and set-up. Customer pays freight company directly for shipping costs.

Directions: From I-40, take exit #123 and drive north on Hwy. 321 to Granite Falls. Turn left on 321-A North, and go into downtown Granite Falls. 321-A will become Main St. Mackie Furniture is on the left.

Mackie Furniture Co. (cont.)

Mackie Furniture Co.

Maitland-Smith Factory Outlet

Furniture Clearance Center
66 Hwy. 321 NW
Hickory, NC 28601

Phone:	**(828) 323-1558**	**Hours:**	**M-F 9:00-6:00, Sat 9:00-5:00**
Toll Free:	**None**	**E-mail:**	**None**
Fax:	**(828) 326-9846**	**Web site:**	**None**

The Furniture Clearance Center in Hickory, NC, is a combined factory-owned factory outlet for Drexel-Heritage, La Barge, Maitland-Smith, Sedgewick Rattan, Carrington Court, and Craftique. It occupies a huge warehouse building.

The stock consists of floor samples, customer returns, photography samples, and discontinued styles. Virtually all of the furniture here is in new first-quality condition. The discounts run from 50%-70% off retail, with most pieces around 60% off. They usually have a big sale every January and May when they mark most pieces an extra 10%-20% off.

If you travel to Hickory to shop for high-end traditional furniture, this outlet is a "must visit"!

Phone orders accepted:	**No**
Discount:	**50%-70% off mfrs. suggested retail**
Payment methods:	**VISA, MC, personal checks**
In-house financing available:	**No**
Deposits required:	**Not applicable**
Catalog available:	**Not applicable**
Clearance center:	**Not applicable**
Delivery:	**Full service in-home delivery and set-up. Customer pays freight company directly for shipping costs.**

Directions: From I-40, take exit #123 and drive north on Hwy. 321 into Hickory.

Maitland-Smith Factory Outlet

Level 1 & 2
Hickory Furniture Mart
U. S. Hwy. 70 SE
Hickory, NC 28602

Phone:	**(828) 324-2220**	**Hours:**	**M-Sat 9:00-6:00**
Toll Free:	**None**	**E-mail:**	**info@hickoryfurniture.com**
Fax:	**(828) 323-8445**	**Web site:**	**www.hickoryfurniture.com**

The Drexel-Heritage/Maitland-Smith Factory Outlet at the Hickory Furniture Mart is huge, covering over one-eighth of the entire square footage of the Mart between its two levels. This outlet also serves as a factory-owned factory outlet for Drexel-Heritage, La Barge, Baldwin Brass, and Beacon Hill.

Most of the stock here is in new first-quality condition: floor samples, customer returns, discontinued items, and stock overruns. There is a fairly even mix of case goods and upholstery.

Their normal discount runs between 50% to 80%. In January, the outlet runs a month long sale with even bigger discounts. During the sale, all items are 75% to 80% off retail. The outlet also runs shorter sales in May and September with the same discounts.

The outlet will not take phone orders for new furniture from Maitland-Smith's current lines, but if you know exactly which item you want, they will see if they have that particular style in stock at the outlet and allow you to order it by phone. They do accept credit cards for payment, and they will arrange shipping.
They do require you to pay in full for the item when your order is placed, but they also ship almost immediately.

This outlet, along with the Hickory Furniture Mart in general, is a "must-visit" on any trip to Hickory, NC. If you don't find exactly what you want at this outlet, Drexel Heritage/Maitland-Smith does have another outlet nearby in Hickory that is also very impressive.

Please also see the listings under Hickory Furniture Mart for more information on travel bargains to the Mart and ways of saving money on shipping.

Phone orders accepted:	**Yes**
Discount:	**50%-80% off mfrs. suggested retail**
Payment methods:	**VISA, MC, AMEX, personal checks**
In-house financing available:	**No**
Deposits required:	**Full payment due with order**
Catalog available:	**No**
Clearance center:	**Not applicable**
Delivery:	**Full service in-home delivery and set-up.** **Customer pays freight company directly for shipping costs.**

Directions: Please see *Hickory Furniture Mart* for complete directions.

Maitland-Smith Factory Outlet

411 Tomlinson St.
High Point, NC 27260

Phone:	(336) 812-2417	**Hours:**	M-F 9:00-5:00
Toll Free:	None	**E-mail:**	None
Fax:	(336) 887-2625	**Web site:**	None

This outlet is amazing. It's huge, adjoining Maitland-Smith's main wholesale showroom in High Point. There are two huge connected warehouses filled with traditional and oriental style furniture and accessories. Maitland-Smith is a very, very high-end line, and the furniture here is exceptional. There are also some La Barge occasional tables here.

Most of the furniture in stock is in new first-quality condition. The discounts range from 50%-75% off retail, with most pieces priced about 65% off. There are a few seconds and damaged returns mixed in.

On my most recent visit here, I found an amazing deal on a leather-topped game table. This table has an insert that lifts out of the top to display a checkerboard and a backgammon board. The retail on this piece is normally $4,326.00, but this table was only $595.00. It was a slightly damaged piece with two superficial scratches about a centimeter long each.

A local refinisher told me that the scratches would cost no more than $150.00 to invisibly repair. So, you save $3,731.00 off retail and pay back $150.00 to restore it to perfect condition. This the kind of fixer-upper that you should be on the lookout for.

This is an amazing outlet. Anyone visiting the High Point area should make a point of stopping in here.

Phone orders accepted:	**No**
Discount:	**50%-75% off mfrs. suggested retail**
Payment methods:	**Personal checks. No credit cards.**
In-house financing available:	**No**
Deposits required:	**Not applicable**
Catalog available:	**Not applicable**
Clearance center:	**Not applicable**
Delivery:	**Customer must make own arrangements to take furniture home.**

Directions: From I-85, take exit #111 (Hwy. 311), and head northwest into High Point. After several miles, when you reach downtown High Point, Hwy. 311 will become S. Main St. When you reach downtown High Point, turn left on Grimes Ave. After a block, turn left on Tomlinson St. The Maitland-Smith Factory Outlet is immediately on the right.

Maitland-Smith Factory Outlet (cont.)

Maitland-Smith Factory Outlet in High Point, NC

Leather-topped game table from Maitland-Smith

Retail: $4,326.00   Discounted price: $595.00
Savings at the Maitland-Smith Factory Outlet: $3,731.00 = 86% off retail

Maitland-Smith Factory Outlet

146 West Ave.
Kannapolis, NC 28081

Phone:	(704) 938-9191	**Hours:**	M-Sat 9:00-6:00
Toll Free:	None	**E-mail:**	None
Fax:	(704) 932-2503	**Web site:**	None

The Maitland-Smith Factory Outlet is located inside the Village Furniture House in Cannon Village. It isn't as extensive as Maitland-Smith's main outlet in High Point, but they do have some terrific deals here.

Most of the stock here are floor samples and discontinued styles in new first-quality condition. There's a nice selection of desks, tables, and other small occasional furniture.

On my most recent visit here, I found a Maitland-Smith console table (pictured on the following page) that normally retails for $2,324.00 marked down to $1,199.00. It was a discontinued style in brand-new first-quality condition.

If you are traveling to North Carolina to buy furniture, you really should consider taking one extra day to visit Cannon Village in Kannapolis. In addition to the Maitland-Smith outlet, there are also true factory outlets for Baker and Century here that are well worth a visit. Kannapolis is about one half hour's drive north of Charlotte, one hour's drive south of High Point, and one hour's drive east of Hickory.

Phone orders accepted:	No
Discount:	60%-75% off mfrs. suggested retail
Payment methods:	Personal checks. No credit cards.
In-house financing available:	No
Deposits required:	Not applicable
Catalog available:	Not applicable
Clearance center:	Not applicable
Delivery:	Full service in-home delivery and set-up. Customer pays freight company directly for shipping costs.

Directions: From I-85, take exit #63, and follow the signs to Cannon Village. The Century Factory Outlet is accessible through the Village Furniture House on West Ave. inside Cannon Village.

Maitland-Smith Factory Outlet (cont.)

Maitland-Smith Factory Outlet in Kannapolis, NC

Console table from Maitland-Smith

Retail: $2,324.00   Discounted price: $1,199.00
Savings at the Maitland-Smith Factory Outlet: $1,125.00 = 48% off retail

Mallory's Fine Furniture
2153 LeJeune Blvd.
Jacksonville, NC 28541

Phone:	(910) 353-1828	**Hours:**	M-F 10:00-6:00
Toll Free:	None	**E-mail:**	mallorys@mallorys.com
Fax:	(910) 353-3348	**Web site:**	www.mallorys.com

Mallory's Fine Furniture is located in Jacksonville, NC, near the Atlantic coast. They have a 40,000 square-foot store with a good selection of medium to high-end lines, including Lexington, Wellington Hall, Classic Leather, and Hooker.

They don't have a clearance center or any floor samples or discontinued pieces on display. For this reason, there is no monetary advantage to visiting in person. They do have good deals on many lines sold over the phone, though. So, if you're planning to order your furniture by phone, give this source a call to compare their prices.

Lines carried:	Please see page 228
Phone orders accepted:	Yes
Discount:	35%-50% off mfrs. suggested retail
Payment methods:	VISA, MC, personal checks
In-house financing available:	No
Deposits required:	40% deposit when order is placed, balance due when furniture is ready to be shipped
Catalog available:	No
Clearance center:	No
Delivery:	Full service in-home delivery and set-up. Customer pays freight company directly for shipping costs.

Directions: From I-40, take exit #364, and follow Hwy. 24 to Jacksonville, NC.

Mallory's Fine Furniture (cont.)

Lines carried:

Accentrics By Pulaski
Action By Lane
Alexander Julian
American Drew
American Of Martinsville
Arnold Palmer Collection
Athol
Baldwin Brass
Bassett
Betsy Cameron
Braxton Culler
Broyhill
Carsons
Casa Bique
Chapman Lamps
Charleston Forge
Chatham County
Chromcraft
Classic Leather
Clayton Marcus
Cochrane
Colonial Furniture
Councill Craftsmen
Cox
Craftique
Crawford Of Jamestown
CTH Sherrill
Dinaire
Eddie Bauer By Lane
Ekornes
Emerson Leather
Entree by La Barge
Fairfield Chair
Friedman Brothers
Habersham Plantation
Hammary
Hancock & Moore
Hekman
Henkel-Harris
Henkel-Moore
Henry Link
Hickory Chair
Highland House
Hooker
Howard Miller
J. Royale
Jasper Cabinet
Jessica Charles
Johnston Casuals

Karges
Kessler
Kincaid
La Barge
Lane
Lane/Venture
Lexington
Lillian August
Link Taylor
Lloyd/Flanders
Lyon Shaw
Madison Square
Maitland Smith
Marbro Lamps
McKay Table Pad
Michael Thomas
Millender
Motioncraft By Sherrill
Nichols & Stone
Ohio Table Pad
Pearson
Pennsylvania House
Pulaski
Richardson Brothers
Ridgeway Clocks
Ridgewood By Broyhill
Riverside
Sam Moore
Sedgefield By Adams
Sherrill
Simmons Beautyrest
Southern Reproductions
Southampton
Southmark Leather
Southwood Reproductions
Stanley
Stiffel Lamps
Sumter Cabinet
Taylor King
Tradition House
Tropitone
Universal
Venture By Lane
Virginia Metalcrafters
Waterford Furniture
Weiman
Wellington Hall
Wesley Allen
Whitmore Leather

Wildwood Lamps
Winston
Woodmark Originals

Manufacturer-Owned Factory Outlets (Lenoir Mall)

1031 Morganton Blvd.
Lenoir, NC 28645

Lenoir Mall, just north of Hickory, NC, is in the process of being transformed into a furniture factory outlet center. It already houses the only true factory outlets for Bernhardt, Broyhill, Highland House, Kincaid, La-Z-Boy, and one of only two true factory outlets in the country for Thomasville. Please check the individual listings for each of these factory outlets for details on their stock, discounts, and store policies. As new outlets are added, I will post announcements at www.smartdecorating.com.

If you are in the Lenoir or Hickory area, you should absolutely make a stop at Lenoir Mall. This outlet center is a "must-visit".

Directions: **From I-40, take exit #123 (Hwy. 321) and head north through Hickory toward Lenoir. Turn left on Hwy. 64, then turn left again on the Hwy. 18S Bypass. Lenoir Mall will be several miles down on your left.**

Mecklenburg Furniture

520 Providence Rd.
Charlotte, NC 28207

Phone:	(704) 376-8401	**Hours:**	M-Wed, Fri, & Sat 9:00-5:30
Toll Free:	None		Thurs 9:00-8:00
Fax:	(704) 347-0499	**E-mail:**	None
		Web site:	None

Mecklenburg Furniture is located in Charlotte, NC, about an hour south of Charlotte. They have a very nice selection of high-end lines, including Lexington, Broyhill, Stanley, and Hooker.

They don't have a clearance center or any floor samples or discontinued pieces on display. For this reason, there is no monetary advantage to visiting in person. They do have great deals on many lines sold over the phone, though. So, if you're planning to order your furniture by phone, definitely give this source a call to compare their prices.

Lines carried:

Accentrics By Pulaski	Bassett Mirror	Carolina Mirror	Clayton Marcus
Action By Lane	Bevan Funnell	Carsons	Colonial
Alexvale	Bigelow Carpet	Carvers Guild	Corsican
American Drew	Blacksmith Shop	Casa Bique	Councill Craftsmen
American Of Martinsville	Boos Co.	Casa Stradivari	Couristan Rugs
Armstrong Vinyl	Borkholder	Century	Courtleigh
Artisan House	Bradington Young	Chapman Lamps	Cowtan & Tout
As You Like It Lamps	Braxton Culler	Charleston Forge	Cox
Austin Sculpture	Brown Street	Chelsea House/Port Royal	Craftique
Baker	Broyhill	Christelle Collection	Craftwork Guild
Baldwin Brass	Brunschwig & Fils	Chromcraft	Crestline
Barcalounger	Buccola	CJC Decorative Pillows	Crystal Clear Lighting
Barlow Tyne	Butler Specialty	Clarence House	CTH Sherrill
Bashian Oriental Rugs	C. R. Laine	Clark Casual	D & F Wicker and Rattan
Bassett	Cal-Style	Classic Rattan	Dansen Contemporary

Phone orders accepted:	Yes
Discount:	30%-70% off mfrs. suggested retail
Payment methods:	Personal checks. No credit cards.
In-house financing available:	No
Deposits required:	1/3 deposit when order is placed, balance due when furniture is ready to be shipped
Catalog available:	No
Clearance center:	No
Delivery:	Full service in-home delivery and set-up. Customer pays freight company directly for shipping costs.

Directions: From I-77 in Charlotte, take the Providence Rd. exit, and head southeast. Mecklenburg Furniture is a few miles down on the right.

Mecklenburg Furniture (cont.)

Lines carried (cont.):

Dapha
Davis & Davis Rugs
Daystrom
Decorative Crafts
Dillon
Dinaire
Distinction Leather
DMI
Duralee Fabrics
Elan International
Elements By Grapevine
Ello
Emerson Leather
Englander Bedding
Fairfield Chair
Fashion Bed Group
Ficks Reed
Fine Art Lamps
Fitz & Floyd
Flexsteel
Frederick Cooper Lamps
Frederick Edward
Friedman Brothers
Fritz & LaRue Rugs
George Kovacs Lamps
Garcia Imports
Georgian Reproductions
Glass Arts
Great City Traders
Guildmaster
Habersham Plantation
Hammary
Hancock & Moore
Hekman
Helios Carpet
Hen Feathers
Hickory Chair
Hickory Fry
Hickory Hill
Hickory Leather
Highland House
High Point Desk
Hitchcock Chair
Hobe Sound Lamps
Hood
Hooker
House Of France
House Parts
Hyundai Furniture

JSF Industries
Jasper Cabinet
Johnston Casuals
John Richard Lamps
John Widdicomb
Karges
Kay Lyn
Keller
Kessler
Key City
Kimball
Kinder-Harris
Kincaid
Kingsdown Mattress
Kirk Steiff
Kittinger
La Barge
L & S Imports
Lane
Lane/Venture
Lea
Lees Carpet
Lenox Lamps
Lexington
Lloyd/Flanders
Lyon Shaw
Mannington Vinyl
Madison Square
Maitland Smith
Marbro Lamps
Masland Carpet
Masterlooms Carpet
McGuire
McKay Table Pad Co.
McKinley Leather
Michael Thomas
Michaels Co.
Millender
Millennium
Milliken Carpets
Mirror Fair
Moosehead
Motion Craft
Mottahedeh
Nathan Hale
Nichols & Stone
Norman Perry Lamps
O'Asian
Ohio Table Pad Co.

Old Hickory Tannery
Palazzetti
PAMA
Paoli
Pande Cameron Rugs
Paul Roberts
Payne Fabrics
Pearson
Pennsylvania Classics
Pennsylvania House
Port Royal
Pulaski
Rex
Ridgeway Clocks
Riverside
Robert Allen Fabrics
Rowe
Rustic Crafts
        Fireplaces
Salem Square
Saloom
Sarreid
Scalamandre Fabrics
Schumacher Fabrics
Sedgefield Lamps
SEE Imports
Selig
Shoal Creek Lighting
Shuford
Silvestri
Simply Southern
Sligh Furniture
Southampton
Southern
        Reproductions
Southwood
        Reproductions
Speer Lamps
Stanford
Stanley
Stanton Cooper
Stark Carpet
Statesville Chair
Statton
Stein World
Stiffel Lamps
Stoneleigh
Stroheim and Romann
Swaim Originals

Swan Brass Beds
Taylorsville
Taylor Woodcraft
Thayer Coggin
Thonet
Tianjin Philadelphia
        Carpets
Touch Of Brass
Tropitone
Trosby
Union National
Universal
Vanguard
Venture By Lane
Virginia House
Virginia Metalcrafters
Waterford Furniture
Waterford
        Crystal Lamps
Waverly Fabrics
Weathercraft By Lane
Weiman
Wellington Hall
Wesley Allen
        Brass Beds
Wesley Hall
Westgate Fabrics
Whitecraft Rattan
Wildwood Lamps
Winston
Woodard
Woodmark
Wright Table

Mitchell Gold Factory Outlet

Furniture Factory Outlet Shoppes
930 Hwy. 70 SW
Hickory, NC 28602

Phone:	(828) 261-0051	**Hours:**	M-Sat 9:30-5:00
Toll Free:	None	**E-mail:**	None
Fax:	None	**Web site:**	None

This is a true factory outlet for Mitchell Gold upholstery. Unfortunately, this source just isn't worth a visit. The upholstery here isn't very well made, and most of it is encased in horrible ill-fitting slipcovers. The furniture here is just a mess. If you want upholstery, you'd be far better off visiting just about any other source in the Hickory, NC, area.

Phone orders accepted:	No
Discount:	50%-60% off mfrs. suggested retail
Payment methods:	VISA, MC, personal checks
In-house financing available:	No
Deposits required:	Not applicable
Catalog available:	Not applicable
Clearance center:	Not applicable
Delivery:	Full service in-home delivery and set-up. Customer pays freight company directly for shipping costs.

Directions: From I-40, take exit #123 (Hwy. 321), and go north toward Hickory. After a few miles, take the Hwy. 70 exit, and go east. The Furniture Factory Outlet Shoppes is immediately on your left as you exit onto Hwy. 70.

Monroe's Furniture

I-95, Exit 77
Reevesville, SC 29471

Phone:	(843) 563-6300	**Hours:**	M-F 9:00-6:00, Sat 9:00-2:00
Toll Free:	None	**E-mail:**	monroes@mindspring.com
Fax:	(843) 563-3160	**Web site:**	www.monroesfurniture.com

Monroe's Furniture is located in Reevesville, SC, about an hour and a half drive southeast of Columbia, SC. They have a good selection of medium to high-end lines, including Lexington, Bradington Young, Henry Link, La Barge, and Hooker.

They don't have a clearance center or any floor samples or discontinued pieces on display. For this reason, there is no monetary advantage to visiting in person. They do have good deals on many lines sold over the phone, though. So, if you're planning to order your furniture by phone, definitely give this source a call to compare their prices.

Lines carried:	Please see page 234
Phone orders accepted:	Yes
Discount:	35%-50% off mfrs. suggested retail
Payment methods:	VISA, MC, personal checks
In-house financing available:	No
Deposits required:	1/3 deposit when order is placed, balance due when furniture is ready to be shipped
Catalog available:	No
Clearance center:	No
Delivery:	Full service in-home delivery and set-up. Customer pays freight company directly for shipping costs.

Directions: From I-95, take exit #77, and follow Hwy. 78 to Reevesville. Turn left at the first yellow light onto Rigby St. Monroe's Furniture is just beyond the railroad tracks on the left side of the road.

Monroe's Furniture (cont.)

Lines carried (cont.):

Acacia
Accentrics By Pulaski
Action By Lane
American Drew
American Heritage
Athens
Athol Table
Atlanta Glass
Baldwin Brass
Bard
Bassett
Benicia Beds
Bernard's
Bernhardt
Berryhill Prints
Best Chairs
Blacksmith Shop
Bob Timberlake
Bradington Young
Brown Street
Broyhill
Builtright Chair
Butler Specialty
Cambridge
Carlton McLendon
Carolina Furniture
Carolina Mirror
Carsons
Cebu
Century
Charles Sadek
Charleston Forge
Chromcraft
Classic Leather
Cochrane
Colonial
Cooper Classics
Corolla
Councill Craftsmen
Cox
Craftique
Craftmaster
Craftwork
Dinaire
Distinction Leather
Entree
Fairfield Chair
Fashion Bed Group
Fashion House

Fitz & Floyd
Georgia Chair
Glass Arts
Greene Brothers
Habersham Plantation
Hammary
Hancock & Moore
Harden
Hekman
Henkel-Harris
Henkel-Moore
Henry Link
Hickory Branch Lamps
Hickory Chair
Hickory White
Homecrest
Hooker
Howard Miller Clocks
Hunt Country
Hyundai Furniture
Jasper Cabinet
Jay Wilfred
Johnston Casuals
Karges
Kimball
Koch Originals
La-Z-Boy
La Barge
Lane
Lea
Leathercraft
Lee Table Pad
Lehigh
Leisters
Lexington
Lloyd/Flanders
Madison Square
Mobel
Nichols & Stone
Null Industries
P & P Chair
Parker Southern
Peters Revington
Powell
Pulaski
Rex
Riverside
Sam Moore
Sarreid

Sedgefield Lamps
Serta Bedding
Skillcraft
Sligh
South Cone Trading
Southern Craftsmen's Guild
Southwood Reproductions
Spring Air
Stanley
Statesville Chair
Statton
Stiffel Lamps
Sumter Cabinet
Superior
Taylor King
Temple
U. S. Furniture
Vanguard
Vaughan
Vaughan Bassett
Venture
Victorian Classics
Virginia House
Virginia Metalcrafters
Webb
Weiman
Wesley Allen Brass Beds
Wesley Hall
Wildwood
Willow Creek
Winston
Woodard

Morgan Stewart Galleries

Level 3
Hickory Furniture Mart
U. S. Hwy. 70 SE
Hickory, NC 28602

Phone:	**(828) 324-4040**	**Hours:**	**M-Sat 9:00-6:00**
Toll Free:	**(877) SOFA2GO**	**E-mail:**	**netsales@msgalleries.com**
Fax:	**(828) 324-4366**	**Web site:**	**www.msgalleries.com**

Morgan Stewart Galleries discounts their own line of upholstery every day, along with a number of other popular lines such as Richardson Brothers. Their standard discount on all lines is 40% off the mfrs. suggested retail, which really isn't as impressive as most of the other discounters in the Hickory area.

All of the furniture at this showroom is new first-quality. Rarely, they will put a floor sample or discontinued item on sale for about 50% off retail. Despite being factory-owned, this store is not a factory outlet for Morgan Stewart Upholstery.

There are many other stores in and around Hickory, NC, that will give you a much better deal on the brands carried here.

Lines carried:

Artistica	Great City Traders	Richardson Brothers	Sealy Mattress
Cambridge	Kingsdown	Ridgeway Clocks	
Coja Leather	Montaage	Robert Allen Fabrics	
Graham Thomas Classics	Morgan Stewart	Sarreid	

Phone orders accepted:	**Yes**
Discount:	**40% off mfrs. suggested retail**
Payment methods:	**VISA, MC, Discover, personal checks**
In-house financing available:	**No**
Deposits required:	**1/3 deposit when order is placed, balance due when furniture is ready to be shipped**
Catalog available:	**No**
Clearance center:	**No**
Delivery:	**Full service in-home delivery and set-up. Customer pays freight company directly for shipping costs.**

Directions: Please see *Hickory Furniture Mart* for complete directions.

Morgan Stewart Galleries

4316 Electric Rd.
Roanoke, VA 24018

Phone:	**(540) 989-8200**	**Hours:**	**M-Sat 9:00-6:00**
Toll Free:	**(877) SOFA2GO**	**E-mail:**	**netsales@msgalleries.com**
Fax:	**(540) 989-8400**	**Web site:**	**www.msgalleries.com**

Morgan Stewart Galleries discounts their own line of upholstery every day, along with a number of other popular lines such as Richardson Brothers. Their standard discount on all lines is 40% off the mfrs. suggested retail, which really isn't as impressive as most of the other discounters.

All of the furniture at this showroom is new first-quality. Rarely, they will put a floor sample or discontinued item on sale for about 50% off retail. Despite being factory-owned, this store is not a factory outlet for Morgan Stewart Upholstery.

There are many other discounters that will give you a much better deal on the brands carried here.

Lines carried:

Artistica	Great City Traders	Richardson Brothers	Sealy Mattress
Cambridge	Kingsdown	Ridgeway Clocks	
Coja Leather	Montaage	Robert Allen Fabrics	
Graham Thomas Classics	Morgan Stewart	Sarreid	

Phone orders accepted:	**Yes**
Discount:	**40% off mfrs. suggested retail**
Payment methods:	**VISA, MC, Discover, personal checks**
In-house financing available:	**No**
Deposits required:	**1/3 deposit when order is placed, balance due when furniture is ready to be shipped**
Catalog available:	**No**
Clearance center:	**No**
Delivery:	**Full service in-home delivery and set-up. Customer pays freight company directly for shipping costs.**

Directions: Please see *Hickory Furniture Mart* for complete directions.

Murrow Furniture Galleries

3514 S. College Rd.
Wilmington, NC 28406

Phone:	(910) 799-4010	**Hours:**	M-F 8:30-5:30, Sat 9:00-5:30
Toll Free:	None	**E-mail:**	None
Fax:	(910) 791-2791	**Web site:**	None

Murrow Furniture Galleries has a huge 45,000 square-foot store in Wilmington, NC, near the Atlantic coast. They have a very impressive stock of high-end lines such as Bernhardt, Lexington, Baker, Century, Thomasville, and others. Their discounts generally run from 40%-50% off retail.

The store doesn't have any floor samples or discontinued styles on display. This, combined with the fact that the store is more than a three-hour drive away from the main concentration of factory outlets and discounters in central North Carolina, make a personal visit impractical and unnecessary unless you live close by.

However, their prices on furniture sold by phone are quite good, and they have an excellent reputation for customer service. If you plan to order furniture by phone, definitely give this source a call and compare their prices.

Lines carried:	Please see page 238
Discount:	40%-50% off mfrs. suggested retail
Payment methods:	VISA, MC, personal checks
In-house financing available:	No
Deposits required:	50% deposit when order is placed, balance due when furniture is ready to be shipped
Catalog available:	No
Clearance center:	No
Delivery:	Full service in-home delivery and set-up. Customer pays freight company directly for shipping costs.

Directions: From I-40, take exit #420, and head south on Hwy. 132. After a few miles, Hwy. 132 will change name to S. College Rd. Murrow Furniture Galleries is about 10 miles south of the interstate on the right side of the road.

Murrow Furniture Galleries (cont.)

Lines carried:

Action By Lane
Ambiance
American Drew
American Heritage
Artistica
Artmark
Asmara Rugs
Baker
Baldwin Brass
Barcalounger
Bassett Mirror
Bernhardt
Bevan Funnell
Blacksmith Shop
Bob Timberlake
Bradington Young
Brass Beds Of Virginia
Braxton Culler
British Collectors Edition
Broyhill Premier
Cambridge
Canadel
Canterbury
Carolina Mirror
Carson's
Carver's Guild
Casa Bique
Casa Stradivari
Century
Charleston Forge
Chapman Lamps
Chelsea House
Chromcraft
Clark Casual
Classic Leather
Classic Rattan
Colonial Furniture
Councill Craftsmen
Cooper Classics
Country Affair
Cox
Craftique
Craftwork Guild
Crawford of Jamestown
Crystal Clear Lighting
Clyde Pearson
Design South
Decorative Crafts
Dillon

Distinction Leather
DSF Scandinavian Furn.
Dutailier
Ekornes
Ello
Elements By Grapevine
Emerson Et Cie
Emerson Leather
Fairfield Chair
Fashion Bed Group
Ficks Reed
Fine Arts Lamps
Frederick Cooper Lamps
Friedman Brothers
Garcia Imports
Georgian Furnishings
Glass Arts
Glober
Grace
Guildmaster
Habersham Plantation
Hammary
Hancock & Moore
Hart Country Shop
Hekman
Hen Feathers
Henry Link
Hickory Chair
Hickory White
Hill Mfg.
Hooker
Howard Miller Clocks
Hyundai Furniture
Jasper Cabinet
Jeffco
John Richard Lamps
John Widdicomb
Johnston Casuals
Jon Elliott
JTB
Kaiser Kuhn Lamps
Karges
Keller
Kimball
Kincaid
King Hickory
Knob Creek
Koch Originals
Koch & Lowy

Kravet Fabrics
La Barge
Lane
Lane/Venture
Lea
Leathermen's Guild
Lexington
Lillian August
Lloyd/Flanders
Lyon Shaw
McGuire
McKay Table Pads
Madison Square
Maitland Smith
Marbro Lamps
Maryland Classics
Masland Carpets
Mastercraft
Michaels
Michael Thomas
Motioncraft
Murray Feiss Lamps
National Mt. Airy
Natural Light
Nathan Hale
Nichols & Stone
Norman Perry Lamps
Ohio Table Pad Co.
Pande Cameron Rugs
Parker Southern
Paul Hansen Lamps
Pennsylvania House
Platt
Pulaski
Reliance Lamp
Rex
Ridgewood Furniture
Riverside
Robert Allen Fabrics
Royal Patina
Salem Square
Saloom
Sam Moore
Sarreid
S. Bent
Schott
Schumacher
Seabrook Wallcoverings
Sedgefield Lamps

Serta Mattress
Sherrill
Shuford
Sligh
Southern Furniture
Southampton
Southwood Reproductions
Speer Lamps
Stanley
Statesville Chair
Statton
Stiffel Lamps
Stroheim & Romann
Superior
Swaim
Taylor King
Taylorsville
Taylor Woodcraft
Temple Stewart
Thayer Coggin
Thomasville
Tianjin Philadelphia
   Carpets
Tradition France
Tradition House
Tropitone
Trosby
Universal
Vanguard
Vaughan
Venture By Lane
Vermont Tubbs
Villageois
Virginia House
Virginia Metalcrafters
Waterford Furniture
Wedgewood/Waterford
Weiman
Wellesley Guild
Wellington Hall
Wesley Allen Brass Beds
Wesley Hall
Whittemore-Sherrill
Wildwood
William Alan
Winston
Woodard
Woodmark
Wright Table Co.

Nite Furniture Co.

611 S. Green St.
Morganton, NC 28680

Phone:	(828) 437-1491	**Hours:**	M-Sat 9:00-6:00
Toll Free:	None	**E-mail:**	nite@ncnet.com
Fax:	(828) 437-1578	**Web site:**	www.ncnet.com/ncnw/nite.html

Nite Furniture Co. in Morganton, NC, has an enormous three story showroom covering one full city block. The main showroom has gorgeous high-end galleries for Councill-Craftsmen, Bernhardt, Thayer-Coggin, Hooker, Hekman, Classic Leather, Century, Sherrill, Henredon, and many other lines. There's also a smaller showroom across the street that has entertainment centers and some upholstery.

Nite Furniture will special order almost any brand over the phone at 30% to 50% off retail. They also sell furniture off the sales floor. New first-quality furniture in-stock is priced at 50%-60% off retail. There are also some floor samples and discontinued styles scattered around at 60%-75% off retail.

On my most recent visit here, I found a gorgeous discontinued sideboard from Councill-Craftsmen (pictured on the following page). This piece normally retails for $5,012.00, but Nite had this one for only $1,289.00, 74% off retail. It was brand-new and in first-quality condition.

If you plan to travel to North Carolina to shop, and you're looking for very high-end furniture, they have some terrific deals here on furniture you can take home that day. This store is definitely worth a visit. If you're planning to buy furniture over the phone, particularly very high-end lines, definitely give this source a call and compare their prices.

Lines carried:	**Please see page 241**
Phone orders accepted:	**Yes**
Discount:	**30%-75% off mfrs. suggested retail**
Payment methods:	**Personal checks. No credit cards.**
In-house financing available:	**No**
Deposits required:	**50% deposit when order is placed, balance due when furniture is ready to be shipped**
Catalog available:	**No**
Clearance center:	**No**
Delivery:	**Full service in-home delivery and set-up. Customer pays freight company directly for shipping costs.**

Directions: From I-40, take exit #105, and go north on Hwy. 18. After about 3 miles, you'll see Nite Furniture on your right in downtown Morganton, NC.

Nite Furniture Co. (cont.)

Nite Furniture Co.

Sideboard from Councill-Craftsmen

Retail: $5,012.00   Discounted price: $1,289.00
Savings at Nite Furniture: $3,723.00 = 74% off retail

Nite Furniture Co. (cont.)

Lines carried:

A La Carte
American Drew
American Leather
Andrew Pearson Designs
Ardley Hall
Arlington House
Artistica Metal Designs
Baldwin Brass
Baldwin Wood Products
Barcalounger
Bassett
Bernhardt
Bradington Young
Brass Beds Of America
Brasscrafters
Broyhill
Butler Specialty
C. R. Laine
Cal-Style
Carolina Mirror
Casa Bique
Casa Stradivari
Century
Chapman
Charleston Forge
Chromcraft
Classic Leather
Clark Casual
Clayton Marcus
Coja Leatherline
Councill Craftsmen
Councill Desk
Corsican
Cox
Craftique
Craftwork Guild
Crawford Of Jamestown
Crystal Clear Lighting
Davis & Davis Rugs
Decorative Crafts
Design South Furniture
Dinaire
Distinction Leather
Dresher Brass Beds
Elements By Grapevine
Emerson Et Cie
Fairfield Chair
Fashion Bed Group
Fine Arts Lamps

Flexsteel
Frederick Cooper Lamps
Fremarc
French Heritage
Friedman Brothers
George Kovacs
Georgian Reproductions
Glass Arts
Great City Traders
Gros Fillex
Guildmasters
Habersham Plantation
Hammary
Hancock & Moore
Hekman
Henry Link
Hickory Chair
Hickory Leather
Highland House
Hooker
Howard Miller Clocks
Iron Classics
J. Royale Furniture
Jasper Cabinet
Key City Furniture
Kincaid
Kinder Harris
Kingsdown
La Barge
Le Meuble Villabeois
Leathercraft
Lexington
Link Taylor
Lloyd/Flanders
Lyon Shaw
Masland Carpets
McKay Table Pads
Meadowcraft
Med Lift Chairs
Michael Thomas
Millennium
Moosehead
Motioncraft By Sherrill
Nichols & Stone
Noble Mission Solid Oak
Norman Perry Lamps
Old Hickory Tannery
Palecek
Parlance

Paul Hansen
Pavilion
Pennsylvania Classics
Pennsylvania House
Pulaski
Regency Leather
Rex
Richardson Brothers
Ridgeway Clocks
Riverside
Rowe
Royal Patina
Sam Moore
Sarreid
Schoonbeck
Sedgefield Lamps
Sherrill
Sligh
Skillcraft
Southern Furniture Co.
Southern Reproductions
Southwood Reproductions
Speer Lamps
Stanley
Statesville Chair
Stiffel Lamps
S. Bent
Style
Sumter Cabinet
Telescope
Thayer Coggin
The Hide Company
Tom Seeley Furniture
Tropitone
Universal
Vanguard
Vaughan
Venture By Lane
Virginia House
Virginia Metalcrafters
Vogue Rattan
Waterford Crystal
Waterford Furniture
Weiman
Wellington Hall
Wesley Allen
Wesley Hall
Westwood Lighting
Wildwood

Winners Only
Winston
Woodard
Woodmark
Wright Table Co.

Pennsylvania House Gallery

The Atrium
430 S. Main St.
High Point, NC 27260

Phone:	**(336) 886-5200**	**Hours:**	**M-F 9:00-6:00, Sat 9:00-5:00**
Toll Free:	**None**	**E-mail:**	**collgall@northstate.net**
Fax:	**(336) 886-5204**	**Web site:**	**www.theatrium.com**

The Pennsylvania House Gallery at the Atrium Furniture Mall in High Point isn't a factory outlet, although it is factory-owned. They have no floor samples or discontinued furniture here. However, they will special order any Pennsylvania House furniture at 50% off the retail price.

If you're interested in ordering Pennsylvania House over the phone, you should definitely check the prices here.

Phone orders accepted:	**Yes**
Discount:	**50% off mfrs. suggested retail**
Payment methods:	**VISA, MC, personal checks**
In-house financing available:	**No**
Deposits required:	**50% deposit when order is placed, balance due when furniture is ready to be shipped**
Catalog available:	**No**
Clearance center:	**No**
Delivery:	**Full service in-home delivery and set-up. Customer pays freight company directly for shipping costs.**

Directions: **Pennsylvania House Gallery is located inside the Atrium complex in downtown High Point. Please see *The Atrium* for complete directions.**

Pennsylvania House Factory Outlet

2629 Ramada Rd.
Burlington, NC 27215

Phone:	**(336) 226-8466**	**Hours:**	**M-F 9:00-5:30, Sat 9:00-5:00**
Toll Free:	**None**	**E-mail:**	**None**
Fax:	**(336) 226-8468**	**Web site:**	**None**

The Pennsylvania House Factory Outlet is in Burlington, NC, about an hour's drive east of High Point, NC. The outlet has a nice selection of case goods and upholstery. There is also quite a bit of Lexington and Stanley furniture in stock. Lexington and Stanley have no factory-owned factory outlets of their own, so this is one of the outlets they use to liquidate floor samples and discontinued pieces.

The discounts here run from 40%-52% off retail. Most of the furniture in stock is new and first-quality, and priced at about 50% off retail. Don't forget to check the back room where the seconds and some discontinued styles are kept. The discounts there run 75%-80% off retail.

On my most recent visit here, I found a great deal on a Pennsylvania House solid cherry chest on chest (pictured on the following page). This piece normally retails for $1,890.00, but the outlet had this one for $980.00. It was a stock overrun in new first-quality condition.

The outlet does accept phone orders for a variety of lines. If you plan to be in the High Point area, this outlet (along with the Hickory White and Classic Leather outlets right next door) is well worth a visit. If you plan to order furniture over the phone, particularly Pennsylvania House, you should definitely compare prices here.

Lines carried:

American Drew	Cox	Hammary	Parker Southern
Art Gallery	Craftique	Hekman	Pennsylvania House
Athens	Crawford	Henry Link	Riverside
Barcalounger	Design South	Howard Miller Clocks	Sealy Upholstery
Bassett	Ducks Unlimited	Lexington	Stanley
Bob Timberlake	Flexsteel	Ligo	Universal
Butler Specialty	Grace Iron	Nord	Woodmere Upholstery

Phone orders accepted:	**Yes**
Discount:	**40%-80% off mfrs. suggested retail**
Payment methods:	**VISA, MC, personal checks**
In-house financing available:	**No**
Deposits required:	**50% deposit when order is placed, balance due when furniture is ready to be shipped**
Catalog available:	**No**
Clearance center:	**Not applicable**
Delivery:	**Full service in-home delivery and set-up. Customer pays freight company directly for shipping costs.**

Directions: From I-85, take exit #143. The Pennsylvania House Factory Outlet is right off the interstate on the frontage road.

Pennsylvania House Factory Outlet (cont.)

Pennsylvania House Factory Outlet in Burlington, NC

Solid cherry chest-on-chest from Pennsylvania House

Retail: $1,890.00   Discounted price: $980.00
Savings at the Pennsylvania House Factory Outlet: $910.00 = 48% off retail

Plaza Furniture Gallery

241 Timberbrook Lane
Granite Falls, NC 28630

Phone:	(828) 396-8150		**Hours:**	M-Sat 9:00-5:00
Toll Free:	None		**E-mail:**	None
Fax:	(828) 396-8151		**Web site:**	None

Plaza Furniture Gallery doesn't have much in stock, but they are a good source to compare by phone.

Lines carried:

Action By Lane	Clark Casual	Kroehler	Richardson Brothers
American Drew	Clayton Marcus	Lane	Riverside
American Impressions	Cochrane	Lea	Robert Abbey
American Of Martinsville	Comfort Designs	Leather Mark	Salterini
Andrea By Sadek	Cooper Classics	Leathermen's Guild	Sam Moore
Arthur Court	Craftmaster	Lexington	Sarreid
Artistry Designs	Crawford	Marlo	Seay Furniture
Athens	Elements By Grapevine	McKay Table Pad	South Sea Rattan
Austin	Fairfield Chair	Miller Desk	Straits
Barcalounger	Fairmont Designs	Morgan Stewart	Stylecraft Lamps
Bassett	Flexsteel	Napp Deady	Taylorsville Upholstery
Bassett Mirror	Fortune Wicker	Null Industries	Temple
Berkline	Grace	Old Hickory Tannery	U. S. Furniture
Blacksmith Shop	Great City Traders	Orderest Bedding	Universal
Bob Timberlake	Hammary	Palecek	Uwharrie Chair
Bon Art	Hen Feathers	Paragon Pictures	Vaughan
Brasscrafters	Henry Link	Park Place Furniture	Vaughan Bassett
Broyhill	Hickory Hill	Passport	Walker Marlen
Cape Craftsmen	Hyundai Furniture	Peters Revington	Weiman
Carolina Mirror	Interior Images By Salterini	Phillip Reinisch	Willow Creek Collection
Charleston Forge	Jasper Cabinet	Powell	Winners Only
Chatham County	Johnston Casuals	Pulaski	Yesteryear Wicker
Chromcraft	Keller	Rex	

Phone orders accepted:	Yes
Discount:	35%-50% off mfrs. suggested retail
Payment methods:	VISA, MC, personal checks
In-house financing available:	No
Deposits required:	50% deposit when order is placed, balance due when furniture is ready to be shipped
Catalog available:	No
Clearance center:	No
Delivery:	Full service in-home delivery and set-up. Customer pays freight company directly for shipping costs.

Directions: From I-40, take exit #123 and drive north on Hwy. 321 to Granite Falls. Plaza Furniture Gallery is on the left side of the road.

Priba Furniture Sales and Interiors

210 Stage Coach Trail
Greensboro, NC 27415

Phone:	**(336) 855-9034**	**Hours:**	**M-F 9:00-5:30, Sat 9:00-5:00**
Toll Free:	**(800) 296-7977**	**E-mail:**	**pribafurniture@worldnet.att.net**
Fax:	**(336) 855-1370**	**Web site:**	**None**

Priba Furniture Sales and Interiors is located in Greensboro, NC, just north of High Point. They have a good selection of medium to high-end lines, including Wellington Hall, Century, and Bernhardt.

They don't have a clearance center or any floor samples or discontinued pieces on display. For this reason, there is no monetary advantage to visiting in person. They do have great deals on many lines sold over the phone, though. So, if you're planning to order your furniture by phone, definitely give this source a call to compare their prices.

Phone orders accepted:	**Yes**
Discount:	**35%-48% off mfrs. suggested retail**
Payment methods:	**VISA, MC, personal checks**
In-house financing available:	**No**
Deposits required:	**50% deposit when order is placed, balance due when furniture is ready to be shipped**
Catalog available:	**No**
Clearance center:	**No**
Delivery:	**Full service in-home delivery and set-up. Customer pays freight company directly for shipping costs.**

Directions: **From I-40, take exit #212, and go north 1/2 mile on Chimney Rock Rd. Turn right on Market St. Go 3/10 of a mile, and turn left on Stage Coach Trail. Priba Furniture Sales and Interiors is on the right.**

Priba Furniture Sales and Interiors (cont.)

Lines carried:

Action By Lane
American Drew
American Of High Point
Ardley Hall
Artistica Metal Designs
As You Like It Lamps
Baldwin Brass
Barcalounger
Bassett
Bernhardt
Bevan Funnell
Blacksmith Shop
Bradburn Gallery
Bradington Young
Braxton Culler
Brown Jordan
Broyhill
CBS
CEBU
C. R. Laine
Carver's Guild
Century
Cal-Style
Canal Dover
Carolina Tables
Carousel
Carsons
Carter
Casa Bique
Casa Stradivari
Chapman Lamps
Charleston Forge
Chatham County
Chelsea House
Chromcraft
Clark Casual
Classic Gallery
Classic Leather
Clayton Marcus
Conover
Councill Craftsmen
Cox
Craftique
Craftwork Guild
Creative Metal
Customcraft
Davis & Davis Rugs
Designs South
Dillon

Dinaire
Directional
Distinction Leather
Ekornes
Ello
Emerson et Cie
Emerson Leather
Fairfield Chair
Fashion Bed Group
Ficks Reed
Flat Rock
Frederick Cooper Lamps
Fremarc
Friedman Brothers
Froelich Company
Glass Arts
Guy Chaddock
Habersham Plantation
Hamilton Hall
Hammary
Hekman
Henry Link
Hickory Chair
Hickory Hill
Hickory White
Highborn Manor
Hitchcock Chair
Hobe Sound
Hood
Hooker
HTB
Hyundai Furniture
Jasper Cabinet
Johnston Casuals
John Richards
John Widdicomb
Kaiser Kuhn Lamps
Karges
Kessler
Kincaid
Kingsdown
La Barge
Lane
Lane/Venture
Leathercraft
Leathermen's Guild
Leather Shop
Lee Industries
Lennox

Lexington
Lillian August
Lloyd/Flanders
Lowenstein
Lyon Shaw
Madison
Madison Square
Maitland Smith
Marboro Lamps
Mar-Kel Lighting
Maryland Classics
Masland Carpets
McGuire
McKay Table Pad
McKinley Leather
Meadowcraft
Motioncraft
Murray Feiss
Nathan Hale
National Mt. Airy
Natuzzi Leather
Nichols & Stone
Nora Fenton
Norman Perry
North Hickory
Ohio Table Pad
Old Hickory Furniture
Old Hickory Tannery
PAMA
Paul Hansen
Pearson
Pennsylvania Classics
Peters Revington
Pinetique
Plant Plant
Port Royal
Porter
Pouliot Designs
Pulaski
Quoizel
Rembrandt
Remington Lamps
Reprodux
Rex
Richardson Brothers
Ridgeway Clocks
Rosecore
Royal Patina
Sedgefield Leather

Salem Square
Sam Moore
Samsonite
Sarreid
Sealy Mattress
Serta Mattress
Sherrill
Shuford
Sligh
Southampton
Southwood
        Reproductions
Spring Air
Stanford
Stanley
Stanton Cooper
Stark Carpets
Statesville Chair
Statton
Stiffel Lamps
Stone International
St. Timothy
Style Upholstery
Swaim
Thayer Coggin
Theodore & Alexander
Thomasville
Tradition House
Tropitone
Trosby
Trouvailles
Universal
Vanguard
Venture By Lane
Virginia House
Virginia Metalcrafters
Waterford
Weiman
Wellington Hall
Wesley Allen
Wesley Hall
Wildwood Lamps
William Alan
Winston
Woodard
Woodmark Originals
Yorkshire House

Pulaski Furniture Factory Outlet

3012 Parquet Rd.
Dalton, GA 30720

Phone:	**(706) 259-1824**	**Hours:**	**M-Sat 9:00-6:00**
Toll Free:	**None**	**E-mail:**	**None**
Fax:	**(706) 259-3404**	**Web site:**	**None**

The Pulaski Furniture Factory Outlet is located in Dalton, GA, the carpet factory outlet capital of the world. Dalton is about an hour's drive northwest of Atlanta on I-75.

This outlet has primarily case goods: bedroom sets, dining room sets, chests, etc. There is a small amount of upholstery, primarily occasional chairs. There is also some wrought iron, primarily end tables and dining room sets.

The discounts here run from 60%-75% off retail. The stock is primarily floor samples, discontinued styles, overruns, customer returns, and a very limited number of seconds. The vast majority of the furniture here is in new first-quality condition.

Although it isn't as well known as some of its competition, Pulaski Furniture has a very nice product. If you're ever in the Atlanta area, this outlet is well worth a side trip.

Phone orders accepted:	**No**
Discount:	**60%-75% off mfrs. suggested retail**
Payment methods:	**Personal checks. No credit cards.**
In-house financing available:	**No**
Deposits required:	**Not applicable**
Catalog available:	**Not applicable**
Clearance center:	**Not applicable**
Delivery:	**Customer must make own arrangements to take furniture home.**

Directions: From I-75, take exit #135, and go one block west. When the road dead-ends after about 100 yards, turn right. After another 100 yards, turn left on Parquet Rd. The Pulaski Furniture Factory Outlet is about 1/2 mile down on the right.

Quality Furniture Market Of Lenoir

2034 Hickory Blvd. SW
Lenoir, NC 28645

Phone:	(828) 728-2946	**Hours:**	M-Sat 8:30-5:00
Toll Free:	None	**E-mail:**	qualityfurniture@twave.net
Fax:	(828) 726-0226	**Web site:**	www.qualityfurnituremarket.com

Quality Furniture Market Of Lenoir has been in business for over forty years in Lenoir, NC. They have a huge store. In fact, it's a lot bigger than it looks from the outside. There is a huge basement gallery that extends under the building and most of the parking lot.

They do sell furniture off the floor, but you generally don't receive any better discount in person than you do by phone. They do have a very few floor samples and discontinued pieces scattered around priced at about 60%-70% off retail, but there really aren't enough to justify a personal visit.

Should you decide to stop in, you should know that they do not allow children in the galleries. They do have a nice, supervised play area in the front lobby of the store for children to stay in while you shop. This is the only North Carolina discounter I'm aware of who has this policy.

Another drawback with this source is the fact that they require full payment with all orders rather than going by the standard procedure with North Carolina furniture discounters of paying 1/3 to 1/2 up front and the remainder when your furniture is ready to be shipped to you. Paying the entire order in advance leaves the discounter with no financial incentive to speed your order and should be normally be avoided.

One saving grace in this particular instance, though, is that this source does accept credit cards. If you do decide to order from this source, be sure to get a written delivery date. If the furniture is not delivered on time for any reason, your credit card issuer should allow you to contest the charge on your credit card in accordance with federal law. This leverage is frequently sufficient to ensure on-time delivery.

This source has been in business for many years and has an excellent reputation for service. They do also have excellent bargains. Anyone ordering furniture by phone should definitely compare prices here.

Lines carried:	Please see page 251
Phone orders accepted:	Yes
Discount:	50%-70% off mfrs. suggested retail
Payment methods:	VISA, MC, Discover, personal checks
In-house financing available:	No
Deposits required:	Full payment required with order
Catalog available:	Yes
Clearance center:	No
Delivery:	Full service in-home delivery and set-up. Customer pays freight company directly for shipping costs.

Directions: From I-40, take exit #123 and drive north on Hwy. 321 toward Lenoir, NC. Quality Furniture Market is on the left side of the highway just before you get into Lenoir.

Quality Furniture Market Of Lenoir (cont.)

Quality Furniture Market Of Lenoir

Quality Furniture Market Of Lenoir (cont.)

Lines carried:

Action By Lane
A La Carte
Alexander Julian
Allusions
Ambiance Imports
American Drew
American Of Martinsville
Andrew Pearson Designs
Ardley Hall
Arnold Palmer Collection
Artisan House
Artistica
Artmark Fabrics
Artmax
Aston Garrett
Austin Sculptures
Baldwin Brass
Barcalounger
Bassett
Bassett Mirror
Bean Station
Bernhardt
Best Chair
Blacksmith Shop
Bob Timberlake
Boling Chair
Bradburn Galleries
Brett Austin
British Traditions
Broyhill
Builtright
Butler Specialty
Cambridge Lamps
Carlton McLendon
Carolina Mirror
Carson's Of High Point
Carver's Guild
Casa Bique
Casa Rustica
Casual Lamps
Chapman Lamps
Charleston Forge
Chatham County
Chrishawn
Chromcraft
Clark Casuals
Classic Leather
Clayton Marcus
Cochrane

Comfort Designs
Conover Chair
Correll
Cox
Craftique
Crawford Of Jamestown
Creative Wood & Metal
Crystal Clear Lamps
Customcraft
D & F Wicker
Dale Tiffany Lamps
Davis & Davis Rugs
Decorative Arts
Decorative Crafts
Design Guild
Design South
Dinaire
Distinctive Designs
Dillon
Ekornes
Elements By Grapevine
Emerson et Cie
European Pine
Fabrica
Fairfield Chair
Fashion Bed Group
Fiam
Ficks Reed
Fine Art Lamps
Fitz & Floyd China
Frederick Cooper
Fur Designs
Gaby's Shoppe
Garcia Imports
Georgia Art Lighting
Glass Arts
Grace
Great City Traders
Guild Master
Hart Associates
Hammary
Hekman
Highland House
Hitchcock Chair
Homecrest
Hooker
Howard Miller Clocks
JSF Industries
J. Royale

James R. Cooper, Ltd.
Jamestown Manor
        By Statton
Jasper Cabinet
Jeffco
John Richards Collection
Kimball
Kinder Harris
Kingsley-Bates
Koch & Lowy
La Barge
Lane
Lane/Venture
Lexington
Lloyd/Flanders
Lyon Shaw
M & H Seating
MER Rugs
Mikhail Darafeev
Miller Desk
Minoff Lamps
Mirror Fair
Montaage
Murray Feiss
NDI
Natural Light Lamps
Nautica By Lexington
New River Artisans
Norman Perry
Oklahoma Imports
Old Hickory Tannery
Ohio Table Pad Co.
Oriental Lacquer
Osborne & Little
Pacific Rim
Palecek
Paper White
Payne
Pearson
Pennsylvania Classics
Pennsylvania House
Peters Revington
Phillip Jeffries
Plant Plant
Pompeii
Powell
Pulaski
Raymond Waites
        By Lane

Reliance Lamps
Remi
Rex
Ridgeway Clocks
Riverside
Robert Allen Fabrics
SEE Imports
Sagefield Leather
St. Timothy
Sarreid
2nd Ave.
Sedgefield Lamps
Serta Bedding
Sherrill
Sidney Arthur
Skillcraft
Sligh
South Sea Rattan
Speer Lamps
Spinning Wheel Rugs
Spring Air
Stanley
Statesville Chair
Stiffel Lamps
Style Seating
Sustainable Lifestyles
Tapestries Ltd.
Thayer Coggin
Thief River Linens
Tomlin Lamps
Trica
Tropitone
Universal
Uttermost
Uwharrie Chair Co.
Vanguard
Velco
Venture By Lane
Virginia Metalcrafters
Visions
Waterford
Weiman
Wellington Hall
Wesley Allen Brass Beds
Wildwood
Winners Only
Winston
Woodard
Younger

Randy's Furniture Gallery

U. S. Hwy. # 21 N.
Troutman, NC 28010

Phone:	**(704) 873-5162**	**Hours:**	**M-F 9:00-5:30, Sat 9:00-4:00**
Toll Free:	**(800) 873-5162**	**E-mail:**	**None**
Fax:	**None**	**Web site:**	**None**

Randy's Furniture Gallery is located in Troutman, NC, about one half-hour's drive east of Hickory, NC. They have a good selection of medium to high-end lines, including Lexington, Lane, American Drew, and Stanley.

They don't have a clearance center or any floor samples or discontinued pieces on display. For this reason, there is no monetary advantage to visiting in person. They do have great deals on many lines sold over the phone, though. So, if you're planning to order your furniture by phone, definitely give this source a call to compare their prices.

Lines carried:

Action By Lane	Fairfield Chair	Lane	Pulaski
American Drew	Five Rivers Craft	Lane/Venture	Rex
Bassett	Flexsteel	Lea	Riverside
Bassett Juvenile	Florida Furniture	Lexington	SK Furniture
Broyhill	Hekman	Ligo	Somma
Carolina Mirror	Henry Link	Link Taylor	Stanley
Cambridge Chair	High Point Furniture	Masterfield	Stiffel Lamps
Chatham County	Hood	Mersman	Taylorsville Upholstery
Cochrane	Hooker	M & H Seating	Universal
Craftique	Howard Miller Clocks	Miller Desk	Vaughan
Craftmaster	Jasper Cabinet	Morgan Stewart	Vaughan Bassett
Denny Lamps	Jetton	National Mt. Airy	Virginia House
Emerald Craft	Johnston Bench Works	Null Industries	
England/Corsair	Kimball	Ohio Table Pads	
Fashion House	Kingsdown	Palliser	

Phone orders accepted:	Yes
Discount:	35%-50% off mfrs. suggested retail
Payment methods:	VISA, MC, personal checks
In-house financing available:	No
Deposits required:	20% deposit when order is placed, balance due when furniture is ready to be shipped
Catalog available:	No
Clearance center:	No
Delivery:	Full service in-home delivery and set-up. Customer pays freight company directly for shipping costs.

Directions: From I-77, take exit #42, and go 4 1/2 miles east on Hwy. 21 N. into downtown Troutman. Randy's Furniture Gallery is on the left.

Repete's

Furniture Factory Outlet Shoppes
930 Hwy. 70 SW
Hickory, NC 28602

Phone:	(828) 328-9440	**Hours:**	M-Sat 9:30-5:00
Toll Free:	None	**E-mail:**	repetes@twave.net
Fax:	None	**Web site:**	www.hfnet.com/repetes/

Repete's specializes in upholstery, although they do have some case goods in stock as well. They have a nice selection of medium to high-end chairs and sofas in stock at good prices: about 50% off retail. If you're looking for a wing-back chair you can pick up today, this is a good source to visit. Virtually all of their stock is in new first-quality condition.

They will also special order, again at about 50% off retail for the brands they carry. This source is worth a visit if you're traveling to Hickory, NC, to buy upholstery.

Lines carried:

Alexvale
Bassett Mirror
C. R. Laine
Capri
Lee
Southwood

Phone orders accepted:	Yes
Discount:	50% off mfrs. suggested retail
Payment methods:	VISA, MC, personal checks
In-house financing available:	Yes
Deposits required:	50% deposit when order is placed, balance due when furniture is ready to be shipped
Catalog available:	No
Clearance center:	No
Delivery:	Full service in-home delivery and set-up. Customer pays freight company directly for shipping costs.

Directions: From I-40, take exit #123 (Hwy. 321), and go north toward Hickory. After a few miles, take the Hwy. 70 exit, and go east. The Furniture Factory Outlet Shoppes is immediately on your left as you exit onto Hwy. 70.

Rhoney Furniture Clearance Center

2401 Hwy. 70 SW
Hickory, NC 28602

Phone:	**(828) 328-2034**	**Hours:**	**M-Sat 9:00-5:00**
Toll Free:	**None**	**E-mail:**	**rhoney@abts.net**
Fax:	**(828) 328-2036**	**Web site:**	**www.hickoryonline.com/rhoneyfurniture**

Rhoney Furniture Clearance Center has a nice stock of floor samples, discontinued styles, and returns from their showrooms next door and at the Hickory Furniture Mart. They have good selection of upholstery and case goods.

The discounts run about 60%-70% off retail. On my most recent visit here, I found a great deal on a Thomasville wing-back chair (pictured on the following page). It normally retails for $792.00, but this one was on sale for only $297.00. This chair was on sale because the fabric (but not the style) had been discontinued. It was in perfect first-quality condition.

This outlet, though small compared to many others in the area, has some very good deals. It's worth a visit if you're traveling to the Hickory, NC, area.

Lines carried:	**Please see page 256**
Phone orders accepted:	**No**
Discount:	**60%-70% off mfrs. suggested retail**
Payment methods:	**Personal checks. No credit cards.**
In-house financing available:	**No**
Deposits required:	**Not applicable**
Catalog available:	**Not applicable**
Clearance center:	**Not applicable**
Delivery:	**Full service in-home delivery and set-up. Customer pays freight company directly for shipping costs.**

Directions: From I-40, take exit #123 (Hwy. 321), and head north. Take the Hwy. 64-70 exit, and head west on Hwy. 64-70. Rhoney Furniture Clearance Center will be about one mile down on the left side of the road, just to the left of the main store.

Rhoney Furniture Clearance Center (cont.)

Rhoney Furniture Clearance Center

Wing-back chair from Thomasville

Retail: $792.00   Discounted price: $297.00
Savings at Rhoney Furniture Clearance Center: $495.00 = 63% off retail

Rhoney Furniture Clearance Center (cont.)

Lines carried:

Accentrics By Pulaski
Action By Lane
American Drew
American Of Martinsville
Artmaster
Artisans Brass
As You Like It Lamps
Austin
Barcalounger
Bassett
Bassett Mirror
Berkshire
Beth Wiseman
Blacksmith Shop
Bob Timberlake
Bradington Young
Brass Beds Of America
Broyhill
C. R. Laine
Caro-Craft
Carolina Mirror
Carolina Table
Casa Bique
Casa Stradivari
Castilian
Chatham County
Chelsea House
Chromcraft
Clayton Marcus
Clover Lamps
Clyde Pearson
Cochrane
Comfort Designs
Councill Craftsmen
Cox
Craftique
Craftwork Guild
Creative Accents
Daystrom
Decorative Crafts
Distinction Leather
Dixie
Dresher
Emerson Leather
Entree By La Barge
Ficks Reed
Fine Arts Lamps
Floral Arts
Freeman

Gerald Stein
Georgian Reproductions
Hale
Hammary
Hekman
HTB Contemporaries
Henry Link
Hickory Leather
Hickory Tavern
Hickory White
Highland House
Hitchcock Chair
Hooker
Howard Miller Clocks
Interlude
Jasper Cabinet
Jeffco
Keller
Key City
Kimball
Kincaid
King Hickory
Lane
Lane/Venture
Lea
Leathercraft
Leathermen's Guild
Leisters
Lenox Lamps
Lexington
Lyon Shaw
Maddox
Madison Square
Mersman
Morgan Stewart
Morris Greenspan
McKay Table Pad
Nichols & Stone
North Hickory
Ohio Table Pad
Old Hickory Tannery
Pulaski
Remington
Riverside
Rosenthal Netter
Sarreid
Selig
Serta
Sierra Arts

Sligh
Stakmore
Stanley
Stanton Cooper
Statton
Stiffel Lamps
Stoneville
Stratford
Style Upholstery
Swann Brass
Temple
Thayer Coggin
Thomasville
Timmerman
Toyo
Tropitone
Universal
Vanguard Studios
Vaughan
Venture By Lane
Virginia House
Weiman
Wellington Hall
Wesley Allen Brass Beds
Whitecraft
Wildwood Lamps
William Alan
Windsor Art
Woodmark

Rhoney Furniture House

Level 2
Hickory Furniture Mart
U. S. Hwy. 70 SE
Hickory, NC 28602

Phone:	**(828) 328-8688**	**Hours:**	**M-Sat 9:00-6:00**
Toll Free:	**None**	**E-mail:**	**rhoney@abts.net**
Fax:	**(828) 328-2036**	**Web site:**	**www.hickoryonline.com/rhoneyfurniture**

Rhoney Furniture House at the Hickory Furniture Mart has large galleries for Clayton Marcus and American Drew. They carry many other lines, too, all discounted 40%-50% off retail.

They charge the same price for furniture purchased over the phone as they do for furniture purchased in person, so there isn't much reason to travel directly to the store.

They do have a nice clearance center next door to their other showroom a few miles away, where they sell off floor samples, discontinued styles, and returns from their showrooms here and at the Hickory Furniture Mart. It's definitely worth a visit if you're traveling to the Hickory, NC, area.

Lines carried:	Please see page 258
Phone orders accepted:	Yes
Discount:	40%-50% off mfrs. suggested retail
Payment methods:	Personal checks. No credit cards.
In-house financing available:	No
Deposits required:	25% deposit when order is placed, balance due when furniture is ready to be shipped
Catalog available:	No
Clearance center:	Yes -- See *Rhoney Furniture Clearance Center*
Delivery:	Full service in-home delivery and set-up. Customer pays freight company directly for shipping costs.

Directions: Please see *Hickory Furniture Mart* for complete directions.

Rhoney Furniture House (cont.)

Lines carried:

Accentrics By Pulaski
Action By Lane
American Drew
American Of Martinsville
Artmaster
Artisans Brass
As You Like It Lamps
Austin
Barcalounger
Bassett
Bassett Mirror
Berkshire
Beth Wiseman
Blacksmith Shop
Bob Timberlake
Bradington Young
Brass Beds Of America
Broyhill
C. R. Laine
Caro-Craft
Carolina Mirror
Carolina Table
Casa Bique
Casa Stradivari
Castilian
Chatham County
Chelsea House
Chromcraft
Clayton Marcus
Clover Lamps
Clyde Pearson
Cochrane
Comfort Designs
Councill Craftsmen
Cox
Craftique
Craftwork Guild
Creative Accents
Daystrom
Decorative Crafts
Distinction Leather
Dixie
Dresher
Emerson Leather
Entree By La Barge
Ficks Reed
Fine Arts Lamps
Floral Arts
Freeman

Gerald Stein
Georgian Reproductions
Hale
Hammary
Hekman
HTB Contemporaries
Henry Link
Hickory Leather
Hickory Tavern
Hickory White
Highland House
Hitchcock Chair
Hooker
Howard Miller Clocks
Interlude
Jasper Cabinet
Jeffco
Keller
Key City
Kimball
Kincaid
King Hickory
Lane
Lane/Venture
Lea
Leathercraft
Leathermen's Guild
Leisters
Lenox Lamps
Lexington
Lyon Shaw
Maddox
Madison Square
Mersman
Morgan Stewart
Morris Greenspan
McKay Table Pad
Nichols & Stone
North Hickory
Ohio Table Pad
Old Hickory Tannery
Pulaski
Remington
Riverside
Rosenthal Netter
Sarreid
Selig
Serta
Sierra Arts

Sligh
Stakmore
Stanley
Stanton Cooper
Statton
Stiffel Lamps
Stoneville
Stratford
Style Upholstery
Swann Brass
Temple
Thayer Coggin
Thomasville
Timmerman
Toyo
Tropitone
Universal
Vanguard Studios
Vaughan
Venture By Lane
Virginia House
Weiman
Wellington Hall
Wesley Allen Brass Beds
Whitecraft
Wildwood Lamps
William Alan
Windsor Art
Woodmark
Young-Hinkle

Rhoney Furniture House

2401 Hwy. 70 SW
Hickory, NC 28602

Phone:	**(828) 328-2034**	**Hours:**	**M-Sat 9:00-5:00**
Toll Free:	**None**	**E-mail:**	**rhoney@abts.net**
Fax:	**(828) 328-2036**	**Web site:**	**www.hickoryonline.com/rhoneyfurniture**

Rhoney Furniture House in Hickory has a very nice store with a large Thomasville gallery. They carry many other lines, too, all discounted 40%-50% off retail.

They charge the same price for furniture purchased over the phone as they do for furniture purchased in person, so there isn't much reason to travel directly to the store.

They do have a nice clearance center right next door, where they sell off floor samples, discontinued styles, and returns from their showrooms here and at the Hickory Furniture Mart. It's worth a visit if you're traveling to the Hickory, NC, area.

Lines carried:	**Please see page 260**
Phone orders accepted:	**Yes**
Discount:	**40%-50% off mfrs. suggested retail**
Payment methods:	**Personal checks. No credit cards.**
In-house financing available:	**No**
Deposits required:	**25% deposit when order is placed, balance due when furniture is ready to be shipped**
Catalog available:	**No**
Clearance center:	**Yes -- See *Rhoney Furniture Clearance Center***
Delivery:	**Full service in-home delivery and set-up. Customer pays freight company directly for shipping costs.**

Directions: From I-40, take exit #123 (Hwy. 321), and head north. Take the Hwy. 64-70 exit, and head west on Hwy. 64-70. Rhoney's will be about one mile down on the left side of the road.

Rhoney Furniture House (cont.)

Lines carried:

Accentrics By Pulaski
Action By Lane
American Drew
American Of Martinsville
Artmaster
Artisans Brass
As You Like It Lamps
Austin
Barcalounger
Bassett
Bassett Mirror
Berkshire
Beth Wiseman
Blacksmith Shop
Bob Timberlake
Bradington Young
Brass Beds Of America
Broyhill
C. R. Laine
Caro-Craft
Carolina Mirror
Carolina Table
Casa Bique
Casa Stradivari
Castilian
Chatham County
Chelsea House
Chromcraft
Clayton Marcus
Clover Lamps
Clyde Pearson
Cochrane
Comfort Designs
Councill Craftsmen
Cox
Craftique
Craftwork Guild
Creative Accents
Daystrom
Decorative Crafts
Distinction Leather
Dixie
Dresher
Emerson Leather
Entree By La Barge
Ficks Reed
Fine Arts Lamps
Floral Arts
Freeman

Gerald Stein
Georgian Reproductions
Hale
Hammary
Hekman
HTB Contemporaries
Henry Link
Hickory Leather
Hickory Tavern
Hickory White
Highland House
Hitchcock Chair
Hooker
Howard Miller Clocks
Interlude
Jasper Cabinet
Jeffco
Keller
Key City
Kimball
Kincaid
King Hickory
Lane
Lane/Venture
Lea
Leathercraft
Leathermen's Guild
Leisters
Lenox Lamps
Lexington
Lyon Shaw
Maddox
Madison Square
Mersman
Morgan Stewart
Morris Greenspan
McKay Table Pad
Nichols & Stone
North Hickory
Ohio Table Pad
Old Hickory Tannery
Pulaski
Remington
Riverside
Rosenthal Netter
Sarreid
Selig
Serta
Sierra Arts

Sligh
Stakmore
Stanley
Stanton Cooper
Statton
Stiffel Lamps
Stoneville
Stratford
Style Upholstery
Swann Brass
Temple
Thayer Coggin
Thomasville
Timmerman
Toyo
Tropitone
Universal
Vanguard Studios
Vaughan
Venture By Lane
Virginia House
Weiman
Wellington Hall
Wesley Allen Brass Beds
Whitecraft
Wildwood Lamps
William Alan
Windsor Art
Woodmark
Young-Hinkle

Robert Bergelin Co.

Level 3
Hickory Furniture Mart
U. S. Hwy. 70 SE
Hickory, NC 28602

Phone:	**(828) 345-1500**	**Hours:**	**M-Sat 9:00-6:00**
Toll Free:	**(800) 345-1599**	**E-mail:**	**rbcfurn@hci.net**
Fax:	**(828) 345-0203**	**Web site:**	**www.rbcfurn.com**

The Robert Bergelin Company is a small 3rd generation family-owned furniture factory in Morganton, NC, that sells directly to the public through their two showrooms at the Hickory Furniture Mart in Hickory and the Atrium Furniture Mall in High Point. They also accept phone orders and ship nationwide.

You can call either showroom for a color brochure showing all of their available styles, or you can view a complete catalog with photos on their Web site.

Most of their furniture is case goods. Their only upholstered items are a mission-style sofa and chair and two upholstered dining room chair styles. They don't have a wide variety of styles, but they do carry the most popular pieces on the market: mission-style beds, poster-beds, pedestal dining room tables, sleigh beds, etc. You'll notice pieces in their catalog that are nearly identical to some of the most popular styles from Stickley, Lexington, and Alexander Julian, among others.

Their quality is quite good. Their prices, while generally a bit better than retail, aren't necessarily as good as the prices you'll get on comparable items from major manufacturers such as Lexington and Alexander Julian that can be purchased at deep discounts. The savings here vary a lot depending on the particular piece you're looking at and the alternatives to that particular piece that are available on the market.

This source may or may not save you any money. The quality and service certainly won't let you down. It is well worth anyone's time to request a free copy of their brochure or check their Web site and compare their prices with other manufacturers.

Warning: in any discussion of price comparisons to other manufacturers, I have found that the staff at this source consistently evades answering any questions about price and instead gives lectures on how much better their quality is than any other manufacturers. You should know that while the Robert Bergelin Co. certainly has very fine quality products, they are no better than similar products available from Stickley, Richardson Bros., Lexington, and other comparable high-end lines. Focus your decisions on price alone.

Phone orders accepted:	**Yes**
Discount:	**Varies**
Payment methods:	**Personal checks. No credit cards.**
In-house financing available:	**No**
Deposits required:	**50% deposit when order is placed, balance due when furniture is ready to be shipped**
Catalog available:	**Yes**
Clearance center:	**No**
Delivery:	**Full service in-home delivery and set-up. Customer pays freight company directly for shipping costs.**

Directions: Please see *Hickory Furniture Mart* for complete directions.

Robert Bergelin Co.

The Atrium
430 S. Main St.
High Point, NC 27260

Phone:	**(336) 889-2189**	**Hours:**	**M-F 9:00-6:00, Sat 9:00-5:00**
Toll Free:	**(888) 296-7977**	**E-mail:**	**rbcfurn@hci.net**
Fax:	**(336) 889-2190**	**Web site:**	**www.rbcfurn.com**

The Robert Bergelin Company is a small 3rd generation family-owned furniture factory in Morganton, NC, that sells directly to the public through their two showrooms at the Hickory Furniture Mart in Hickory and the Atrium Furniture Mall in High Point. They also accept phone orders and ship nationwide.

You can call either showroom for a color brochure showing all of their available styles, or you can view a complete catalog with photos on their Web site.

Most of their furniture is case goods. Their only upholstered items are a mission-style sofa and chair and two upholstered dining room chair styles. They don't have a wide variety of styles, but they do carry the most popular pieces on the market: mission-style beds, poster-beds, pedestal dining room tables, sleigh beds, etc. You'll notice pieces in their catalog that are nearly identical to some of the most popular styles from Stickley, Lexington, and Alexander Julian, among others.

Their quality is quite good. Their prices, while generally a bit better than retail, aren't necessarily as good as the prices you'll get on comparable items from major manufacturers such as Lexington and Alexander Julian that can be purchased at deep discounts. The savings here vary a lot depending on the particular piece you're looking at and the alternatives to that particular piece that are available on the market.

This source may or may not save you any money. The quality and service certainly won't let you down. It is well worth anyone's time to request a free copy of their brochure or check their Web site and compare their prices with other manufacturers.

Warning: in any discussion of price comparisons to other manufacturers, I have found that the staff at this source consistently evades answering any questions about price and instead gives lectures on how much better their quality is than any other manufacturers. You should know that while the Robert Bergelin Co. certainly has very fine quality products, they are <u>no better</u> than similar products available from Stickley, Richardson Bros., Lexington, and other comparable high-end lines. Focus your decisions on price alone.

Phone orders accepted:	**Yes**
Discount:	**Varies**
Payment methods:	**Personal checks. No credit cards.**
In-house financing available:	**No**
Deposits required:	**50% deposit when order is placed, balance due when furniture is ready to be shipped**
Catalog available:	**Yes**
Clearance center:	**No**
Delivery:	**Full service in-home delivery and set-up. Customer pays freight company directly for shipping costs.**

Directions: Please see *The Atrium* for complete directions.

Rooms Now

Furnitureland South
4th Floor
5635 Riverdale Dr.
Jamestown, NC 27282

Phone:	**(336) 841-4328**	**Hours:**	**M-W & Sat 8:30-5:30, Th-F 8:30-8:30**
Toll Free:	**None**	**E-mail:**	**Dick_Cottam@furniturelandsouth.com**
Fax:	**(336) 841-7026**	**Web site:**	**www.furniturelandsouth.com**

Rooms Now is the clearance center for Furnitureland South. It occupies the entire fifth floor of the new Furnitureland South building.

It's huge, and it has an enormous selection of overstocks, floor samples, customer returns, and discontinued styles from all of the lines carried by Furnitureland South at 60%-70% off retail. Virtually all of the furniture here is in new first-quality condition. There's an even mix of upholstery and case goods.

This is a terrific source to visit if you plan to be in High Point personally to shop for furniture.

Phone orders accepted:	**Yes**
Discount:	**60%-70% off mfrs. suggested retail**
Payment methods:	**Personal checks. No credit cards.**
In-house financing available:	**No**
Deposits required:	**Not applicable**
Catalog available:	**Not applicable**
Clearance center:	**Not applicable**
Delivery:	**Full service in-home delivery and set-up. Customer pays freight company directly for shipping costs.**

Directions: From I-85, take exit #118, and turn west on Business 85. Furnitureland South will be about one mile down on your right at the Riverdale Rd. exit.

Rose Furniture

916 Finch Ave.
High Point, NC 27261

Phone:	(336) 886-6050	**Hours:**	M-F 8:30-5:00, Sat 8:30-4:00
Toll Free:	None	**E-mail:**	None
Fax:	(336) 886-5055	**Web site:**	www.rosefurniture.com

Rose Furniture is one of the oldest and best-established furniture discounters in the High Point area, if not the entire state of North Carolina. Their discounts are quite good, about 30%-50% off retail, depending on the line. They also have periodic sales throughout the year, including their annual winter sale each February when they discount everything an extra 10% off.

There are no discontinued items or floor samples at this location. All such clearance furniture is sent to their two nearby clearance centers.

If you plan to order your furniture by phone, you may wish to compare prices here. If you plan to visit the High Point area to shop, you'll get a better deal at Rose's two clearance centers nearby.

Lines carried:	**Please see pages 266-269**
Phone orders accepted:	Yes
Discount:	30%-50% off mfrs. suggested retail
Payment methods:	Personal checks. No credit cards.
In-house financing available:	No
Deposits required:	30% deposit when order is placed, balance due when furniture is ready to be shipped
Catalog available:	No
Clearance center:	Yes-See *Rose Furniture Main Clearance Ctr.* and *Rose Furniture Leather & Office Clearance Ctr.*
Delivery:	Full service in-home delivery and set-up. Customer pays freight company directly for shipping costs.

Directions: From Business I-85, take the Surrett Dr. exit in High Point. Go south about 100 yards, and turn right on Finch Ave. Rose Furniture will be immediately on your right.

Rose Furniture (cont.)

Rose Furniture

Rose Furniture (cont.)

Lines carried:

A Thing Of Beauty
A. A. Laun
AGI Industries
AKKO
Acacia Furniture
Accents By Gary Parlin
Accessories Abroad
Accessories International
Action By Lane
Aesthetics & Artifacts
Alan White
Alexandra Diez
Albert's Art & Mirror
Allan Copley
Allibert
Alliston Dize
Allusions
Ambience Lighting
American Drew
American Heritage
American Of High Point
American Impressions
American Mirror
Amish Country Collection
Andrew Knob & Son Ltd.
Andrew Pearson Design
Ann Gish
Arbek
Ardley Hall
Arlington House
Art Gallery
Art Image
Arte De Mexico
Arte Lore
Artisian House Inc.
Artistica Metal Designs
Artmark Fabrics
As You Like It Lamps
Ashley Furniture
Ashley Manor
Athens Furniture
Austin Sculptures
BDT Furniture Dist.
B. Berger
Bacon & Wing
Balangier
Baldwin Brass
Banks Coldstone
Barcalounger

Barn Door
Barrow
Bashian Rugs
Bassett Mirror
Basta Sole
Bauer Lamp
Beach Manufacturing
Bean Station
Benchcraft Rattan
Benchcraft
Benecia Beds
Bentwood
Berkline
Bernhardt
Best Chairs
Bestar
Bevan Funnell
Bob Timberlake
Boling
Botanica
Boyd
Bradburn Gallery
Bradington Young
Brady
Brasscrafters
Braxton Culler
Brett Austin Ltd.
British Traditions
Brown Jordan
Broyhill
Brunschwig & Fils
Builtright
Bush
Butler Specialty
CBS Imports
C. R. Laine
CSD Furniture
CTH Sherrill
Cal-Bear
Cal-Style
Cambridge Lamps
Canadel
Canal Dover
Candella Lighting Co.
Canterbury
Cape Craftsmen
Capel Rugs
Capital Garden Products
Capitol Leather

Carlton McLendon
Carolina Mirror
Carolina Table
      Of Hickory
Carolina's Choice
Carson's
Carter
Carver's Guild
Casa Bique
Casa Rustica
Casa Stradivari
Cassady
Cassidy West
Cast Classics
Castilian Imports
Casual Creations
Casual Lamps
Century
Chapman
Chairworks
Charleston Forge
Chatham County
Chatham Reproductions
Chelsea House
Chrishawn Distinctive Art
Christian Aubrey
Chromcraft
Czech Point
Claire Murray
Clark Casual
Classic Gallery
Classic Georgian
Classic Leather
Classic Rattan
Classic Traditions
Clayton Marcus
Coach House Antiques
Cochrane
Coco Island
Collections 85 Inc.
Collezione Europa
Colonial Furniture
Comfort Designs
Conant Ball
Conestoga Wood
Conover
Cooper Classics
Corsican
Councill Craftsmen

Cowtan & Tout
Cox
Craftique
Craftwork Guild
Crawford
Creations By Hill
Creative Elegance
Creative Expressions
Creative Metal & Wood
Crown Crafts
Cruzer Enterprises
Crystal Clear Lamps
Curry & Co.
Custom Style
D & F Wicker & Rattan
DMI Furniture
D-Scan/Danwood
Dale Tiffany
Dar/Ran
Dauphine Mirror
Davis Conference Group
Davis & Davis Rugs
Dawson
Decorative Arts
Decorative Crafts
Del Jour Art
Denunzio
Design Guild Lamps
Designmaster
Design Systems
Dillon
Dinaire
Directional
Distinction Leather
Double D Home Coll.
Double R Leather
Douglas
Dr. Livingstone
Dreamweavers Rugs
Ducks Unlimited
Duralee Fabrics
Dura-Wicker
Dutailier
E. R. Buck
Eagle Craft
Ecco
Edward Art
Ekornes
Elements By Grapevine

Rose Furniture (cont.)

Lines carried (cont.):

Elizabeth Marshall
Elliott's Designs
Ellis Home Furnishings
Ello
Emerson Et Cie
Entree
Ercole
Excel Office
Excelsior
Executive Furniture
525
Fald
Fairfield Chair
Fashion Bed Group
Feizy
Fer Forge
FIAM/FORMA Designs
Ficks Reed
Fine Arts Lamps
Fitz & Floyd
Flat Rock
Flexsteel
Floral Art
Florita Nova
Frank & Son
Franklin Chairs
Frederick Cooper Lamps
Fremarc
Friedman Brothers Mirrors
Friendship Upholstery
Froelich Corporation
Fun With Furs Inc.
Gaby's Shoppe
Gaines Mfg. Co.
Game Room
Garcia Imports
Gatco Brass
General Store
George Kovacs
Georgian Furnishings
Giovanni Turano
Glass Arts
Glen Allen
Global Views
Glober
Golden Rabbit
Great City Traders
Greene's Handtied Canopies
Greeff Fabrics

Guild Master
Guildmaster Art
H & H Furniture Mfg.
HZD Collections
H. Potter
Habersham Plantation
Habitat International
Hale
Hale Of Vermont
Hammary
Harris Marcus
Harris Strong
Hart
Hatteras Hammocks
Hearthside Classics
Hekman
Hen Feathers
Henkel Harris
Henkel Moore
Henry Link
Heritage Haus Furniture
Historic Golf Prints
Hickory Chair
Hickory Hill
Hickory Leather
Hickory White
Hide Company
High Point Desk
Hilda Flack
Hollywoods
Homecrest Aluminum
Homefront
Home Treasures
Hooker
Howard Miller Clocks
Hoyle Industries
Hunt Courtry
Hunter Douglas
Hyundai Furniture
Inter Art
Interline Italia
Intrada
Italmond
JDI
JSF
Jasper Cabinet
Jasper Desk
Jay Willifred
Jeffco

Jenigere
John Boos & Co.
John McGill
John Richard Collection
Johnston Casuals
Johnston Tombigbee
    Furniture
J. D. Originals
J. K. Reed
J. Royale
J. Sidney Smith
JRW Contemporary
Kaiser Kuhn Lighting
Karges
Karress Fine Linens
Kaywood Shutter Co.
Kennebunk Weavers
Kessler
Kimball
Kinder Harris
Kings Antique
Kingsdown
Kingsley Bate
Klaussner
Koch & Lowy
Koch Originals
Koko Linens
Kravet Fabrics
Kushwood
La Barge
Lady Bug
Lane
Lane/Venture
Lawrence Unlimited
Lea
Leathermen's Guild
Leatherworks
Lee Jofa Fabrics
Leeazanne Lamps
Legacy Designs
Leisters
Lennox
Lexington
Ligo
Linon Imports
Linrene
Lister By GeeBro
Lloyd/Flanders
Lotus Arts

Lucia Designs
LUI Corporation
Luigi Bormioli
Luminart Pictures
Lyon Shaw
Madison Furniture
Madison Square
Mahogany Heirlooms
Maitland Smith
Majestic Mirror
Mallin
Manchester Wood
Manor Traditions
Marbro Lamp
Mario Industries
Markel Lighting
Marshall James
Maryland Classics
Masland Carpets
Massoud
Master Design
Masterfield
McEnroe
McGuire
McKay Table Pad
McKinley Leather
Mer Corp.
Meadowcraft
Merit Wish
Miami Metal
Michael Showalter
    Designs
Michael Thomas
Mikhail Darafeev
Milano Sculpture
Millennium
Miller Desk
Minoff Lamps
Mirror Fair
Mobel
Montaage
Montibello Collection
Moon Collections
Moosehead
Morgan & Co.
Morgan Stewart
Motioncraft
Mottahedeh
Murray Feiss

Rose Furniture (cont.)

Lines carried (cont.):

Mystic Valley Traders
NDI
Nagykery Imports
Najarian
Natural Light
Natuzzi Leather
Nessen
New River Artisan
Nichols & Stone
Nora Fenton
Nord
Norman Perry Lamps
Null Industries
OEM
Oak Heritage
Oggetti
Ohio Table Pad
Oklahoma Importing
Old Hickory Furniture
Old Hickory Tannery
Oriental Lacquer
Otto Zenke
Outdoor Lifestyle
P. Collins
P & P Chair Co.
Pace
Pacific Coast Lighting
Palazetti
Palecek
Paper White
Peoli
Paragon Pictures
Parker Southern
Paul Robert
Paul Robinson
Pawley's Island Co.
Payne Fabrics
Payne Street
Peacock Alley
Pearson
Pennsylvania Classics
Pentaura Limited
Peoplelounger
Peters Revington
Phillip Reinisch Co.
Phillips Collection
Phillips Furniture Co.
Phoenix Art Group
Piage Elite Mirrors

Pine-tique
Pinnacle
Plant Plant
Plantation Comfort
Platt Collection
Powell Collections
Precedent
Presidential
Preview
Privilege House
Profile Lighting
Pulaski
Raymond Waites
       Collection
Regency Furnishings
Reliance Lamps
Rembrandt Lamp
Remington Lamps
Reprocrafters Inc.
Rex
Richardson Brothers
Richmond Lighting
Ridgeway Clocks
Ridgewood
Riverbend Ironworks
Riverside
Robert Allen Fabrics
Robert M. Weiss
Robinson Furniture
Rosalco
Rosenbaum Fine Arts
Rowe
Royal Haeger Lamp
Royal Patina Inc.
Royce Corporation
Rug Barn
Rug Market
SEE Imports
S. Harris & Co.
Salem Square
Sam Moore
Samsonite
Samuel Lawrence
San Diego Designs
San Miguel Trading
Sanderson
Sarreid
Scalamandre
Scangift Ltd.

Scheibe Co.
Schnadig
Schumacher
Schweiger
Seay
Sealy
Second Impressions
Sedgefield
Sedgewick
Serta
Shady Lady
Sharut
Shelter
Shuford
Sigla
Signature Rugs
Silvestri
Sinclair-Burke
Skillcraft
Sligh
Soicher-Marin Fine Arts
South Sea Rattan
Southampton
Southern Craftsmen Guild
Southern Of Conover
Southern Reproductions
Southern Table
Southwood Reproductions
Spectrum Ltd.
Speer
Spring Air
St. Timothy
Stakmore
Stanford
Stanley
Statesville Chair
Statton
Stein World
Stewart Furniture
Stiffel Lamps
Stone Art
Stone County Ironworks
Stone International
Stoneville Furniture
Straits
Stratford
Stratolounger
Stroheim & Romann
Style Upholstery Co.

Summer Classics
Superior
Swaim
Sylvan Lake
Tapestries Ltd.
Taylorsville Upholstery
Telescope
Temple
Temple Stuart
Thayer Coggin
Tianjin-Philadelphia
Timmerman
Tomlin
Toulemond Bochart
Town Square Furniture
Toyo
Traditional Heirlooms
Triune
Tropitone
Trowbridge Gallery
Tufenkian
       Tibetan Carpets
Tyndale
U. S. Furniture
Ultimate Lamps
Union City CHair
Unique Originals
Universal
Uttermost Mirrors
Uwharrie Chair
Van Teal
Vanguard
Vaughan
Vaughan Bassett
Veneman
Venetian Traders
Venture By Lane
Vietri
Villageois
Virginia Galleries
Virginia House
Virginia Metalcrafters
Visual Comfort
W. King Ambler
Walker Marlen
Wallstreet Design
Wambold Furniture
Waterford Lamps
Waterford Furniture

Rose Furniture (cont.)

Lines carried (cont.):

Waverly
Wellington Hall
Wesley Allen Brass Beds
Wesley Hall
Westgate Fabrics
Westwood Lighting
Whitaker Furniture
Whitecraft
Wildwood Lamps
William Alan
Windsor Designs
Winners Only
Winston
Woodard
Woodmark Originals
World Glass
Yesteryear Wicker
Younger
Zrike Co.

Rose Furniture Main Clearance Center

1813 S. Main St.
High Point, NC

Phone:	(336) 886-8525	**Hours:**	**M-F 9:00-5:30, Sat 9:00-5:00**
Toll Free:	**None**	**E-mail:**	**None**
Fax:	**None**	**Web site:**	**www.roseclearance.com**

This is the main clearance center for nearby Rose Furniture. It's huge. Rose's clearance center is much larger than many discounters' entire operations.

They have a good selection of medium to high-end from all the lines Rose carries. The discounts here generally run about 40%-50% off retail. Virtually all of the furniture here are floor samples, discontinued styles, or customer returns. Most of it is in first-quality condition.

On my last visit here, I found a good deal on a Hekman china cabinet (pictured on the following page). The retail on this piece is normally $9,175.00, but this piece was on sale for only $5,646.00. It was a floor sample in first-quality condition.

If you're in the High Point area, this clearance center is worth a look. Do be sure to check out the other factory outlets and clearance centers in High Point and nearby Thomasville before you buy here, though. The prices here are good, but not great. Many other sources nearby will offer you a better bargain.

Lines carried:	**Please see pages 266-269**
Phone orders accepted:	**No**
Discount:	**40%-60% off mfrs. suggested retail**
Payment methods:	**Personal checks. No credit cards.**
In-house financing available:	**No**
Deposits required:	**Not applicable**
Catalog available:	**Not applicable**
Clearance center:	**Not applicable**
Delivery:	**Full service in-home delivery and set-up. Customer pays freight company directly for shipping costs.**

Directions: **From I-85, take exit #111 (Hwy. 311), and head northwest into High Point. After several miles, when you reach downtown High Point, Hwy. 311 will become S. Main St. Rose Furniture Main Clearance Center is on the right side of Main St., across from Kagan's Furniture.**

Rose Furniture Main Clearance Center (cont.)

Rose Furniture Main Clearance Center

China cabinet from Hekman

Retail: $9,175.00   Discounted price: $5,646.00
Savings at Rose Furniture Main Clearance Center: $3,529.00 = 38% off retail

Rose Furniture Leather & Office Clearance Center

2017 S. College Dr.
High Point, NC 27261

Phone:	**(336) 886-6092**	**Hours:**	**M-F 9:00-5:00, Sat 9:00-5:30**
Toll Free:	**None**	**E-mail:**	**None**
Fax:	**None**	**Web site:**	**www.roseclearance.com**

    This is the leather and office furniture clearance center for nearby Rose Furniture. It has quite a good selection of leather sofas and chairs, office groups, and executive desks. Most of the stock here is high-end from brands such as Flexsteel, Woodmark, and Distinctive Designs.

    Virtually all of the furniture here are floor samples, discontinued styles, or customer returns. Most of it is in first-quality condition.

    If you're in the High Point area, this clearance center is worth a look. Do be sure to check out the other factory outlets and clearance centers in High Point and nearby Thomasville before you buy here, though. The prices here are good, but not great. Many other sources nearby will offer you a better bargain.

Lines carried:	**Please see pages 266-269**
Phone orders accepted:	**No**
Discount:	**50%-60% off mfrs. suggested retail**
Payment methods:	**Personal checks. No credit cards.**
In-house financing available:	**No**
Deposits required:	**Not applicable**
Catalog available:	**Not applicable**
Clearance center:	**Not applicable**
Delivery:	**Full service in-home delivery and set-up. Customer pays freight company directly for shipping costs.**

Directions: **From I-85, take exit #111 (Hwy. 311), and head northwest into High Point. After several miles, when you reach downtown High Point, Hwy. 311 will become S. Main St. Rose Furniture Leather & Office Clearance Center is on the left side of Main St., next to Kagan's Furniture.**

Seconds & Samples

Furniture Factory Outlet Shoppes
930 Hwy. 70 SW
Hickory, NC 28602

Phone:	(828) 267-2108	**Hours:**	M-Sat 9:30-5:00
Toll Free:	None	**E-mail:**	None
Fax:	None	**Web site:**	None

Seconds & Samples carries medium to high-end case goods and upholstery purchased at area factories and trade shows. The discounts run from 60%-70% off retail. The brands here vary widely and change constantly.

The quality and prices here are a bit uneven. There are some really great bargains mixed in with the so-so deals. This source is worth a visit if you're in the Hickory, NC, area.

Lines carried:	**Varies**
Phone orders accepted:	**No**
Discount:	**60%-70% off mfrs. suggested retail**
Payment methods:	**VISA, MC, personal checks**
In-house financing available:	**No**
Deposits required:	**Not applicable**
Catalog available:	**Not applicable**
Clearance center:	**Not applicable**
Delivery:	**Full service in-home delivery and set-up. Customer pays freight company directly for shipping costs.**

Directions: From I-40, take exit #123 (Hwy. 321), and go north toward Hickory. After a few miles, take the Hwy. 70 exit, and go east. The Furniture Factory Outlet Shoppes is immediately on your left as you exit onto Hwy. 70.

Sedgewick Rattan Factory Outlet

Furniture Clearance Center
66 Hwy. 321 NW
Hickory, NC 28601

Phone:	**(828) 323-1558**	**Hours:**	**M-F 9:00-6:00, Sat 9:00-5:00**
Toll Free:	**None**	**E-mail:**	**None**
Fax:	**(828) 326-9846**	**Web site:**	**None**

The Furniture Clearance Center in Hickory, NC, is a combined factory-owned factory outlet for Drexel-Heritage, La Barge, Maitland-Smith, Sedgewick Rattan, Carrington Court, and Craftique. It occupies a huge warehouse building.

The stock consists of floor samples, customer returns, photography samples, and discontinued styles. Virtually all of the furniture here is in new first-quality condition. The discounts run from 50%-70% off retail, with most pieces around 60% off.   They usually have a big sale every January and May when they mark most pieces an extra 10%-20% off.

If you travel to Hickory to shop for high-end traditional furniture, this outlet is a "must visit"!

Phone orders accepted:	**No**
Discount:	**50%-70% off mfrs. suggested retail**
Payment methods:	**VISA, MC, personal checks**
In-house financing available:	**No**
Deposits required:	**Not applicable**
Catalog available:	**Not applicable**
Clearance center:	**Not applicable**
Delivery:	**Full service in-home delivery and set-up. Customer pays freight company directly for shipping costs.**

Directions: From I-40, take exit #123 and drive north on Hwy. 321 into Hickory.

Shaw Furniture Clearance Center

131 W. Academy St.
Randleman, NC 27317

Phone:	**(336) 498-2628**	**Hours:**	**M-F 9:00-5:30, Sat 9:00-5:00**
Toll Free:	**None**	**E-mail:**	**None**
Fax:	**(336) 498-2439**	**Web site:**	**None**

Shaw Furniture Clearance Center liquidates floor samples, discontinued items, and customer returns from the two main Shaw's showrooms and their huge telephone sales operation.

The clearance center occupies an enormous warehouse right behind the two main showrooms. Most items are in new first-quality condition, and the discounts run about 60%-70% off retail. On my most recent visit here, I found a great deal on a Councill Craftsmen solid mahogany dresser (pictured on the following page). The normal retail on this piece is $3,830.00, but this one was marked down to $1,299.00. It was brand new and in perfect condition. This particular piece was ordered incorrectly for a customer who refused to accept it. It had no damage or flaws whatsoever.

Shaw Furniture Clearance Center has pieces from Thomasville, Hooker, Hekman, Harden, Bernhardt, Century, Hickory White, and most of the over 300 other lines they carry. If you are traveling to Hickory or Thomasville to shop for furniture, a side trip to this clearance center is a must.

Lines carried:	**Over 300 lines carried. Please call for details.**
Phone orders accepted:	**No**
Discount:	**50%-70% off mfrs. suggested retail**
Payment methods:	**VISA, MC, personal checks**
In-house financing available:	**Yes**
Deposits required:	**Not applicable**
Catalog available:	**Not applicable**
Clearance center:	**Not applicable**
Delivery:	**Full service in-home delivery and set-up. Customer pays freight company directly for shipping costs.**

Directions: From I-85, take exit #122, and head south on Hwy. 220. After about 13 miles, you'll come to Randleman. Follow the signs to Shaw's. The clearance center is behind the two main showrooms.

Shaw Furniture Clearance Center (cont.)

Shaw Furniture Clearance Center

Solid mahogany dresser from Councill-Craftsmen

Retail: $3,830.00   Discounted price: $1,299.00
Savings at Shaw Furniture Clearance Center: $2,531.00 = 66% off retail

Shaw Furniture Galleries

131 W. Academy St.
Randleman, NC 27317

Phone:	**(336) 498-2628**	**Hours:**	**M-F 9:00-5:30, Sat 9:00-5:00**
Toll Free:	**None**	**E-mail:**	**shaw@northstate.net**
Fax:	**(336) 498-2439**	**Web site:**	**www.shawfurniture.com**

Shaw's is one of the best-established, and most interesting, furniture discounters you'll ever come across. They have an excellent reputation for good prices and customer service. I receive letters every day from readers who want to give their opinion of a particular discounter. Shaw's has consistently gotten high votes from readers all over the U. S. They have an very good reputation for going out of their way to make sure their customers are happy with their furniture.

The main store is located in the old Randleman schoolhouse. Mr. Shaw went to school here himself, and when he heard later on that the building might be torn down, he bought it and moved his original store inside. The store has a nice selection of Lexington, Hooker, Hekman, Harden, and many other high-end lines. Shaw's doesn't publish a list of the lines they carry, but I've found they can order just about anything.

There is also a new showroom next door with extensive galleries for Thomasville, Bernhardt, Century, Hickory Chair, and Hickory White.

Most of the furniture inside the main galleries is new first-quality. The discounts run about 30%-50% off retail. Most lines run from 40%-50% off retail. There are a few discontinued styles and floor samples scattered around priced at 60%-70% of retail.

On my most recent visit here, I found a terrific deal on a discontinued Lexington solid maple and cherry "Victorian Mansions" bedroom set (pictured on the following pages). The bed, nightstand, dresser, mirror, and armoire normally retail together for $11,089.00. Shaw's had this set for only $4,992.00.

Most of the discontinued styles, floor samples, and customer returns are kept in Shaw's huge warehouse clearance center right behind the two main showrooms.

If you will be in the Hickory, NC, area to shop for furniture, you should definitely make the 10 minute drive to Randleman to check out Shaw's. If you plan to order your furniture by phone, you should definitely compare Shaw's prices.

Lines carried:	**Over 300 lines carried. Please call for details.**
Phone orders accepted:	**Yes**
Discount:	**30%-50% off mfrs. suggested retail**
Payment methods:	**VISA, MC, personal checks**
In-house financing available:	**Yes**
Deposits required:	**30% deposit when order is placed, balance due when furniture is ready to be shipped**
Catalog available:	**No**
Clearance center:	**Yes - See *Shaw Furniture Clearance Center***
Delivery:	**Full service in-home delivery and set-up. Customer pays freight company directly for shipping costs.**

Directions: From I-85, take exit #122, and head south on Hwy. 220. After about 13 miles, you'll come to Randleman. Follow the signs to Shaw's.

Shaw Furniture Galleries (cont.)

Shaw Furniture Galleries main showroom -- the old Randleman schoolhouse

Shaw Furniture Galleries new showroom

Shaw Furniture Galleries (cont.)

Shaw Furniture Galleries entrance sign

Victorian Mansions solid maple and cherry bedroom set from Lexington

Retail: $11,089.00   Discounted price: $4,992.00
Savings at Shaw Furniture Galleries: $6,097.00 = 55% off retail

Skyland Furniture Galleries

Hwy. 321 N.
Blowing Rock, NC 28661

Phone:	(828) 758-4580	**Hours:**	M-Sat 9:00-5:00
Toll Free:	None	**E-mail:**	None
Fax:	None	**Web site:**	None

Skyland Furniture Galleries is located about an hour's drive north of Hickory, NC, in Blowing Rock. They have a good selection of medium to high-end lines, including Lexington, Bernhardt, Universal, and Hooker.

They don't have a clearance center or any floor samples or discontinued pieces on display. For this reason, there is no monetary advantage to visiting in person. They do have good deals on many lines sold over the phone, though. So, if you're planning to order your furniture by phone, definitely give this source a call to compare their prices.

Phone orders accepted:	Yes
Discount:	40%-60% off mfrs. suggested retail
Payment methods:	VISA, MC, personal checks
In-house financing available:	No
Deposits required:	50% deposit when order is placed, balance due when furniture is ready to be shipped
Catalog available:	No
Clearance center:	No
Delivery:	Full service in-home delivery and set-up. Customer pays freight company directly for shipping costs.

Directions: From I-40, take exit #123 and drive north on Hwy. 321 about 44 miles to Blowing Rock. Skyland Furniture Galleries is on the right side of the road.

Skyland Furniture Galleries (cont.)

Lines carried:

Action By Lane
American Drew
American Furniture
       Galleries
American Heritage
American Of Martinsville
Athol
Austin Sculptures
Bassett
Benicia Beds
Berkline
Bernhardt
Bob Timberlake
Brown Street
Broyhill
Builtright Chair
C. R. Laine
Carlton McLendon
Capitol Victorian
Carolina Mirror
Casa Bique
Castilian Imports
Charleston Forge
Chromcraft
Classic Rattan
Clayton Marcus
Clyde Pearson
Cochrane
Craftique
Denny Lamps
Dinaire
Distinctive Designs
Dresher Brass
Eagle Craft
Emerson Leather
Fairfield Chair
Fashion Bed Group
Flexsteel
Frederick Cooper Lamps
Genesis Lamps
Georgian Furnishings
HTB Contemporary
Hammary
Hanover Cherry Tables
Hanover Craftsmen
Hekman
Henry Link
Hickory Hill
Hickory Leather

Hickory Tavern
Highland House
High Point Furniture
High Point Woodworking
Hood
Hooker
Interline
Jasper Cabinet
Johnston Benchworks
Keller
King Hickory
Kingsdown
Lane
Lane/Venture
Lea
Leather Shop
Leathermen's Guild
Leister Furniture
Lexington
Link Taylor
Lloyd/Flanders
Lynn Holland
Markel Lighting
Masterfield Upholstery
Moosehead Furniture
Nathan Hale
National Mt. Airy
Nichols & Stone
Northwood
Null Industries
Ohio Table Pad
Old Hickory Tannery
Old Salem
Park Place
Paul Roberts Chair
Pearson Upholstery
Pinnacle
Pymouth Harlee Lamps
Pouliot
Pulaski
Rex
S. K. Products
Sarreid
Sealy Bedding
Seay
Serta Bedding
Shelby Williams
Skillcraft
Speer Lighting

Stakmore
Stanley
Stanton Cooper
Taylorsville Upholstery
Temple Stuart
Tradition House
Tropitone
Universal
Vaughan
Vaughan Bassett
Venture By Lane
Victorian Classics
Virginia House
Virginia Metalcrafters
Weathercraft
Weathermaster
Weekend Retreat
Wellington Hall
Wesley Allen
Woodmark
Yesteryear Wicker
Young Hinkle

Smokey Mountain Furniture

3281 Hickory Blvd.
Hudson, NC 28638

Phone:	(828) 726-1434	**Hours:**	M-Sat 9:00-6:00
Toll Free:	None	**E-mail:**	None
Fax:	(828) 726-1152	**Web site:**	None

Smokey Mountain Furniture is located just a few miles north of Hickory, NC. They have a limited selection of lines in stock (American Drew, Lexington, Pulaski, etc.), but they can special order many more.

They don't have a clearance center or any floor samples or discontinued pieces on display. For this reason, there is no monetary advantage to visiting in person. They do have good deals on many lines sold over the phone, though. So, if you're planning to order your furniture by phone, give this source a call to compare their prices.

Lines carried:

Action By Lane	Broyhill	Jetton	Riverside
American Drew	Chromcraft	Kingsdown	Universal
Athens	England Corsair	Lexington	Vaughan
Benchcraft	Hood	Null Industries	
Bob Timberlake	Howard Miller	Pulaski	

Phone orders accepted:	Yes
Discount:	35%-50% off mfrs. suggested retail
Payment methods:	VISA, MC, personal checks
In-house financing available:	No
Deposits required:	50% deposit when order is placed, balance due when furniture is ready to be shipped
Catalog available:	No
Clearance center:	No
Delivery:	Full service in-home delivery and set-up. Customer pays freight company directly for shipping costs.

Directions: From I-40, take exit #123 and drive north on Hwy. 321 to Hudson. Smokey Mountain Furniture is on the right side of the road.

Sobol House

Richardson Blvd.
Black Mountain, NC 28711

Phone:	(828) 669-8031	**Hours:**	M-F 9:00-5:00, Sat 9:00-5:30
Toll Free:	None	**E-mail:**	None
Fax:	(828) 669-7969	**Web site:**	None

Sobol House is located in Black Mountain, NC, just east of Asheville. They have a good selection of medium to high-end lines, including Lexington, Lane, Hekman, and Councill Craftsmen.

They don't have a clearance center or any floor samples or discontinued pieces on display. For this reason, there is no monetary advantage to visiting in person. They do have great deals on many lines sold over the phone, though. So, if you're planning to order your furniture by phone, definitely give this source a call to compare their prices.

Lines carried:	Please see page 284
Phone orders accepted:	Yes
Discount:	40%-50% off mfrs. suggested retail
Payment methods:	VISA, MC, personal checks
In-house financing available:	No
Deposits required:	50% deposit when order is placed, balance due when furniture is ready to be shipped
Catalog available:	No
Clearance center:	No
Delivery:	Full service in-home delivery and set-up. Customer pays freight company directly for shipping costs.

Directions: From I-40, take exit #64, and go north on Hwy. 9. Turn left on Sutton Ave. Sobol House is about a mile down on the left.

Sobol House (cont.)

Lines carried:

Alexvale
American Drew
American of Martinsville
Amyx
Arbek
Ashley
Athol
Barcalounger
Bassett
Bassett Mirror
Bevan Funnell
Bradington Young
Braxton Culler
Blackhawk
Brady
Brown Jordan
Casa Bique
Casa Rustica
Century
Chromcraft
Clark Casuals
Colonial
Councill Craftsmen
Cox
Craftique
Crawford
Davis
Dillon
Ecco
Eclexion
Elliott's
Ello
Fashion Bed Group
Fauld
Froelich
Generations
Georgian Furnishings
Glass Arts
Hekman
Hickory White
Hyundai Furniture
Jamestown
Jasper Cabinet
Johnston Casuals
Karges
Keller
Kessler
Lane
Lane/Venture

Lea
Lexington
Master Design
Millennium
Millender
Mobel
Myrtle Desk
Nathan Hale
Oakwood Interiors
Old Hickory Tannery
Pompeii
Pennsylvania Classics
Pine-tique
Pulaski
Richardson Brothers
Riverside
Rowe
Saloom
Sealy
Sligh
Southampton
Southern Craftsmen
Southern Of Conover
Southwood
Stakmore
Stanley
Stone International
Stoneleigh
Straits
Sumter Cabinet
Superior
Swaim
Tradition House
U. S. Furniture
Universal
Vaughan
Vaughan Bassett
Varges
Wambold
Waterford Furniture
Weiman
Wesley Allen Brass Beds
Whitaker
Yorkshire House

Southern Designs

Level 3
Hickory Furniture Mart
U. S. Hwy. 70 SE
Hickory, NC 28602

Phone:	**(828) 328-8855**	**Hours:**	**M-Sat 9:00-6:00**
Toll Free:	**None**	**E-mail:**	**info@hickoryfurniture.com**
Fax:	**(828) 328-1806**	**Web site:**	**www.hickoryfurniture.com**

Southern Designs in the Hickory Furniture Mart has good bargains on a number of high-end lines, such as Jasper Cabinet and Hitchcock Chair.

They also have a number of high-quality manufacturers which produce knock-offs of better known brands. Richardson Brothers and Chatham County each produce very nice arts & crafts style furniture similar to Stickley. Brown Street produces a line almost identical to the Bob Timberlake signature series from Lexington. The quality is identical in my experience, but the prices on the lesser-known lines are quite a bit cheaper.

If you're shopping for any of the current "in" styles, such as mission or arts & crafts, you should check with this source to see what they may have from a lesser-advertised brand that may be identical to the heavily advertised pieces you originally chose.

Lines carried:

Ashton Pictures	Distinction Leather	Lighting Enterprises	Stone County Ironworks
Big Sky Carvers	Eagle Craft Desks	Lt. Moses Willard Lamps	Superior
Brown Street	Heritage Haus	Mobel	Today's Home Upholstery
Chatham County	Hitchcock Chair	Null Industries	2 Day Designs
Cherry Pond	Huntington House	Oriental Accents	Van Patten Curios
Conover Chair	Jasper Cabinet	Richardson Brothers	Virginia House
Cooper Classics	Key City	Shady Lady	Wisconsin Furniture
Craft-Tex	Leather Comfort	Skillcraft	
Crawford of Jamestown	By Viewpoint	Southern Craftsmen's Guild	

Phone orders accepted:	**Yes**
Discount:	**40%-60% off mfrs. suggested retail**
Payment methods:	**VISA, MC, personal checks**
In-house financing available:	**No**
Deposits required:	**50% deposit when order is placed, balance due when furniture is ready to be shipped**
Catalog available:	**No**
Clearance center:	**No**
Delivery:	**Full service in-home delivery and set-up. Customer pays freight company directly for shipping costs.**

Directions: Please see *Hickory Furniture Mart* for complete directions.

Southland Furniture Galleries

1244 Hwy. 17
Little River, SC 29566

Phone:	**(843) 280-9342**	**Hours:**	**M-Sat 9:00-5:30**
Toll Free:	**None**	**E-mail:**	**None**
Fax:	**(843) 249-4527**	**Web site:**	**None**

Southland Furniture Galleries has a huge 30,000 square-foot store in Little River, SC, near Myrtle Beach. They have a very impressive stock of high-end lines such as La Barge, Lexington, Baker, Century, Thomasville, Hickory White, and others. Their discounts generally run from 40%-50% off retail.

The store doesn't have any floor samples or discontinued styles on display. This, combined with the fact that the store is so far from the main concentration of factory outlets and discounters in central North Carolina, make a personal visit impractical and unnecessary unless you live close by.

However, their prices on furniture sold by phone are quite good, and they have an excellent reputation for customer service. If you plan to order furniture by phone, definitely give this source a call and compare their prices.

Phone orders accepted:	Yes
Discount:	**40%-50% off mfrs. suggested retail**
Payment methods:	**VISA, MC, personal checks**
In-house financing available:	No
Deposits required:	**50% deposit when order is placed, balance due when furniture is ready to be shipped**
Catalog available:	No
Clearance center:	No
Delivery:	**Full service in-home delivery and set-up. Customer pays freight company directly for shipping costs.**

Directions: **From I-95, take the Hwy. 9 exit at Florence, SC, and head east. After about 20 miles, turn southeast on Hwy. 501. After about 60 miles, when you near Myrtle Beach, turn north on Hwy. 17. Southland Furniture Galleries is about 20 miles north of Myrtle Beach in Little River, SC, right near the NC/SC state line.**

Southland Furniture Galleries (cont.)

Lines carried:

A La Carte
Action By Lane
Alock Furniture
American Drew
American Heritage
American Of Martinsville
Amisco
Arte de Mexico
Artistica
Artmark
Asmara Rugs
Baker
Baldwin Brass
Barcalounger
Bassett
Bassett Mirror
Bernhardt
Bevan Funnell
Blacksmith Shop
Bob Timberlake
Bradington Young
Brass Beds Of Virginia
Braxton Culler
Broyhill
Burton Reproduction
Butler Specialty
Canadel
Carolina Mirror
Carson's
Carvers Guild
Casa Bique
Casa Stradivari
Century
Chapman Lamps
Chelsea House
Chromcraft
Clark Casual
Classic Leather
Classic Rattan
Colonial Furniture
Councill Craftsmen
Cooper Classics
Country Affair
Cox
Craftique
Craftwork Guild
Crawford of Jamestown
Crescent
Crystal Clear Lighting

Clyde Pearson
Dansen Contemporary
Decorative Crafts
Design South
Dillon
Distinctive Leather
DSF Scandinavian
Duralee Fabrics
Dutailier
Ello
Elements By Grapevine
Emerson Et Cie
Emerson Leather
Excelsior
Fairfield Chair
Fashion Bed Group
Ficks Reed
Fine Arts Lamps
Forbes Brothers Lamps
Frederick Cooper Lamps
Frederick Edward
Friedman Brothers Mirrors
Fritz & LaRue Rugs
Froelich Furniture
Gaines
Garcia Imports
Georgian Furnishings
Glass Arts
Glober
Grace
Greeff Fabrics
Guildmaster
Habersham Plantation
Hammary
Hancock & Moore
Harden
Hart Country Shop
Hekman
Hen Feathers
Henry Link
Hickory White
Hill Mfg.
Hitchcock Chair
Hood
Hooker
Howard Miller Clocks
Hyundai Furniture
Jasper Cabinet
Jeffco

John Widdicomb
Johnston Casuals
Jon Elliott
J. Royale
Kaiser Kuhn Lamps
Karges
Keller
Kimball
Kincaid
King Hickory
Knob Creek
Koch Originals
Koch & Lowy
Kravet Fabrics
La Barge
Lane
Lane/Venture
Lea
Leathermen's Guild
Lexington
Lillian August
Lloyd/Flanders
Lyon Shaw
McGuire
McKay Table Pads
Madison Square
Maitland Smith
Marbro Lamps
Maryland Classics
Masland Carpets
Mastercraft
Michael Thomas
Montaage
Motioncraft
Murray Feiss Lamps
National Mt. Airy
Natural Light
Nathan Hale
Nichols & Stone
Norbar Fabrics
Norman Perry Lamps
Ohio Table Pad
Old Hickory Tannery
Old Waverly By JTB
Pande Cameron Rugs
Parker Southern
Paul Hansen Lamps
Paul Robert
Pavillion

Pennsylvania House
Platt
Pompeii
Precedent
Pulaski
Reliance Lamp
Rex
Ridgewood Furniture
Riverside
Robert Allen Fabrics
Salem Square
Saloom
Sarreid
S. Bent
Schott
Schumacher/Waverly
Seabrook Wallcoverings
Sedgefield Lamps
Serta Mattress
Sherrill
Shuford
Sligh
Southern Furniture
Southampton
Southwood Reproductions
Speer Lamps
Stanley
Stanton Cooper
Statesville Chair
Statton
Stiffel Lamps
Stoneleigh
Stroheim & Romann
Superior
Swaim
Temple Stewart
Thayer Coggin
Thomasville
Tianjin Philadelphia Carpets
Tradition France
Tradition House
Transpacific
Tropitone
Tyndale Lamps
Universal
Vanguard
Vaughan
Venture By Lane

Southland Furniture Galleries

Lines carried (cont.):

Vermont Tubbs
Virginia House
Virginia Metalcrafters
Wara Tapestries
Waterford Furniture
Wedgewood/Waterford
Weiman
Wellington Hall
Wesley Allen Brass Beds
Wesley Hall
Westgate Fabrics
Wisconsin
Wildwood
William Alan
Winston Furniture
Woodard
Woodmark
Yorkshire Leather

Stevens Furniture

Hwy. 105 S.
Boone, NC 28607

Phone:	(828) 264-3993	**Hours:**	M-Sat 9:00-5:30
Toll Free:	None	**E-mail:**	sales@stevensfurniture.com
Fax:	(828) 262-3530	**Web site:**	www.stevensfurniture.com

Stevens Furniture in Boone, NC, has been discounting furniture by phone since 1964. They have a very impressive showroom with large galleries for Stanley, Broyhill, and Lexington, among other lines.

You can buy furniture off the floor if you wish, but the discount you receive in person is no better than the discount you receive over the phone. Their discounts run about 40%-50% off retail.

They do have a small "Value Center" with discounts of up to 75% off retail on floor samples and discontinued styles at their other location about 15 minutes away in Lenoir, NC, but it has a very sparse selection.

If you're planning to order furniture over the phone, you may wish to compare prices with this source, but it really isn't worth a personal visit. Other outlets in the Hickory area have more to choose from.

Lines carried:	Please see page 290
Phone orders accepted:	Yes
Discount:	40%-50% off mfrs. suggested retail
Payment methods:	VISA, MC, personal checks.
In-house financing available:	Yes
Deposits required:	50% deposit when order is placed, balance due when furniture is ready to be shipped
Catalog available:	No
Clearance center:	Yes
Delivery:	Full service in-home delivery and set-up. Customer pays freight company directly for shipping costs.

Directions: From I-40, take exit #123 and head north into Hickory, NC, on Hwy. 321. Go 25 miles north on Hwy. 321 to Boone, and turn left on Hwy. 105. Stevens Furniture is about two miles down on the left side of the road.

Stevens Furniture (cont.)

Lines carried:

Action By Lane
American Drew
Arnold Palmer Collection
Austin Sculpture
Baldwin Brass
Barcalounger
Bard
Bassett
Bevan Funnell
Bob Timberlake
Brady
Broyhill
Butler Specialty
Canadel
Carolina Mirror
Carver's Mirror
Charleston Forge
Chelsea House
Clark Casuals
Classic Leather
Classic Rattan
Councill Craftsmen
Cochrane
Cooper Classics
Corsican
Cox
Craftique
Craftwork Guild
Crystal Clear Lighting
Decorative Crafts
Ducks Unlimited
Entree
Fashion Bed Group
Hammary
Hekman
Henry Link
Hickory Chair
Hickory Hill
Hickory Tavern
High Point Furniture
Hitchcock Chair
Hooker
Howard Miller Clocks
Hyundai Furniture
J. Royale
Jasper Cabinet
Jeral
John Richard Collection
Kaiser Kuhn Lamps

Keller
Kincaid
Kinder Harris
Koch
Lane
Lane/Venture
Lea
Lexington
Link Taylor
Lloyd/Flanders
Lyon Shaw
Maitland Smith
McKay Table Pads
Madison Square
Meadowcraft
Michael Thomas
Millender
Morganton Chair
Nichols & Stone
Ohio Table Pad
Pennsylvania Classics
Pennsylvania House
Phillip Reinisch
Port Royal
Pulaski
Reflections
Reprodux
Rex
Ridgeway
Riverside
S. Bent
Salem Square
Sarreid
Sedgefield
Serta
Simmons Bedding
Skillcraft
Speer Lamps
St. Timothy Chair
Stanford
Stanley
Statesville Chair
Statton
Stiffel Lamps
Swan Brass Beds
Tradition House
Tropitone
Universal
Vanguard

Virginia House
Virginia Metalcrafters
Weiman
Wellington Hall
Wesley Allen Brass Beds
Westwood Lighting
Wildwood
Willow Creek
Winners Only
Winston
Woodard

Stevens Furniture

1258 Hickory Blvd. SW
Lenoir, NC 28645

Phone:	**(828) 728-5511**	**Hours:**	**M-Sat 9:00-5:30**
Toll Free:	**None**	**E-mail:**	**sales@stevensfurniture.com**
Fax:	**(828) 728-5518**	**Web site:**	**www.stevensfurniture.com**

Stevens Furniture in Lenoir, NC, has been discounting furniture by phone since 1964. They have a huge store with large galleries for Stanley, Broyhill, Lexington, and Hickory White, among other lines.

Although you can buy furniture off the floor if you wish, the discount you receive in person is no better than the discount you receive over the phone. Their discounts run about 40%-50% off retail.

There is a small "Value Center" in the basement with some discontinued styles and floor samples discounted up to 75% off retail, but there really isn't much selection. Routinely, they might have a few odd dining room tables, a few occasional tables and chairs, and a desk or two.

If you're planning to order furniture over the phone, you may wish to compare prices with this source, but it really isn't worth a personal visit. Other outlets in the Hickory area have much broader selections.

Phone orders accepted:	**Yes**
Discount:	**40%-50% off mfrs. suggested retail**
Payment methods:	**VISA, MC, personal checks.**
In-house financing available:	**Yes**
Deposits required:	**50% deposit when order is placed, balance due when furniture is ready to be shipped**
Catalog available:	**No**
Clearance center:	**Yes**
Delivery:	**Full service in-home delivery and set-up. Customer pays freight company directly for shipping costs.**

Directions: From I-40, take exit #123 and head north into Hickory, NC, on Hwy. 321. Go about 10 miles north on Hwy. 321 to Lenoir, NC. Stevens is on the left side of the highway right past Quality Furniture Market of Lenoir.

Stevens Furniture (cont.)

Lines carried:

Action By Lane
American Drew
Arnold Palmer Collection
Art Forms
Austin Sculpture
Baldwin Brass
Barcalounger
Bard
Bassett
Bernhardt
Bevan Funnell
Bob Timberlake
Brady
Broyhill
Butler Specialty
Canadel
Carolina Mirror
Carver's Mirror
Charleston Forge
Chelsea House
Clark Casual
Classic Leather
Classic Rattan
Councill Craftsmen
Cochrane
Cooper Classics
Corsican
Cox
Craftique
Craftwork Guild
Crawford Of Jamestown
Crystal Clear Lighting
Decorative Crafts
Distinctive Designs
Ducks Unlimited
Entree
Fashion Bed Group
Hammary
Hekman
Henry Link
Hickory Chair
Hickory Hill
Hickory Tavern
High Point Furniture
Hitchcock Chair
Hooker
Howard Miller Clocks
Hyundai Furniture
J. Royale

Jasper Cabinet
Jeral
John Richard Collection
Kaiser Kuhn Lamps
Keller
Kincaid
Kinder Harris
Koch
Lane
Lane/Venture
Lea
Lexington
Link Taylor
Lloyd/Flanders
Lyon Shaw
Maitland Smith
McKay Table Pads
Madison Square
Meadowcraft
Michael Thomas
Millender
Morganton Chair
Nichols & Stone
Ohio Table Pad
Pennsylvania Classics
Pennsylvania House
Phillip Reinisch
Port Royal
Pulaski
Reflections
Reprodux
Rex
Ridgeway
Ridgewood
Riverside
S. Bent
Salem Square
Samsonite
Sarreid
Sedgefield
Serta
Simmons Bedding
Skillcraft
Speer Lamps
St. Timothy Chair
Stanford
Stanley
Statesville Chair
Statton

Stiffel Lamps
Swan Brass Beds
Tradition House
Tropitone
Universal
Uwharrie Chair
Vanguard
Virginia House
Virginia Metalcrafters
Weiman
Wellington Hall
Wesley Allen Brass Beds
Westwood Lighting
Wildwood
Willow Creek
Winners Only
Winston
Woodard

Stickley Factory Sale

300 Orchard St
Fayetteville, NY 13066

Phone:	(315) 637-2278	**Hours:**	Not open every day. Occasional sales.
Toll Free:	None	**E-mail:**	None
Fax:	None	**Web site:**	None

The sales that take place every six weeks or so at Stickley Furniture's original factory in Fayetteville, NY, are the only place you can purchase discontinued styles or floor samples from Stickley. Fortunately, there's always a lot to choose from here. The sales always take place on a Saturday, usually from 9:00-5:00.

The discounts range from 40%-65% off retail, with most pieces marked at a straight 50% discount. They have a very wide selection of beds, office furniture, dining room sets, entertainment centers, and some upholstery.

On my most recent visit to a Stickley factory sale, I found a great deal on a three-piece mission cherry entertainment center (pictured on the following page). The two bookcases and the middle entertainment center normally retail together for $7,983.00, but this floor sample was tagged at $3,999.00 for all three pieces. It was in perfect condition.

Stickley also offers what they refer to as "vintage" Stickley furniture. Stickley is one of the few furniture manufacturers that will accept their own product as a trade-in. There are customers who will turn in their ten-year old dining room set for a discount on a newer style. Since Stickley furniture is so well-made in the first place, it holds up very well. The "vintage" pieces are then offered at about 65% off the comparable retail at the periodic factory sales. There's a small room in the back where most of the vintage pieces are displayed. These can be really great bargains, so do look out for them.

Please read the entry for *Stickley Factory Showroom* for information on Stickley's unusual policy regarding not knowingly selling to customers outside the Syracuse area. As explained in that entry, this policy is widely ignored by customers who take advantage of the "don't ask, don't tell" attitude of most of the salespeople here. If you look at the tags on the hundreds of cars that surround the original Stickley factory whenever these sales take place, you'll see customers from nearly every state in the Northeast.

This sale is really spectacular. Anyone in the New York area should consider going if they're looking for great deals on Stickley furniture.

The one catch is finding out when they will take place. The Stickley factory office won't usually give out the dates of upcoming sales over the phone. However, there is a newsletter available from my publisher called the *National Home Furnishings Trade Show Newsletter*, which tracks these types of special sales at factory outlets, factories, trade centers, etc. It normally lists the upcoming Stickley sales. There is an order form for the newsletter in the back of this book.

Phone orders accepted:	No
Discount:	40%-65% off mfrs. suggested retail
Payment methods:	VISA, MC, personal checks
In-house financing available:	Yes
Deposits required:	Not applicable
Catalog available:	Not applicable
Clearance center:	Not applicable
Delivery:	Free delivery in the Syracuse, NY area. Other customers must pick up their own furniture.

Directions: From Hwy. 481 around Syracuse, take exit #3, and go east on Hwy. 5.

Stickley Factory Sale (cont.)

Stickley Factory Sale at the original Stickley factory in Fayetteville, NY

Mission Cherry entertainment center from Stickley

Retail: $7,983.00   Discounted price: $3,999.00
Savings at the Stickley Factory Sale: $3,984.00 = 50% off retail

Stickley Factory Sale (cont.)

Shoppers at the Stickley Factory Sale

The "bed room" at the Stickley Factory Sale

Stickley Factory Showroom

1 Stickley Dr.
Manlius, NY 13104

Phone:	**(828) 726-3333**	**Hours:**	**Mon, Wed, Fri, Sat 9:30-5:00,**
Toll Free:	**None**		**Tues, Thurs 9:30-8:30, Sun 1:00-5:00**
Fax:	**None**	**E-mail:**	**None**
		Web site:	**None**

This is Stickley Furniture's only permanent showroom open to the public, although there are also periodic sales at their original factory location in nearby Fayetteville, NY. Manlius is near Syracuse, NY.

The Stickley Factory Showroom has extensive galleries of not only Stickley, but Century, Henredon, Drexel-Heritage, Baker, Hooker, Classic Leather, and Hancock & Moore. The discounts generally run 35%-50% off retail, with most of the furniture around 40% off. You can special order any new furniture from any of these lines. This is the only place you can special order new Stickley furniture at wholesale.

On my most recent visit here, I found a great deal on a Mission Oak armoire from Stickley (pictured on the following page). The regular retail price is $5,892.00, but the price at the Stickley showroom is only $3,830.00.

Stickley has an unusual policy among factory outlets and showrooms. They will only sell to you if you live in the Syracuse, NY, area or if you happen to live in an area which doesn't have a local Stickley dealer.

These "protected areas" for local dealers are pretty large, so it doesn't necessarily matter that there may not be a Stickley dealer right in your hometown. I overheard a woman in the showroom being told that she could not make a purchase because she lived in Orlando, FL, and there was a Stickley dealer in Naples, FL. Naples is about a four-hour drive from Orlando! That's hardly what I would call a "local dealer".

So, the upshot of this is that the Stickley factory has decided that Syracuse area residents may purchase Stickley at a discount, but just about everyone else in the country must pay double for the same product and may be forced to buy from a dealer several hours away from their homes. I find this a very unfair and discriminatory policy. I have never heard of any other factory outlet having a policy like this. At every other furniture factory outlet in the U. S., if you're willing to drive there, you can shop there.

The one saving grace here is that I've found that the commissioned salespeople at this showroom don't ask where you're from. After all, they want to sell as much furniture as possible. One saleswoman actually told me: "Just don't tell me where you're from". So, don't! There's a "don't ask, don't tell" policy in place here, so take advantage of it.

Anyone who wants to buy Stickley at a discount should be able to cruise right in and do so as long as you don't discuss where you're from and you make your own arrangements to pick your furniture up.

Those who aren't able to get to Syracuse have a much better alternative than paying full price through a Stickley dealer. Buy your furniture from one of the many companies that manufacture Stickley knock-offs, such as Richardson Brothers, Kincaid, Arts & Crafts Industries, and many others. The quality is every bit as good, and these lines can all be ordered over the phone at wholesale prices from many North Carolina discounters.

Phone orders accepted:	**No**
Discount:	**35%-50% off mfrs. suggested retail**
Payment methods:	**VISA, MC, personal checks**
In-house financing available:	**No**
Deposits required:	**Not applicable**
Catalog available:	**Not applicable**
Clearance center:	**Yes - See *Stickley Factory Sale***
Delivery:	**Free delivery in the Syracuse, NY area. Other customers must pick up their own furniture.**

Directions: From Hwy. 481 around Syracuse, take exit #3, and go SE on Hwy. 92.

Stickley Factory Showroom (cont.)

Stickley Factory Showroom

Mission oak armoire from Stickley

Retail: $5,892.00   Discounted price: $3,830.000
Savings at the Stickley Factory Showroom: $2,062.00 = 35% off retail

Stuckey Brothers Furniture Company

Route 1
Stuckey, SC 29554

Phone:	**(843) 558-2591**	**Hours:**	**M-F 9:00-6:00, Sat 9:00-5:00**
Toll Free:	**None**	**E-mail:**	**None**
Fax:	**(843) 558-9229**	**Web site:**	**None**

Stuckey Brothers Furniture Company is located in Stuckey, SC, west of Myrtle Beach, SC. They have a good selection of high end lines, including Century, Drexel-Heritage, Sherrill, and Hickory Chair.

They don't have a clearance center or any floor samples or discontinued pieces on display. For this reason, there is no monetary advantage to visiting in person. They do have great deals on many lines sold over the phone, though. So, if you're planning to order your furniture by phone, definitely give this source a call to compare their prices.

Phone orders accepted:	**Yes**
Discount:	**35%-50% off mfrs. suggested retail**
Payment methods:	**Personal checks. No credit cards.**
In-house financing available:	**No**
Deposits required:	**1/3 deposit when order is placed, balance due when furniture is ready to be shipped**
Catalog available:	**No**
Clearance center:	**No**
Delivery:	**Full service in-home delivery and set-up. Customer pays freight company directly for shipping costs.**

Directions: From I-95, take Hwy. 512 east to Stuckey. Stuckey Brothers Furniture is downtown.

Stuckey Brothers Furniture Company (cont.)

Lines carried:

Action By Lane
Allibert
American Drew
Artisans Brass Beds
Athol
Bassett
Barcalounger
Benecia Brass Beds
Berkline
Bernhardt
Best Chairs
Blacksmith Shop
Boling Chair
Bradington Young
Braxton Culler
Broyhill
Capris
Carlton McLendon
CTH Sherrill Occasional
Century
Chapmen Lamps
Chatham County
Charleston Forge
Chromcraft
Clark Casual
Classic Leather
Classic Rattan
Corsican Brass Beds
Councill Craftsmen
Cox
Craftique
Crescent
Dansen Contemporary
Disque
Drexel Heritage
Durham
Ekornes
Elements By Grapevine
Elliott's Brass Beds
Fairfield Chair
Fine Arts Lamps
Finkel
Friedman Brothers Mirrors
Habersham Plantation
Hammary
Hancock & Moore
Harden
Henkel-Harris
Henkel-Moore

Hekman
Heritage
Hickory Chair
Hickory White
Hitchcock Chair
Holiday House
Hooker
Howard Miller Clocks
Huntington House
J. B. Ross Brass Beds
Jasper Cabinet
Keller
Kessler
Kimball
Kincaid
La Barge
Lane
Lane/Venture
Lea
Lexington
Lloyd/Flanders
McKay Table Pad
Madison Square
Maitland Smith
Meadowcraft
Mobel
Murray Feiss Lamps
Nichols & Stone
Null Industries
Ohio Table Pad Co.
Pearson
Peters Revington
Pulaski
Reinisch
Remington Lamps
Rex
Ridgeway Clock
Riverside
Rowe
Sam Moore
S. Bent
Sealy Mattress
Serta Mattress
Sherrill
Shuford
Sligh
Southampton
Southwood Reproductions
Speer Lamps

Stanley
Stanton Cooper
Statesville Chair
Statton
Stiffel Lamps
Stratolounger
Sumter Cabinet
Superior
Taylor King
Taylor Woodcraft
Temple
Tropitone
Universal
Vanguard
Vaughan
Vaughan Bassett
Venture By Lane
Virginia House
Waterford Lamps
Wellington Hall
Wesley Allen Brass Beds
Whitecraft
Whittemore Sherrill
Wildwood Lamps
Winston
Woodard
Woodmark

Thomas Home Furnishings

4346 Hickory Blvd.
Granite Falls, NC 28630

Phone:	(828) 396-2147	**Hours:**	M-Sat 9:00-5:00
Toll Free:	None	**E-mail:**	None
Fax:	(828) 396-6179	**Web site:**	www.hfnet.com/thf.html

Thomas Home Furnishings in Granite Falls just north of Hickory, NC, has a very nice store with large galleries for Lexington, Pennsylvania House, and Century, among other lines.

The one thing that gets your attention first when you walk in the door, though, is the sound of phones buzzing off the hook. This source does a booming order-by-phone business. They do have good discounts, about 40%-50% off retail on most brands.

All of the furniture in stock is new first-quality. There are no discontinued items or floor samples available, which makes a personal visit unnecessary. This is a great source to compare prices with if you plan to order your furniture over the phone, but if you plan to travel to Hickory to shop, you would be better off visiting the many true factory outlets in the area which have much better discounts for customers who shop in person.

Phone orders accepted:	Yes
Discount:	40%-50% off mfrs. suggested retail
Payment methods:	VISA, MC, personal checks
In-house financing available:	No
Deposits required:	50% deposit when order is placed, balance due when furniture is ready to be shipped
Catalog available:	No
Clearance center:	No
Delivery:	Full service in-home delivery and set-up. Customer pays freight company directly for shipping costs.

Directions: From I-40, take exit #123 and drive north on Hwy. 321 to Granite Falls. Thomas Home Furnishings is on the right side of the road.

Thomas Home Furnishings (cont.)

Lines carried:

American Drew
American Of Martinsville
Arnold Palmer Collection
Athol
Austin Sculptures
Baldwin Brass
Bassett
Bernhardt
Blacksmith Shop
Bob Timberlake
Bradington Young
Carolina Mirror
Carsons
Casa Bique
Century
Chapman
Charleston Forge
Clayton Marcus
Cochrane
Conover Chair
Councill Craftsmen
Cox
Craftique
Designmaster
Ducks Unlimited
Elliott's Designs
Friedman Brothers Mirrors
Great City Traders
Hammary
Hekman
Henry Link
Highland House
Hitchcock Chair
Hooker
Jasper Cabinet
Keller
Kessler
Kimball
Kinder Harris
Knob Creek
Lane
Lane/Venture
La-Z-Boy
Leathercraft
Lexington
Madison Square
Michaels
Moosehead
National Mt. Airy

Nichols & Stone
Palmer Home Collection
Pennsylvania House
Pulaski
Sam Moore
Sedgefield
Serta Mattress
Southampton
Shuford
Southwood Reproductions
Stanford
Statton
Stanley
Statton
Stewart Clocks
Stiffel Lamps
Sumter Cabinet
Universal
Venture By Lane
Virginia Metalcrafters
Waterford
Weiman
Wellington Hall
Wesley Allen Brass Beds
Wildwood Lamps
Woodmark

Thomasville Factory Outlet

Manufacturer-Owned Factory Outlets (Lenoir Mall)
1031 Morganton Blvd.
Lenoir, NC 28645

Phone:	**(828) 757-2711**	**Hours:**	**M-F 10:00-6:30,**
Toll Free:	**None**		**Sat 10:00-5:00, Sun 1:30-5:00**
Fax:	**(828) 757-2702**	**E-mail:**	**info@thomasville.com**
		Web site:	**www.thomasville.com**

This is one of Thomasville's only two factory outlets. The stock here is primarily upholstery from Thomasville's nearby upholstery plant in Hickory. There are some case goods, primarily dining room sets and armoires, but the majority of the furniture here are traditional sofas and chairs. There is also a nice selection of leather furniture from Thomasville's nearby leather furniture manufacturing plant.

They do have some terrific upholstery bargains here. On my most recent visit, I found a living room group in a discontinued fabric (pictured on the following page). The sofa was marked down to $609.00 from a usual retail price of $1,649.00, and the chair was marked down to $389.00 from a retail of $1,069.00. Both pieces were first quality.

The outlet is huge, occupying what was once a small department store in the Lenoir Mall. If you're looking for good deals on high-end upholstery, this is definitely an outlet you should visit.

If you're looking for good deals on armoires, beds, chests, and other case goods from Thomasville, you would be better off to visit their other factory outlet in Thomasville, NC (near High Point). The other outlet is a direct offshoot of Thomasville's main case goods plant, and it has a far better selection of that type of furniture.

Phone orders accepted:	**No**
Discount:	**65%-75% off mfrs. suggested retail**
Payment methods:	**VISA, MC, AMEX, or Discover. No checks.**
In-house financing available:	**Yes**
Deposits required:	**Not applicable**
Catalog available:	**Not applicable**
Clearance center:	**Not applicable**
Delivery:	**Full service in-home delivery and set-up. Customer pays freight company directly for shipping costs.**

Directions:	**From I-40, take exit #123 (Hwy. 321) and head north through Hickory toward Lenoir. Turn left on Hwy. 64, then turn left again on the Hwy. 18S Bypass. The outlet is on the left inside Lenoir Mall.**

Thomasville Factory Outlet (cont.)

Thomasville Factory Outlet at the Manufacturer Owned Furniture Outlets in Lenoir, NC

Sofa and chair from Thomasville

Retail: $2,718.00   Discounted price: $998.00
Savings at the Thomasville Factory Outlet: $1,720.00 = 63% off retail

Thomasville Factory Outlet

401 East Main St.
Thomasville, NC 27361

Phone:	**(336) 476-2371**	**Hours:**	**M-F 9:00-5:30, Sat 9:00-4:00**
Toll Free:	**None**	**E-mail:**	**info@thomasville.com**
Fax:	**(336) 476-2359**	**Web site:**	**www.thomasville.com**

This is one of Thomasville's only two true factory outlets. Most of the furniture in stock here are case goods from Thomasville's main case goods manufacturing plant, right next door to the outlet.

They do have some upholstery in stock here, but most of Thomasville's sample and discontinued upholstery is liquidated through their other outlet in Lenoir, NC, which is closer to their main upholstery and leather manufacturing plants in Hickory, NC. If you are specifically looking for Thomasville upholstery, you would be better off visiting their Lenoir outlet instead.

The outlet is quite large, and they have some very good bargains here. On my most recent visit, I found a great deal on a solid cherry entertainment center (pictured on the following page). The usual retail on this item is $3,045.00, but the outlet had this floor sample marked down to only $1,155.00. It was in new first-quality condition.

Thomasville does a good job of clearly marking which items are first-quality, floor samples, seconds, or irregulars. The majority of the stock here is in new first-quality condition. Even the few seconds I found scattered around the outlet had very small flaws, and these were marked down to about 70% to 80% off retail.

The outlet will not special order furniture from Thomasville's current stock, but they will accept phone orders for any piece that is currently in stock at the outlet. Thomasville has a very strict sign-in policy. Be sure to sign in when you visit. As long as your name is in the registry log, the outlet will accept phone orders from you for up to 90 days.

If you see a Thomasville item in a local retail store, it's worth calling the outlet to see if they might have a floor sample of that item, or a very similar one, in stock. They will also keep an eye out in case the item you want comes in at a later time. The staff is quite cooperative about checking the outlet for these items and allowing you to order them by phone, provided that you have signed in within the last 90 days.

This outlet has a very nice variety of beds, armoires, entertainment centers, chests, bedroom sets, dining room sets, office furniture, and other case goods, as well as some upholstery. This outlet is a "must-visit".

Phone orders accepted:	**Yes**
Discount:	**60%-80% off mfrs. suggested retail**
Payment methods:	**VISA, MC, AMEX, or Discover. No checks.**
In-house financing available:	**Yes**
Deposits required:	**Not applicable**
Catalog available:	**Not applicable**
Clearance center:	**Not applicable**
Delivery:	**Full service in-home delivery and set-up. Customer pays freight company directly for shipping costs.**

Directions: From I-85, take exit #103 and go north on Randolph St. into downtown Thomasville. Just before you reach the railroad tracks, turn right onto E. Main St. The Thomasville outlet will be 4 blocks down on your right.

Thomasville Factory Outlet(cont.)

Thomasville Factory Outlet in Thomasville, NC

Solid cherry entertainment center from Thomasville

Retail: $3,045.00   Discounted price: $1,155.00
Savings at the Thomasville Factory Outlet: $1,890.00 = 62% off retail

Transit Damage Freight

1604 S. Main St.
Lexington, NC 27292

Phone:	(336) 248-2646	**Hours:**	M-Thurs & Sat 9:00-5:30,
Toll Free:	None		Fri 9:00-9:00
Fax:	(336) 243-2168	**E-mail:**	None
		Web site:	None

Transit Damage is much more than just a typical damaged-freight liquidation center. Yes, they do have a small amount of furniture damaged in shipment or separated from it's original paperwork, but most of their stock at this particular location is made up of floor samples, discontinued styles, and seconds.

Lexington (including Henry Link, Bob Timberlake, and Palmer Home Collection), Stanley, and Bassett all have factories nearby, and they use Transit Damage as a quasi-factory outlet. There are no factory-owned factory outlets for these lines, so this is the closest thing available. They have pieces from various other brands here, as well.

This source isn't necessarily worth a separate trip, but if you're in the Lexington area anyway, you may wish to stop in. The prices are good, but not as good as in a typical factory-owned factory outlet. Most of the furniture here is priced at about 40%-50% off retail. The bargains here vary widely from not-so-great to fantastic.

This is not a place for an amateur furniture shopper to start out. If you have a good eye for furniture and you can easily judge what it ought to be worth, you can get some spectacular deals here. If you don't know what to take and what to leave alone, though, you could end up paying more than you should.

Expert furniture shoppers and those with the woodworking skills to make minor touch-ups and repairs: run, don't walk, to this outlet. Average consumers: stick with the many less confusing factory outlets and deep discounters elsewhere in North Carolina.

Lines carried:	Varies
Phone orders accepted:	Yes
Discount:	40%-50% off mfrs. suggested retail
Payment methods:	VISA, MC, personal checks
In-house financing available:	No
Deposits required:	Not applicable
Catalog available:	Not applicable
Clearance center:	Not applicable
Delivery:	Customers must make own arrangements to take furniture home.

Directions: From I-85, take exit #87, and get on Business I-85 north. Take exit #86 off of Business 85, and take a left at the light. Transit Damage Freight is just up the road on the left.

Triad Furniture Discounters

P. O. Box 7505
Myrtle Beach, SC 29577

Phone:	None	**Hours:**	24 hours/7 days a week
Toll Free:	(800) 323-8469	**E-mail:**	None
Fax:	None	**Web site:**	None

Triad Furniture Discounters is located in Myrtle Beach, on the Atlantic coast. They sell by mail order only, but the have very good prices on a wide selection of medium to high-end lines. If you plan to order furniture over the phone, you should give them a call to compare prices.

Lines carried:

Action By Lane	Craftwork	Lane/Venture	Southern Reproduc-
Alexvale	Crawford	Lea	tions
American Drew	CTH/Sherrill	Lexington	Stanley
Barcalounger	Design South	Madison Square	Statesville Chair
Bassett	Distinction Leather	Marbro	Statton
Benchcraft	Entree	Motioncraft-Sherrill	Stiffel
Benecia Beds	Fairfield Chair	Nichols & Stone	Sumter Cabinet
Berkline	Habersham Plantation	Ohio Table Pad	Swaim
Bevan Funnell	Hammary	Pearson	Taylor King
Bradington Young	Hekman	Pennsylvania Classics	Universal
Braxton Culler	Hickory White	Precedent	Vanguard
Broyhill	Highland House	Pulaski	Vaughan
Capel Rugs	Hooker	Rex	Vaughan-Bassett
Casa Bique	Jasper Cabinet	Richardson Brothers	Venture By Lane
Charleston Forge	Johnston Casuals	Rowe	Virginia House
Classic Leather	Kaiser Kuhn Lighting	Salem Square	Weiman
Clayton Marcus	Key City	Sam Moore	Wellington Hall
Cochrane	Kimball	Sedgefield	Wesley Allen Beds
Councill Craftsmen	Kincaid	Serta Mattress	Whittemore-Sherrill
C. R. Laine	La Barge	Simmons	Wildwood
Craftique	Lane	SK Products	

Phone orders accepted:	Yes
Discount:	35%-60% off mfrs. suggested retail
Payment methods:	VISA, MC, Discover, personal checks
In-house financing available:	No
Deposits required:	50% deposit when order is placed, balance due when furniture is ready to be shipped
Catalog available:	No
Clearance center:	No
Delivery:	Full service in-home delivery and set-up. Customer pays freight company directly for shipping costs.

Directions: **Triad Furniture Discounters has no showroom open to the public.**

Triplett's Furniture Fashions

2084 Hickory Blvd. SW
Lenoir, NC 28645

Phone:	**(828) 728-8211**	**Hours:**	**M-Sat 8:30-5:00**
Toll Free:	**None**	**E-mail:**	**None**
Fax:	**(828) 726-0171**	**Web site:**	**None**

Triplett's Furniture Fashions has a very nice store in Lenoir, NC, just north of Hickory. They have a good selection of medium to high-end lines, such as Lexington, Hekman, Hooker, and Universal. They can also special order many lines over the phone.

The discounts on new furniture in first-quality condition, whether purchased in person or over the phone, run from 40%-50% off retail.

They generally don't have any floor samples or discontinued styles on display, with one exception. Triplett's houses a brand-new factory outlet for Clayton-Marcus. This is Clayton Marcus' only factory outlet anywhere. Please see the *Clayton-Marcus Factory Outlet* entry for more information.

If you're in the Lenoir/Hickory area, and you're looking for high-end upholstery, you may wish to stop by here. Clayton-Marcus produces very fine quality upholstery, and the prices at the outlet here are very good. Otherwise, there isn't much reason to go in person. However, anyone planning to buy furniture by phone should make a point of calling here to compare prices. They have great discounts and good service.

Phone orders accepted:	**Yes**
Discount:	**40%-50% off mfrs. suggested retail**
Payment methods:	**VISA, MC, personal checks**
In-house financing available:	**No**
Deposits required:	**50% deposit when order is placed, balance due when furniture is ready to be shipped**
Catalog available:	**No**
Clearance center:	**Yes - See *Clayton-Marcus Factory Outlet***
Delivery:	**Full service in-home delivery and set-up. Customer pays freight company directly for shipping costs.**

Directions: From I-40, take exit #123 and drive north on Hwy. 321 to Lenoir.
Triplett's Furniture Fashions is on the left side of the road.

Triplett's Furniture Fashions (cont.)

Lines carried:

Action By Lane
American Drew
American Impressions
American Leather
American Of Martinsville
Andrea By Sadek
Arnold Palmer Collection
Athol
Austin Sculptures
Betsy Cameron
Blacksmith Shop
Bob Timberlake
Boston Rockers
Builtright Chairs
Caldwell Chair
Cape Craftsmen
Carolina Mirror
Charleston Forge
Chatham County
Chromcraft
Clayton Marcus
Cochrane
Colonial Furniture
Cooper Classics
Cox
Crystal Clear Lighting
Denny Lamps
Design Master
Eddie Bauer
Fashion Bed Group
Fashion House
Frederick Cooper Lamps
Hammary
Hekman
Henry Link
Hollywoods
Hooker
Howard Miller Clocks
Hyundai Furniture
Jasper Cabinet
Johnston Casuals
Keller
Kimball
Lane
Lane/Venture
Lea
Leda
Lexington
Leisters

Meadowcraft
Nichols & Stone
Null Industries
Ohio Table Pad
P & P Chair
Palmer Home Collection
Pennsylvania Classics
Pennsylvania Heirlooms
Pulaski
Regency House
Riverside
Sam Moore
Sarreid
Serta
Skillcraft
Stein World
Straits
Statesville Chair
Sumter Cabinet
Temple
Toyo
Universal
Uwharrie Chair
Villageois
Weathercraft
Weather Master
Weekend Retreat
Wesley Allen Brass Beds
Weiman
Westwood Lamps

Trott Furniture Co.

Hwy. 258
Richlands, NC 28574

Phone:	(910) 324-4660	**Hours:**	M-Sat 9:30-5:00
Toll Free:	None	**E-mail:**	None
Fax:	(910) 324-2515	**Web site:**	None

Trott Furniture Co. is located in Richlands, NC, about three hours east of High Point, NC. They have a good selection of medium to high-end lines, including Lexington, Universal, Hooker, and Pulaski.

They don't have a clearance center or any floor samples or discontinued pieces on display. For this reason, there is no monetary advantage to visiting in person. They do have great deals on many lines sold over the phone, though. So, if you're planning to order your furniture by phone, definitely give this source a call to compare their prices.

Lines carried:

American Drew	Crown Fine Arts	McKinley Leather	Sligh
Arts Uniq'	Distinction Leather	Moosehead	Skillcraft
Bob Timberlake	Fritz & LaRue	Nichols & Stone	Somma
Bradington Young	Henry Link	Ohio Table Pad	Stiffel Lamps
Broyhill	Hooker	Old Salem	Statton
Capel Rugs	Jasper Cabinet	Pande Cameron	Sumter Cabinet
Carolina Heritage	Karel Mintjens	Parker Southern	Two Day Designs
Carolina Mirror	Keller	Patch Magic Group	Universal
Chatham County	Lane	Peking Handicrafts	Virginia Metalcrafters
Craftique	Lexington	Pulaski	Waterford Furniture
C. R. Laine	Link Taylor	Robinson	Wayborn
Craftmark	Madison Square	Sedgefield	Wesley Allen Brass Beds
Crescent	Mario Industries	Serta Mattress	

Phone orders accepted:	Yes
Discount:	40%-50% off mfrs. suggested retail
Payment methods:	VISA, MC, personal checks
In-house financing available:	No
Deposits required:	1/3 deposit when order is placed, balance due when furniture is ready to be shipped
Catalog available:	No
Clearance center:	No
Delivery:	Full service in-home delivery and set-up. Customer pays freight company directly for shipping costs.

Directions: From I-40, take exit #364, and head east for about an hour on Hwy. 24 into Richlands, NC. Hwy. 24 will run into Hwy. 258. The store is on Hwy. 258 in downtown Richlands.

Tyson Furniture Company

109 Broadway
Black Mountain, NC 28711

Phone:	**(828) 669-5000**	**Hours:**	**M-Sat 9:00-5:00**
Toll Free:	**None**	**E-mail:**	**None**
Fax:	**(828) 669-8292**	**Web site:**	**None**

Tyson's Furniture Company in Black Mountain, NC, just east of Asheville, is huge. It occupies about a dozen interconnected buildings covering more than a city block in downtown Black Mountain. They have huge galleries for many high-end lines, including Hickory White, Baker, Century, Henredon, and others.

On my most recent visit here, I found a terrific deal on a Hickory White solid cherry highboy (pictured on the following page). It normally retails for $5,264.00, but Tyson's had this one in stock for only $2,099.00. It was brand-new and in perfect condition.

Most of the furniture here is new first-quality, priced at about 40%-50% off retail. All lines can be ordered over the phone at about 5%-10% less than the regular showroom prices, plus phone customers don't have to pay North Carolina sales tax, so there's really no reason to travel here in person. Should you decide to shop here in person for any reason, though, be sure to ask for their extra 10% discount for cash purchases made in-person at the store.

However, anyone shopping by phone should definitely call this source to compare their prices. They don't publish a list of the lines they carry, but I've found that they can order just about anything.

Lines carried:	**Please call for information**
Phone orders accepted:	**Yes**
Discount:	**40%-60% off mfrs. suggested retail**
Payment methods:	**VISA, MC, personal checks**
In-house financing available:	**Yes**
Deposits required:	**50% deposit when order is placed, balance due when furniture is ready to be shipped**
Catalog available:	**No**
Clearance center:	**No**
Delivery:	**Full service in-home delivery and set-up. Customer pays freight company directly for shipping costs.**

Directions: From I-40, take exit #64, and go north one mile into Black Mountain, NC. Tyson's Furniture Company is right downtown on Broadway.

Tyson Furniture Company (cont.)

Tyson Furniture Company

Solid cherry highboy from Hickory White

Retail: $5,264.00   Discounted price: $2,099.00
Savings at Tyson Furniture Company: $3,165.00 = 60% off retail

Utility Craft Fine Furniture

2630 Eastchester Dr.
High Point, NC 27265

Phone:	**(336) 454-6153**	**Hours:**	**M-F 9:00-5:30, Sat 9:00-5:00**
Toll Free:	**None**	**E-mail:**	**None**
Fax:	**(336) 454-5065**	**Web site:**	**None**

Utility Craft Fine Furniture on the north side of High Point has a very nice store with a good selection of high-end lines: Hickory White, La Barge, Wellington Hall, Lexington, etc.

All of the furniture here is in new first-quality condition. The discounts run from 40%-50% off retail. There are no floor samples or discontinued styles here. These are all sent to their clearance center downtown.

On my most recent visit here, I found a great deal on a Hickory White dining room set (pictured on the following page). The hutch, table, and six chairs normally retail as a group for $18,060.00, but Utility Craft's price on the same set was only $7,345.00. The set was brand-new and in first-quality condition.

Since you save just as much over the phone as you do in person, there really isn't much reason to travel here in person to shop. However, if you plan to order furniture by phone, you really should call here to compare prices. Utility Craft has some great deals.

If you do travel directly to High Point to shop, don't miss Utility Craft's clearance center downtown. There's more information about that source under the listing for *Furniture Clearance Center -- High Point*.

Lines carried:	**Please see page 315**
Phone orders accepted:	**Yes**
Discount:	**40%-50% off mfrs. suggested retail**
Payment methods:	**VISA, MC, personal checks**
In-house financing available:	**No**
Deposits required:	**50% deposit when order is placed, balance due when furniture is ready to be shipped**
Catalog available:	**No**
Clearance center:	**Yes - See *Furniture Clearance Center - High Pt.***
Delivery:	**Full service in-home delivery and set-up. Customer pays freight company directly for shipping costs.**

Directions: **From I-85, take exit #111 (Hwy. 311), and head northwest into High Point. After several miles, when you reach downtown High Point, Hwy. 311 will become Main St. Follow Main St. north all the way through High Point. When you come to the intersection of Eastchester, turn right. Go about 10 miles, and turn left on Penny Rd. Utility Craft Furniture is on the corner.**

Utility Craft Fine Furniture (cont.)

Utility Craft Fine Furniture

Dining room set from Hickory White

Retail: $18,060.00   Discounted price: $7,345.00
Savings at Utility Craft Fine Furniture: $10,715.00 = 60% off retail

Utility Craft Fine Furniture (cont.)

Lines carried:

Action By Lane	Hitchcock Chair	Statesville Chair
American Drew	Hollywoods	Statton
American Of Martinsville	Hooker	Stiffel Lamps
Ardley Hall	Jasper Cabinet	Superior
As You Like It Lamps	John Richards Collection	Swan Brass Beds
Baldwin Brass	Kaiser Kuhn Lighting	Taylor Woodcraft
Barcalounger	Kimball	Tell City
Bassett	King Hickory	Universal
Benecia Brass Beds	Kingsdown	Uttermost
Blacksmith Shop	Knob Creek	Vanguard
Bob Timberlake	La Barge	Venture By Lane
Bradington Young	La-Z-Boy	Viewpoint
Broyhill	Lane	Waterford Furniture
Canadel	Lane/Venture	Weiman
Carolina Mirror	Lexington	Wellington Hall
Carson's	Link Taylor	Wesley Allen Brass Beds
Casa Bique	Lloyd/Flanders	Wesley Hall
Casa Stradivari	Lyon Shaw	Winston
Century	Madison Square	Woodard
Charleston Forge	Michael Thomas	Woodmark Originals
Chatham County	Miles Talbott	
Chromcraft	Moosehead	
Clark Casual	Motioncraft	
Classic Leather	National Mt. Airy	
Classic Rattan	Nichols & Stone	
Clayton Marcus	Pearson	
Cochrane	Pennsylvania Classics	
Corsican Brass Beds	Pulaski	
Cox	Rex	
C. R. Laine	Richardson Brothers	
Craftmark	Riverside	
Craftwork	Rowe	
Crawford	S. K. Products	
Crescent	S. Bent	
CTH Sherrill	Salem Square	
Dinaire	Sam Moore	
Distinction Leather	Sarreid	
Emerson Leather	Sealy Mattress	
Fashion Bed Group	Sedgefield/Woodcraft	
Ficks Reed	Serta Mattress	
Frederick Cooper Lamps	Sherrill	
Great City Traders	Shuford	
Guildmaster	Sligh	
Habersham Plantation	Somma	
Hadley Pottery	Southampton	
Hammary	Southern Reproductions	
Hekman	Southwood Reproductions	
Henry Link	Stanford	
Hickory White	Stanley	

Vanguard Furniture Factory Outlet

Furniture Factory Outlet Shoppes
930 Hwy. 70 SW
Hickory, NC 28602

Phone:	**(828) 261-0051**	**Hours:**	**M-Sat 9:30-5:00**
Toll Free:	**None**	**E-mail:**	**None**
Fax:	**None**	**Web site:**	**None**

This is a true factory outlet for Vanguard upholstery. The entire stock is sofas and chairs, most about 60% off retail.

They don't have a huge selection here, but they do have some nice pieces. The quality is about medium, and the prices are fairly good.

They won't special order from their current lines, but they will let you select from samples of their discontinued fabrics and have a sofa or chair custom made in any frame style you choose at the 60% off outlet price.

If you're looking for medium-quality upholstery, this source is worth a visit.

Phone orders accepted:	**No**
Discount:	**60% off mfrs. suggested retail**
Payment methods:	**VISA, MC, personal checks**
In-house financing available:	**No**
Deposits required:	**Not applicable**
Catalog available:	**Not applicable**
Clearance center:	**Not applicable**
Delivery:	**Full service in-home delivery and set-up. Customer pays freight company directly for shipping costs.**

Directions:	**From I-40, take exit #123 (Hwy. 321), and go north toward Hickory. After a few miles, take the Hwy. 70 exit, and go east. The Furniture Factory Outlet Shoppes is immediately on your left as you exit onto Hwy. 70.**

Village Furniture House

146 West Ave.
Kannapolis, NC 28081

Phone:	**(704) 938-9171**	**Hours:**	**M-Sat 9:00-6:00**
Toll Free:	**None**	**E-mail:**	**None**
Fax:	**(704) 932-2503**	**Web site:**	**None**

Village Furniture House in Cannon Village has a very good selection of high-end lines. They have furniture in stock from Lane, Lexington (including Bob Timberlake), Stanley, Flexsteel, Godfrey Thomas, Broyhill, Kincaid, and others. They can special order many other lines. They also house factory-owned factory outlets for Baker, Century, and Maitland-Smith in another part of the store building.

Most of the furniture in stock is priced at 30%-50% off retail. Usually, the salespeople will tell you as you come in that they are willing to go even lower than the prices marked and that they will beat any competitor's discounts, so take them up on it!

On my most recent visit here, I found a great deal on a Bob Timberlake five-piece bedroom set: queen sleigh bed, dresser, mirror, chest, and nightstand (pictured on the following page). This group normally retails for $9,435.00, but Village Furniture House had this set for only $5,249.00, a discount of 45% off retail. The set was brand-new and in first-quality condition.

If you are traveling to North Carolina to buy furniture, you really should consider taking one extra day to visit Cannon Village in Kannapolis. In addition to the Village Furniture House, there are also true factory outlets for Baker, Century, and Maitland-Smith here that are well worth a visit. Kannapolis is about one half hour's drive north of Charlotte, one hour's drive south of High Point, and one hour's drive east of Hickory.

If you are ordering furniture by phone, definitely give this source a call. They have a very good reputation for customer service, and they do offer to beat any competitor's prices. Take them up on it!

Lines carried:	**Please see page 319**
Phone orders accepted:	**Yes**
Discount:	**30%-50% off mfrs. suggested retail**
Payment methods:	**Personal checks. No credit cards except their own store credit card through GE credit.**
In-house financing available:	**Yes**
Deposits required:	**1/3 deposit when order is placed, balance due when furniture is ready to be shipped**
Catalog available:	**No**
Clearance center:	**No**
Delivery:	**Full service in-home delivery and set-up. Customer pays freight company directly for shipping costs.**

Directions: From I-85, take exit #63, and follow the signs to Cannon Village. Village Furniture House is on West Ave. inside Cannon Village.

Village Furniture House (cont.)

Village Furniture House

Bob Timberlake bedroom set from Lexington

Retail: $9,435.00   Discounted price: $5,249.00
Savings at Village Furniture House: $4,186.00 = 44% off retail

Village Furniture House (cont.)

Lines carried:

Action By Lane
Alexander Julian
Alexvale
American Drew
American Of Martinsville
Ashley
Athol
Baldwin Brass
Barcalounger
Bassett
Benchcraft
Berkline
Bevan Funnell
Bob Timberlake
Blacksmith Shop
Bradington Young
Brady
Braxton Culler
Broyhill
C. R. Laine
Capitol Leather
Carolina Mirror
Carson's
Casa Bique
Casual Concepts
Chapman Lamps
Charleston Forge
Chromcraft
Clayton Marcus
Colonial Solid Cherry
Councill Craftsmen
Craftique
Craftwork Guild
Dansen Contemporary
Design Horizons
Design South
Dillon
Dinaire
Distinction Leather
Ducks Unlimited
Ello
Emerson Leather
Fairfield Chair
Fashion Bed Group
Flexsteel
Friedman Brothers Mirrors
Habersham Plantation
Hammary
Hekman

Henry Link
Hickory Fry
Hickory Hill
Hickory White
Highland House
Hitchcock Chair
Hooker
Howard Miller
J. Royale
Jasper Cabinet
JTB
Keller
Kessler
Key City
Kimball
Kincaid
King Hickory
Kingsdown Bedding
Klaussner
Knob Creek
La Barge
Lane
Lane/Venture
Lea
Lexington
Link Taylor
Lloyd/Flanders
Lyon Shaw
Madison Square
Master Design
Michael Thomas
Millennium
Moosehead
Nathan Hale
National Mt. Airy
Nichols & Stone
Norman Rockwell
Old Hickory Tannery
Pearson
Pennsylvania Classics
Peters Revington
Pulaski
Ridgeway Clocks
Riverside
Rowe
Royal Patina
Salem Square
Saloom
Sam Moore

S. Bent
Schwieger
Shuford
Simply Southern
Singer
Skillcraft
Sligh
S. K. Dinettes
Southern Of Conover
Southwood Reproductions
Stanley
Statesville Chair
Statton
Stiffel Lamps
Swaim
Tradition France
Tradition House
Tropitone
Universal
Vanguard
Vaughan
Vaughan Bassett
Venture By Lane
Virginia House
Waterford Furniture
Weiman
Wellington Hall
Wesley Allen Brass Beds
Wildwood Lamps
Winston
Woodard
Woodmark

Wellington Hall Factory Outlet

Hwy. 70
Lexington, NC 27293

Phone:	**(336) 249-4931**	**Hours:**	**M-F 9:00-5:00**
Toll Free:	**None**	**E-mail:**	**None**
Fax:	**(336) 249-7798**	**Web site:**	**None**

Wellington Hall manufactures absolutely gorgeous high-end traditional furniture. In fact, they even make some styles for Baker and Henredon, two better-known high-quality lines.

The Wellington Hall Factory Outlet is a bit different from the rest, however. It's located in the back of the actual factory, rather than being at a separate location. Many people don't even know that there's an outlet here. You have to go all the way to the back of the factory building (toward the extreme right in the picture on the next page), and ring a bell by a little door. Then, you wait patiently for someone from the front office to walk all the way to the back of the factory to open the little door.

It's well worth the wait, though. The outlet is actually just a back corner of the factory floor itself. It's quite an interesting eyeful to see all of the works in progress further forward in the plant.

The selection of outlet merchandise is pretty good. All of the pieces are case goods, no upholstery. Most are overstocks, floor samples,discontinued styles, and a very few high-quality seconds. Virtually everything in the outlet is first-quality, and marked down 50%-75% off retail.

On my most recent visit here, I found a beautiful mahogany table (pictured on the following page) that normally retails for $1,247.00, marked down to $575.00. It was a discontinued style with no damage.

This is a terrific outlet. If you're traveling to the Lexington area, near Hickory, you have to see this place!

Discount:	**50%-75% off mfrs. suggested retail**
Payment methods:	**VISA, MC, personal checks**
In-house financing available:	**No**
Deposits required:	**Not applicable**
Catalog available:	**Not applicable**
Clearance center:	**Not applicable**
Delivery:	**Customer must make own arrangements to take purchases home**

Directions: The Wellington Hall Factory Outlet is right on Business 85, just north of Lexington, NC.

Wellington Hall Factory Outlet (cont.)

Wellington Hall Factory Outlet

Mahogany table from Wellington Hall

Retail: $1,247.00   Discounted price: $575.00
Savings at the Wellington Hall Factory Outlet: $672.00 = 54% off retail

Wellington's Fine Leather Furniture

7771 Valley Blvd.
Hwy. 321 S.
Blowing Rock, NC 28605

Phone:	**(828) 295-0491**	**Hours:**	**M-Sat 9:00-6:00**
Toll Free:	**(800) 262-1049**	**E-mail:**	**hampwell@fineleatherfurniture.com**
Fax:	**(828) 295-0495**	**Web site:**	**www.fineleatherfurniture.com**

Wellington's Fine Leather Furniture has a very nice leather showroom in Blowing Rock, NC, about 40 miles north of Hickory. They also sell by phone. They guarantee prices of at least 30%-40% off the manufacturers retail price.

All of the furniture displayed in their showroom is new first-quality. There are no floor samples or discontinued styles available, which means there really isn't any reason to travel here in person. Also, this store is quite far from the main cluster of factory outlets and discounters in Hickory and Lenoir, NC.

If you're planning to order leather furniture by phone, you may wish to compare prices here. There are many other discounters, primarily in Hickory and High Point, who generally have better bargains on leather upholstery, though.

Lines carried:

Distinction
McKinley
Palliser

Phone orders accepted:	**Yes**
Discount:	**30%-40% off mfrs. suggested retail**
Payment methods:	**VISA, MC, AMEX, Discover, personal checks**
In-house financing available:	**No**
Deposits required:	**50% deposit when order is placed, balance due when furniture is ready to be shipped**
Catalog available:	**Yes**
Clearance center:	**No**
Delivery:	**Full service in-home delivery and set-up. Customer pays freight company directly for shipping costs.**

Directions: From I-40, take exit #123, and drive north on Hwy. 321 about 40 miles to Blowing Rock. The store is on the left side of the highway.

Wicker Gallery

8009 Raleigh-Durham Hwy.
Raleigh, NC 27612

Phone:	**(919) 781-2215**	**Hours:**	**M-F 9:00-6:00, Sun 1:00-5:00**
Toll Free:	**None**	**E-mail:**	**None**
Fax:	**(919) 781-3520**	**Web site:**	**None**

Wicker Gallery is located in Raleigh, NC, about two hours' drive east of High Point. They have a very nice selection of medium to high-end wicker and rattan.

They don't have a clearance center or any floor samples or discontinued pieces on display. For this reason, there is no monetary advantage to visiting in person. They do have great deals on many lines sold over the phone, though. So, if you're planning to order your furniture by phone, definitely give this source a call to compare their prices.

Lines carried:

American Drew	Clark Casuals	Lane/Venture	Summer Classics
Artisan House	Classic Rattan	Lexington	Sunset Lamps
Ayers Chairmaker	D & F Wicker & Rattan	Link Taylor	United Basket Co.
Bon Art Industries	David Marshall Sculptors	Lloyd/Flanders	Venture By Lane
Bassett	Don Tickle Imports	Michaels Classic Wicker	Vogue Rattan
Benchcraft Rattan	European Imports	O'Asian	Whitecraft Rattan
Braxton Culler	Ficks Reed	Pacific Rattan	Wicker Barn
Cardinal Art	Glass Fashions	Rattan Specialties	Wicker Street
Cebu Imports	Henry Link	Royal Design	Young Hinkle
Carolina Gallery	James Wicker Imports	South Seas Rattan	

Phone orders accepted:	**Yes**
Discount:	**30%-50% off mfrs. suggested retail**
Payment methods:	**VISA, MC, personal checks**
In-house financing available:	**No**
Deposits required:	**25% deposit when order is placed, balance due when furniture is ready to be shipped**
Catalog available:	**No**
Clearance center:	**No**
Delivery:	**Full service in-home delivery and set-up. Customer pays freight company directly for shipping costs.**

Directions: From I-40, turn left onto the I-440 perimeter around Raleigh. Take exit #7, and head northwest on Hwy. 70. Hwy. 70 will become Raleigh-Durham Hwy. Wicker Gallery is a few miles outside the perimeter.

Wildermere Inc.

Level 4
Hickory Furniture Mart
2200 Hwy. 70 SE
Hickory, NC 28602

Phone:	(828) 322-6602	**Hours:**	M-F 9:00-6:00, Sat 9:00-5:00
Toll Free:	None	**E-mail:**	None
Fax:	(828) 322-6433	**Web site:**	None

Wildermere has a several huge showrooms covering over half of the 4th floor of the Hickory Furniture Mart. There are extensive galleries for Universal, Flexsteel, Sam Moore, Kingsdown, Century, Serta Mattress, Highland House, Carson's, Cochrane, and Richardson Brothers. Many more lines are available by special order.

Wildermere will sell directly off the floor, or they will special order by phone. The discount is the same either way: 40%-50% off retail. All of the furniture they stock is new first-quality. They don't have any floor samples or discontinued items available, and they have no clearance center.

This source is well worth checking out if you plan to order your furniture by phone. If you plan to visit North Carolina in person, there are many other sources that will give you a much better deal on furniture purchased directly off the sales floor.

Phone orders accepted:	Yes
Discount:	40%-50% off mfrs. suggested retail
Payment methods:	VISA, MC, personal checks
In-house financing available:	Yes
Deposits required:	50% deposit when order is placed, balance due when furniture is ready to be shipped
Catalog available:	No
Clearance center:	No
Delivery:	Full service in-home delivery and set-up. Customer pays freight company directly for shipping costs.

Directions: Please see *Hickory Furniture Mart* for complete directions.

Wildermere Inc.

Lines carried:

Accentrics By Pulaski
Alexander Julian
Artistica
Ardley Hall
American Decor Mirrors
Athol
Berkshire
Bevan Funnell
Blue Ridge Leather
Bob Timberlake
Brady
Charles Adrian
Carolina Mirror
Carsons
Carvers Guild
Century
CBS Imports
Chapman
Chelsea House
Clark Casual
Cochrane
Courtleigh
Cox
Craftique
Creative Metal & Wood
Crystal Clear Lighting
Decorative Crafts
Denny Lamps
Eldred Wheeler
Entree By La Barge
Excelsior
Executive Leather
Fairfield Chair
Fashion Bed Group
Fine Arts Lamps
Frederick Cooper Lamps
Friedman Mirrors
Furniture Guild
Garcia Imports
Gatco
Georgian Furnishings
Glass Arts
Great City Traders
Greeff Fabrics
Guildmaster
Gulden
Hart Associates
Henry Link
Hickory Leather

Hickory White
High Point Desk
Highland House
Howard Miller Clocks
Jasper Cabinet
John Richard Lamps
John McGill Lamps
John Royale
Johnston Casuals
Karges
Kay-Lyn
Keller
Kingsdown
Lane/Venture
Lexington
Link Taylor
Lloyd/Flanders
Lotus Arts
Madison Square
Maitland Smith
Marbro
McKay Table Pad
Miller Desk
Nagykery Imports
Nathan Hale
Oggetti
Ohio Table Pad
Pulaski
Ralph Lauren Wallpapers
Riverside
Ron Fisher
Sagefield Leather
Sarreid
Schumacher Fabrics
Sedgefield
SEE Imports
Serta Mattress
Shuford
Southampton
Speer Lamps
Stanford Furniture
Stroheim & Romann
Tom Thumb Lighting
Tradition House
Trosby
Universal
Venture By Lane
Virginia Metalcrafters
Victorious

Walker Marlen
Waterford Furniture
Waverly Fabrics
Wellington Hall
Wesley Allen Brass Beds
Wildwood
Woodmark

Wood Armfield Furniture Co.

The Atrium
430 S. Main St.
High Point, NC 27260

Phone:	**(336) 889-6522**	**Hours:**	**M-F 9:00-6:00, Sat 9:00-5:00**
Toll Free:	**None**	**E-mail:**	**woodarmfield@theatrium.com**
Fax:	**(336) 889-5381**	**Web site:**	**www.theatrium.com**

Wood-Armfield Furniture Co. has a very nice store in the Atrium Furniture Mall in High Point. Their stock is an even mix of traditional and contemporary. All stock is new first-quality.

There isn't much reason to shop here in person, but they have great deals on furniture sold over the phone. If you do plan to travel to High Point, NC, to buy furniture, don't miss Wood Armfield's clearance center several blocks away.

Phone orders accepted:	**Yes**
Discount:	**40%-50% off mfrs. suggested retail**
Payment methods:	**VISA, MC, personal checks**
In-house financing available:	**No**
Deposits required:	**50% deposit when order is placed, balance due when furniture is ready to be shipped**
Catalog available:	**No**
Clearance center:	**Yes - See *Furniture Clearance Center - High Pt.***
Delivery:	**Full service in-home delivery and set-up. Customer pays freight company directly for shipping costs.**

Directions: Wood Armfield is located inside the Atrium complex in downtown High Point. Please see *The Atrium* for complete directions.

Wood Armfield (cont.)

Wood Armfield Furniture Co.

Lines carried:

Ambience
Ardley Hall
Arttra
Berkline
Bernhardt
Bob Timberlake
Bradington Young
Broyhill
Cambridge
Canadel
Cape Craftsman
Capel
Carsons
Casa Bique
Casa Stradivari
Century
Chapman
Classic Leather
Councill
Colonial Furniture
Craftwork
Crescent
Designmaster
Florita Nova
Fine Art
Frederick Cooper
Friedman Bros.
Garcia Imports
Great City Traders
Guildmaster

Habersham
Hart
Hekman
Henry Link
Hickory White
Hilda Flack
Hollywoods
Howard Miller
Jasper Cabinet
John Richards
Kinder Harris
Koch
La Barge
La-Z-Boy
Lexington
Ligna
Maitland Smith
Miles Talbott
Montaage
Nichols & Stone
Nora Fenton
O. L. F.
Palecek
Pennsylvania Classics
Phillips Collection
Phoenix Art
Rex
S. Bent
Sarreid
Sedgefield

Shadow Catchers
Silkwood
Soicher Marin
Southwood
Stanley
Statesville Chair
Statton
Swaim
Tapestries Ltd.
Thomasville
Vanguard
Wesley Hall

Worthington Furniture Gallery

237 Timber Brook Place
Granite Falls, NC 28630

Phone:	**(828) 396-6343**	**Hours:**	**M-Sat 9:30-5:30**
Toll Free:	**None**	**E-mail:**	**None**
Fax:	**(828) 396-6345**	**Web site:**	**None**

Worthington Furniture Gallery is located just a few miles north of Hickory, NC. They have a limited selection of medium to high-end lines, including Hammary, Lexington, and Universal.

They don't have a clearance center or any floor samples or discontinued pieces on display. For this reason, there is no monetary advantage to visiting in person. They do have some good deals on the lines they sell by phone, though. So, if you're planning to order your furniture by phone, give this source a call to compare their prices.

Lines carried:

Hammary
Hekman
Leatherworks
Lexington
Sam Moore
Sedona Leather
Universal
Waterford Furniture

Phone orders accepted:	**Yes**
Discount:	**35%-50% off mfrs. suggested retail**
Payment methods:	**Personal checks. No credit cards.**
In-house financing available:	**No**
Deposits required:	**50% deposit when order is placed, balance due when furniture is ready to be shipped**
Catalog available:	**No**
Clearance center:	**No**
Delivery:	**Full service in-home delivery and set-up. Customer pays freight company directly for shipping costs.**

Directions: From I-40, take exit #123 and drive north on Hwy. 321 to Granite Falls. Worthington Furniture Gallery is on the left side of the road.

Young's Furniture and Rug Company

1706 N. Main St.
High Point, NC 27262

Phone:	**(336) 883-4111**	**Hours:**	**M-F 9:00-5:30, Sat 9:00-5:00**
Toll Free:	**None**	**E-mail:**	**None**
Fax:	**(336) 887-2915**	**Web site:**	**None**

Young's Furniture and Rug Company has a nice showroom with a good selection of medium to high-end furniture lines: Century, Hickory Chair, Lexington, Wellington Hall, etc. They also have a nice selection of outdoor and rattan furniture. Discounts here run about 40%-50% off retail on new first-quality furniture, whether you buy it in person or over the phone.

They have a small clearance area in the very back of the store with a small selection of floor samples and discontinued styles priced at about 60% off retail. There really isn't enough selection in the clearance center to justify visiting this store in person. The selection of discontinued styles and floor samples is far better at many other High Point factory outlets and discounters, and the prices are generally better, too.

However, if you plan to order your furniture by phone, you should definitely call this source and compare their prices. They do have some good deals.

Lines carried:	Please see page 330
Phone orders accepted:	Yes
Discount:	40%-50% off mfrs. suggested retail
Payment methods:	VISA, MC, personal checks
In-house financing available:	No
Deposits required:	1/3 deposit when order is placed, balance due when furniture is ready to be shipped
Catalog available:	No
Clearance center:	Yes
Delivery:	Full service in-home delivery and set-up. Customer pays freight company directly for shipping costs.

Directions: From I-85, take exit #111 (Hwy. 311), and head northwest into High Point. After several miles, when you reach downtown High Point, Hwy. 311 will become S. Main St. Continue on through High Point. Young's Furniture is on the north side of town on the right side of the road.

Young's Furniture and Rug Company (cont.)

Lines carried:

Accessories International
Albert's Art & Mirrors
Anichini
Anne David Thomas
Ardley Hall
Art Lore
Artex
Artistica
As You Like It Lamps
Austin Horn
Baldwin Brass
Bevan Funnell
Bob Timberlake
Bradburn Gallery
Bradington Young
Brown Jordan
Cal-Bear
CAP
Capel Rugs
Casa Bique
Casa Stradivari
Century
Chapman
Charleston Forge
Chelsea House
Chelsea Textiles
CJC
Clark Casual
Corsican
Councill Craftsmen
Dar-Ran
Faberge
Ficks Reed
Fine Arts Lamps
Fitz & Floyd
Florita Nova
Frederick Cooper Lamps
Friedman Brothers Mirrors
Garcia Imports
Garden Source
Goodship
Great City Traders
Guildmaster
Habersham Plantation
Hammary
Hancock & Moore
Hart
Hekman
Hen Feathers

Henkel-Harris
Henkel-Moore
Henry Link
Hickory Chair
Hitchcock Chair
Hooker
House Parts
Howard Miller Clocks
Jasper Cabinet
Jay Willfred
Jeffco
John Richard Collection
John Widdicomb
Johnston Casuals
Kaiser Kuhn Lighting
Karess Linens
Karges
Kinder Harris
La Barge
Lane
Lexington
Lotus Arts
Lyon Shaw
Madison Square
Maitland Smith
Majestic Mirror
Marbro
Masland Carpets
McGuire
Meadowcraft
Miller Desk
Mottahedeh
Mystic Valley Traders
Nagykery Imports
Napp Deady
Nichols & Stone
Old Biscayne Designs
PAMA
Paper White
Peacock Alley
Plant Plant
Pompeii
Port Royal
Pulaski
Royal Patina
Sadek
Sarreid
Sealy Mattress
Sedgefield Lamps

Sherrill Occasional
Soicher Marin
Southampton
Southwood Reproductions
Sova & Sova
Speer Lamps
Statesville Chair
Sterling Collection
Stiffel Lamps
Tapestries Ltd.
Theodore & Alexander
Thief River
Tropitone
Trosby
Veneman
Vietri
Virginia Metalcrafters
W. King Ambler
Waterford Lighting
Wellington Hall
Wesley Allen Brass Beds
Wildwood Lamps
Winston
Woodard
Woodmark
Wright Table
Yorkshire House

Zagaroli Classics

Level 3
Hickory Furniture Mart
U. S. Hwy. 70 SE
Hickory, NC 28602

Phone:	**(828) 328-3373**	**Hours:**	**M-Sat 9:00-6:00**
Toll Free:	**(800) 887-2424**	**E-mail:**	**zagaroli@twave.net**
Fax:	**(828) 328-5839**	**Web site:**	**www.zagarolileather.com**

Zagaroli Classics is a family-owned business based in Hickory, NC, that sells high-end custom leather upholstery directly to the public through their two showrooms in the Atrium Furniture mall in High Point and the Hickory Furniture Mart in Hickory, as well as through their catalog. Their prices are typically about half of what a retailer would charge for comparable furniture.

I was very impressed with the service at both showrooms and through their catalog. The furniture is very high quality, with solid maple frames and 8-way hand-tied springs. They use only aniline-dyed leather, which is the best quality you can buy.

It isn't necessary to visit their showrooms in order to buy from them. They have a free full-color catalog showing all of the various sofa and chair styles they manufacture. They have a nice selection of contemporary and traditional styles. They will also send you leather samples in the mail, so you can easily decide in your own home what color and grade of leather you would like. They do require a $10 deposit before sending you a leather sample kit, but this is refunded when you return the leather samples to them.

I was very impressed with the quality and service at this source. Anyone who is considering purchasing new leather upholstery by phone should definitely request their free catalog and compare their prices. You are unlikely to find better prices on leather upholstery without actually traveling to North Carolina and shopping in person for floor samples and discontinued styles.

Phone orders accepted:	**Yes**
Discount:	**Up to 60% off mfrs. suggested retail**
Payment methods:	**VISA, MC, personal checks**
In-house financing available:	**No**
Deposits required:	**50% deposit when order is placed, balance due when furniture is ready to be shipped**
Catalog available:	**Yes**
Clearance center:	**No**
Delivery:	**Full service in-home delivery and set-up. Customer pays freight company directly for shipping costs.**

Directions: Please see *Hickory Furniture Mart* for complete directions.

Zagaroli Classics

The Atrium
430 S. Main St.
High Point, NC 27260

Phone:	**(336) 882-7385**	**Hours:**	**M-F 9:00-6:00, Sat 9:00-5:00**
Toll Free:	**(800) 887-2424**	**E-mail:**	**zagaroli@twave.net**
Fax:	**(336) 882-7386**	**Web site:**	**www.zagarolileather.com**

Zagaroli Classics is a family-owned business based in Hickory, NC, that sells high-end custom leather upholstery directly to the public through their two showrooms in the Atrium Furniture mall in High Point and the Hickory Furniture Mart in Hickory, as well as through their catalog. Their prices are typically about half of what a retailer would charge for comparable furniture.

I was very impressed with the service at both showrooms and through their catalog. The furniture is very high quality, with solid maple frames and 8-way hand-tied springs. They use only aniline-dyed leather, which is the best quality you can buy.

It isn't necessary to visit their showrooms in order to buy from them. They have a free full-color catalog showing all of the various sofa and chair styles they manufacture. They have a nice selection of contemporary and traditional styles. They will also send you leather samples in the mail, so you can easily decide in your own home what color and grade of leather you would like. They do require a $10 deposit before sending you a leather sample kit, but this is refunded when you return the leather samples to them.

I was very impressed with the quality and service at this source. Anyone who is considering purchasing new leather upholstery by phone should definitely request their free catalog and compare their prices. You are unlikely to find better prices on leather upholstery without actually traveling to North Carolina and shopping in person for floor samples and discontinued styles.

Phone orders accepted:	**Yes**
Discount:	**Up to 60% off mfrs. suggested retail**
Payment methods:	**VISA, MC, personal checks**
In-house financing available:	**No**
Deposits required:	**50% deposit when order is placed, balance due when furniture is ready to be shipped**
Catalog available:	**Yes**
Clearance center:	**No**
Delivery:	**Full service in-home delivery and set-up. Customer pays freight company directly for shipping costs.**

Directions: Zagaroli Classics is located inside the Atrium complex in downtown High Point. Please see *The Atrium* for complete directions.

BRAND INDEX

A

A. Locke, 10, 12
A. A. Laun, 10, 12, 21,138, 188, 213, 216, 266
A. L. Shaver, 213
A La Carte,138, 241, 251, 287
A Thing Of Beauty, 266
ABCO, 129
Acacia, 143, 188, 234, 266
Accentrics By Pulaski, 23, 78, 82, 216, 228,
    230, 234, 256, 258, 260, 325
Accents By Gary Parlin, 266
Accents Etc., 184, 186
Accessories Abroad, 266
Accessories International, 14, 184, 186, 266, 330
Acco, 213
Ace Crystal, 175
Action By Lane, 10, 12, 16, 46, 48, 78, 82, 84,
    97, 129, 133, 134, 138, 148, 150, 168, 169,
    175, 180, 182, 188, 191, 193, 194, 197, 205,
    216, 219, 228, 230, 234, 238, 245, 247, 251,
    252, 256, 258, 260, 266, 281, 282, 287, 290,
    292, 299, 307, 309, 315, 319
Aesthetics & Artifacts, 266
AGI Industries, 266
Ainsley, 213
Airguide Weather Instruments, 213
AKKO, 266
Alan White Co., 184, 186, 266
Alexander Julian, 82, 107, 138, 143, 175, 191,
    199, 200, 216, 228, 251, 319, 325
Alexandra Diez, 266
Alexvale, 46, 78, 133, 168, 169, 188, 191, 216,
    230, 253, 284, 307, 319

Albert's Art & Mirror, 266, 330
All Continental Inc., 184, 186
Allan Copley, 266
Alliance Art, 82
Allibert, 71, 118, 266, 299
Alliston Dize, 266
Allusions, 14, 138, 251, 266
Alock Furniture, 287
Alva, 216
Ambiance, 14, 138, 238, 251, 266, 327
American Chair & Table, 21, 82, 188
American Country West, 82
American Decor Mirrors, 325
American Drew, 10, 12, 16, 41, 44, 46, 48, 50,
    51, 53, 64, 72, 74, 75, 78, 82, 84, 97, 100,
    102, 107, 122, 124, 129, 133, 134, 138, 143,
    148, 156, 175, 180, 182, 188, 191, 193, 194,
    197, 198, 205, 209, 212, 213, 216, 219, 228,
    230, 234, 238, 241, 243, 245, 247, 251, 252,
    256, 258, 260, 266, 281, 282, 284, 287, 290,
    292, 299, 301, 307, 309, 310, 315, 319, 323
American Furniture Galleries, 281
American Heritage, 118, 234, 238, 266, 281, 287
American Impressions, 10, 12, 21, 138, 199,
    200, 245, 266, 309
American Leather, 241, 309
American Mirror, 107, 175, 188, 191, 266
American Of High Point, 10, 12, 21, 23, 84, 188,
    213, 216, 247, 266
American Of Martinsville, 10, 12, 41, 46, 48, 50,
    64, 74, 84, 107, 122, 129, 133, 134, 143,
    148, 150, 175, 193, 194, 197, 199, 200, 205,
    209, 212, 213, 216, 228, 230, 245, 251, 256,
    258, 260, 281, 284, 287, 301, 309, 315, 319
American Pacific, 124

B

C

D

E

Excursions By Venture, 138
Executive Furniture, 266
Executive Leather, 11, 13, 21, 180, 182, 188, 216, 325
Expressive Designs Rugs, 138

F

Faberge, 330
Fabric To Frame, 138
Fabrica Rugs, 14, 251
Fabricoate, 175
Fairchild, 46
Fairfax, 11, 13
Fairfield Chair Co., 11, 13, 21, 41, 44, 46, 48, 50, 64, 78, 82, 84, 97, 107, 134, 138, 143, 150, 175, 180, 182, 188, 191, 194, 197, 205, 212, 213, 216, 219, 228, 230, 234, 238, 241, 245, 247, 251, 252, 266, 281, 287, 299, 307, 319, 325
Fairington, 71
Fairmont Designs, 64, 84, 188, 245
Fald, 266
Fancher, 46, 216
Fancy Frames, 184, 186
Fashion Bed Group, 11, 13, 23, 41, 44, 48, 78, 82, 84, 97, 102, 107, 118, 121, 133, 138, 143, 175, 180, 182, 188, 191, 193, 203, 212, 216, 219, 230, 234, 238, 241, 247, 251, 266, 281, 284, 287, 290, 292, 309, 315, 319, 325
Fashion Bedding, 188
Fashion House, 11, 13, 82, 234, 252, 309
Fashioncraft, 46
Fauld, 284
Feathermade Mattress, 216
Feizy Imports, 145, 266
Fer Forge, 266
Ferguson Copeland, 14
Fiam, 251, 266
Ficks-Reed, 11, 13, 44, 46, 48, 71, 74, 84, 118, 138, 145, 175, 180, 182, 188, 216, 230, 238, 247, 251, 256, 258, 260, 266, 287, 315, 323, 330
Fine Arts Lamps, 14, 21, 44, 50, 54, 82, 133, 138, 145, 175, 191, 213, 216, 230, 238, 241, 251, 256, 258, 260, 266, 287, 299, 325, 327, 330
Finkel, 71, 213, 299
Fire Farm Lamps, 14, 138
Five Rivers Craft, 252

"525", 266
Fitz & Floyd, 50, 175, 213, 230, 234, 251, 266, 330
Flair, 46, 107, 138
Flat Rock, 133, 247, 266
Flexsteel, 11, 13, 16, 41, 44, 48, 50, 64, 74, 78, 82, 84, 97, 100, 107, 122, 129, 133, 134, 138, 175, 180, 182, 188, 191, 198, 199, 200, 205, 212, 213, 216, 230, 241, 243, 245, 252, 266, 281, 319
Floral Art, 82, 175, 184, 186, 216, 256, 258, 260, 266
Florida Furniture, 11, 13, 41, 107, 212, 252
Florita Nova, 138, 184, 186, 266, 327, 330
F. O. Moire & Co., 184, 186
Focal Point, 184, 186
Fogle, 46
Forbes Brothers Lamps, 287
Forjo Designs, 184, 186
Forma Design, 138
Fort Steuben, 23
Fortress, 150
Fortune Rattan, 150, 245
Founders, 44
Foundry, 138
Framed Picture Ent., 138
Frames and Arts, 138
Frank & Son, 266
Franklin Chairs, 266
Franklin Pictures, 138, 184, 186
Franklin Recliner, 11, 13, 82, 107, 216
Frederick Cooper Lamps, 11, 13, 23, 44, 46, 48, 50, 54, 74, 78, 102, 138, 149, 175, 180, 182, 188, 191, 197, 213, 216, 230, 238, 241, 247, 251, 266, 281, 287, 309, 315, 325, 327, 330
Frederick Edward, 11, 13, 46, 74, 216, 230, 287
Freeman, 256, 258, 260
Fremarc, 44, 71, 108, 133, 188, 241, 247, 266
French Heritage, 125, 138, 241
Friedman Bros. Mirrors, 44, 46, 71, 74, 78, 102, 138, 145, 149, 175, 191, 228, 230, 238, 241, 247, 266, 287, 299, 301, 319, 325, 327, 330
Friendship Upholstery, 11, 13, 18, 19, 122, 175, 188, 266
Fritz & LaRue Rugs, 230, 287, 310
Froelich, 84, 107, 180, 182, 188, 216, 247, 266, 284, 287
Fun With Furs, 266
Fur Designs, 251
Furniture Guild, 14, 74, 325
Futuristic, 107, 122, 216

G

H

I

J

K

L

M

N

O

P

Q

R

S

Spectrum Ltd., 268
Speer Lamps, 14, 48, 74, 78, 145, 214, 231, 238, 241, 251, 268, 281, 287, 290, 292, 299, 325, 330
Spinning Wheel Rugs, 251
Sprague Carlton, 214
Spiral Collections, 138, 184, 186
Spring Air Mattress, 11, 13, 21, 82, 97, 134, 138, 168, 169, 188, 191, 234, 247, 251, 268
Spring Wall Bedding, 84
St. Timothy, 71, 138, 188, 247, 251, 268, 290, 292
Stainsafe, 184, 186
Stakmore, 11, 13, 44, 48, 64, 82, 107, 138, 191, 256, 258, 260, 268, 281, 284
Stanford, 78, 145, 146, 231, 247, 268, 290, 292, 301, 315, 325
Stanley, 16, 46, 48, 50, 51, 53, 60, 64, 71, 74, 75, 78, 82, 84, 102, 129, 133, 134, 138, 143, 145, 148, 149, 150, 156, 175, 191, 193, 194, 197, 205, 209, 212, 214, 216, 228, 231, 234, 238, 241, 243, 247, 251, 252, 256, 258, 260, 268, 281, 284, 287, 290, 292, 299, 306, 307, 315, 319, 327
Stanton-Cooper, 11, 13, 23, 44, 48, 64, 71, 78, 84, 122, 205, 214, 216, 231, 247, 256, 258, 260, 281, 287, 299
Stark Carpet, 231, 247
Statesville Chair, 11, 13, 44, 46, 64, 71, 78, 82, 84, 100, 108, 138, 150, 188, 191, 216, 231, 234, 238, 241, 247, 251, 268, 287, 290, 292, 299, 307, 309, 315, 319, 327, 330
Statton, 11, 13, 50, 71, 74, 78, 82, 122, 138, 145, 146, 149, 188, 231, 234, 238, 247, 256, 258, 260, 268, 287, 290, 292, 299, 301, 307, 310, 315, 319, 327
Stearns & Foster, 193
Stein World, 78, 107, 118, 188, 231, 268, 309
Sterling Collection, 330
Sterling Taylor, 148
Stewart, 71, 188, 268, 301
Stickley Furniture, 293, 296
Stiffel Lamps, 11, 13, 23, 44, 46, 48, 50, 64, 74, 78, 84, 102, 138, 149, 175, 180, 182, 188, 191, 193, 197, 214, 216, 228, 231, 234, 238, 241, 247, 251, 252, 256, 258, 260, 268, 287, 290, 292, 299, 301, 307, 310, 315, 319, 330
Stone Art, 268
Stone Collection, 133
Stone County Ironworks, 268, 285
Stone International, 133, 138, 247, 268, 284
Stoneleigh, 78, 138, 191, 231, 284, 287
Stoneville, 11, 13, 41, 129, 138, 143, 184, 186, 188, 212, 256, 258, 260, 268

Stout Chair, 191
Straits Furniture, 138, 184, 186, 191, 199, 200, 216, 245, 268, 284, 309
Stratalounger, 11, 13, 82, 138, 143, 175, 188, 191, 205, 214, 216, 268, 299
Stratford, 11, 13, 122, 138, 175, 188, 191, 205, 214, 216, 256, 258, 260, 268
Stroheim & Romann, 231, 238, 287, 325
Strong, 138
Stroupe Mirror, 188
Stuart, 122
Studio International, 184, 186
Studio One Accessories, 82
Style Upholstery, 44, 46, 168, 169, 188, 241, 247, 251, 256, 258, 260, 268
Stylecraft Lamps, 21, 48, 82, 107, 124, 138, 184, 186, 188, 191, 245
Summer Classics, 79, 191, 268, 323
Sumter Cabinet, 11, 13, 50, 64, 84, 133, 138, 193, 197, 228, 234, 241, 284, 299, 301, 307, 309, 310
Sunset Lamps, 46, 214, 323
Superior, 11, 13, 44, 50, 64, 74, 82, 84, 102, 138, 188, 191, 193, 209, 216, 234, 238, 268, 284, 285, 287, 299, 315
Sustainable Lifestyles, 251
Swaim, 11, 13, 14, 44, 74, 78, 138, 175, 188, 191, 199, 200, 214, 216, 231, 238, 247, 268, 284, 287, 307, 319, 327
Swan Brass Beds, 11, 13, 23, 44, 46, 134, 138, 191, 205, 214, 216, 231, 256, 258, 260, 290, 292, 315
Sylvan Lake, 268
Symbol Bedding, 84, 118

T

Table Designs, 138
Tafco, 107
Tapestries Ltd., 23, 251, 268, 327, 330
Taylor-King, 11, 13, 21, 108, 133, 145, 146, 197, 228, 234, 238, 299, 307
Taylor Woodcraft, 46, 64, 214, 216, 231, 238, 299, 315
Taylorsville Upholstery, 11, 13, 46, 64, 78, 84, 107, 122, 175, 180, 182, 184, 186, 188, 231, 238, 245, 252, 268, 281
Telescope, 11, 13, 23, 44, 71, 79, 134, 138, 143, 150, 175, 180, 182, 214, 219, 241, 268
Tell City Chair, 46, 74, 122, 194, 205, 209, 214, 315

U

V

W

X

Y

Z

Order Form

☎ **Telephone orders:** Call Toll Free: 1 (800) 829-1203.
Visa, Mastercard, Discover, and American Express cards accepted.

✉ **Mail orders:** Send to: Home Decor Press
PMB 312
11770 Haynes Bridge Rd., Suite 205
Alpharetta, GA 30004

Please send the books checked below:

☐ The Furniture Factory Outlet Guide $24.95

☐ The Insider's Guide To Buying Home Furnishings $24.95

☐ National Directory of Wholesale Home Furnishings Sources and Showrooms $39.95

☐ The 1997 Decorative Fabrics Cross-Reference Guide $39.95

☐ National Home Furnishings Trade Show Newsletter $18.00
(issued monthly -- price is for a one year subscription)

Subtotal	$
Please add $4.00 shipping for each book ordered	$
GA residents please add 7% sales tax	$

Total amount enclosed $

$ **Payment:** ☐ Check ☐ Mastercard ☐ Visa ☐ Amex ☐ Discover

Card number:_____

Name on card: _____ Expiration date:_____

✉ **Shipping:** Name_____

Address_____

City_____ State_____ Zip_____ Daytime phone_____

Call toll free and order now